Heidegger and the Holy

New Heidegger Research

Series Editors: Gregory Fried, Professor of Philosophy, Boston College, USA and Richard Polt, Professor of Philosophy, Xavier University, USA

The *New Heidegger Research* series promotes informed and critical dialogue that breaks new philosophical ground by taking into account the full range of Heidegger's thought, as well as the enduring questions raised by his work.

Titles in the Series:
Time and Trauma: Thinking Through Heidegger in the Thirties
Richard Polt
Contexts of Suffering: A Heideggerian Approach to Psychopathology
Kevin Aho
Heidegger's Phenomenology of Perception: An Introduction, Volume I
David Kleinberg-Levin
Confronting Heidegger: A Critical Dialogue on Politics and Philosophy
Edited by Gregory Fried
Proto-Phenomenology, Language Acquisition, Orality and Literacy: Dwelling in Speech II
Lawrence J. Hatab
Transcending Reason: Heidegger on Rationality
Edited by Matthew Burch and Irene McMullin
The Fate of Phenomenology: Heidegger's Legacy
William McNeill
Agency, Freedom, and Responsibility in the Early Heidegger
Hans Pedersen
Heidegger's Phenomenology of Perception: Learning to See and Hear Hermeneutically, Volume II
David Kleinberg-Levin
Towards a Polemical Ethics: Between Heidegger and Plato
Gregory Fried
Thought Poems: A Translation of Heidegger's Verse
By Martin Heidegger - Translated by Eoghan Walls
Correspondence: 1919–1973
By Martin Heidegger and Karl Löwith - Translated by J. Goesser Assaiante and S. Montgomery Ewegen
Heidegger and the Holy, Edited by Richard Capobianco
Heidegger in the Literary World
Edited by Florian Grosser and Nassima Sahraoui

Heidegger and the Holy

Edited by
Richard Capobianco

ROWMAN & LITTLEFIELD
Lanham • Boulder • New York • London

Published by Rowman & Littlefield
An imprint of The Rowman & Littlefield Publishing Group, Inc.
4501 Forbes Boulevard, Suite 200, Lanham, Maryland 20706
www.rowman.com

86-90 Paul Street, London EC2A 4NE

Selection and editorial matter © by Richard Capobianco 2022
Copyright in individual chapters is held by the respective chapter authors.

All rights reserved. No part of this book may be reproduced in any form or by any electronic or mechanical means, including information storage and retrieval systems, without written permission from the publisher, except by a reviewer who may quote passages in a review.

British Library Cataloguing in Publication Information Available

Library of Congress Cataloging-in-Publication Data

Names: Capobianco, Richard, 1957- editor.
Title: Heidegger and The Holy / edited by Richard Capobianco.
Description: Lanham : Rowman & Littlefield, [2022] | Series: New Heidegger research | Includes bibliographical references and index.
Identifiers: LCCN 2021058238 (print) | LCCN 2021058239 (ebook) | ISBN 9781538162521 (cloth) | ISBN 9781538162545 (paperback) | ISBN 9781538162538 (epub)
Subjects: LCSH: Heidegger, Martin, 1889-1976—Religion. | Holy, The. Classification: LCC B3279.H49 H342224 2022 (print) | LCC B3279.H49 (ebook) | DDC 193—dc23/eng/20220126
LC record available at https://lccn.loc.gov/2021058238
LC ebook record available at https://lccn.loc.gov/2021058239

Omnia ab uno,
Omnia ad unum

Contents

Introduction: Dwelling in Nearness to the Holy   1
Richard Capobianco

1   The Holy in Heidegger: The Open Clearing as Excess and Abyss   5
    John W.M. Krummel

2   The Unsayable Mystery of the Holy: Hölderlin's Late Poetry   27
    Sazan Kryeziu

3   The Divine as the Origin of the Work of Art   45
    Lawrence Berger

4   Poetic Colors of the Holy: Heidegger on Pindar and Trakl   63
    Ian Alexander Moore

5   Tracing the Holy in Heidegger's *Hölderlin's Hymns "Germania" and "The Rhine"*   85
    Elias Schwieler

6   Heidegger and the Question and the Need of the Holy   105
    Holger Zaborowski

7   Through Being to the Holy: Learning to Ask the Question of Being   117
    Joeri Schrijvers

8   The Holy in Heidegger's Reading of Greek Tragedy: Necessity, Measure, and Law   137
    James M. Magrini

9 Retrieving and Constructing a Spatial-Phenomenology of the
Holy in the Early Heidegger 159
Paul Downes

Notes on the Text and Heidegger's *Gesamtausgabe* 185

Index 191

Contributors 195

Introduction

Dwelling in Nearness to the Holy

Richard Capobianco

> Meditation is not melancholy, but gladsomeness in which everything is gladdened.
>
> Heidegger, "*700 Jahre Messkirch*," (GA 16: 582)

I am delighted to bring together this collection of essays on the topic of "Heidegger and the Holy." The holy (Being-as-the holy) is a distinctive theme in Heidegger's work that is perhaps familiar to readers, yet not attended to sufficiently in the scholarship. There are illuminating studies on Heidegger and "the gods," such as Susanne Claxton's *Heidegger's Gods: An Ecofeminist Perspective*, which was published in the New Heidegger Research series in 2017, and there have also appeared a number of books on Heidegger and "religion." Yet this is the first scholarly collection to explore in depth the topic of Heidegger and "the holy" (*das Heilige*). The essays in this volume, authored by an international group of scholars, offer readers an opportunity to consider the many dimensions and possibilities of the notion of "the holy" in his thought.

By Heidegger's own testimony, the core question of his lifetime of thinking was the question of Being (*die Seinsfrage*). Yet we must take into account his well-known "turn" (*die Kehre*) in thinking after the publication of *Being and Time*, or more broadly, after 1930. In the early work of the 1920s, Heidegger was clearly influenced by the transcendental-phenomenological approach of his teacher Edmund Husserl in framing the question of Being. Nevertheless, after *Being and Time* and into the 1930s, it became clear to Heidegger that he simply could not arrive at his core matter of Being through a transcendental-phenomenological positioning. On further consideration, the philosophical project of "phenomenology" was but another enshrinement of the human "subject" as the measure of all that is, and thus another version of "the forgottenness of Being" (*Seinsvergessenheit*). Heidegger abandoned the fundamental positioning of the phenomenological project, and, not surprisingly, the very term "phenomenology" virtually vanished in the later Heidegger's vast output of lectures and writings from the 1930s to his death in 1976.

After *Being and Time*, Heidegger moved on in his thinking to experiment with a variety of new ways of addressing and expressing the matter of Being. One hallmark of the originality and creativity of his later thinking was that he named Being in a multitude of different ways to make manifest the various features of Being-as-time as the unitary and unifying temporal emerging and unfolding process or "way" (what I refer to as "the Being-way") whereby and wherein all beings come to be. Thus, he looked back to the earliest Greek thinkers Parmenides, Heraclitus, and Anaximander to retrieve what he understood to be the earliest "names" for Being: *physis, aletheia,* the primordial *Logos, hen* (the One), *zoe, kosmos, apeiron*. Or he crafted his own terms of art to name Being: "the clearing" (*die Lichtung*), *Ereignis, Es gibt*—and "the holy" (*das Heilige*).[1] Regarding the holy, he stated in *Letter on Humanism* (1947): "Only from the truth of Being can the essence of the holy be thought" (GA 9: 351).

The authors of the essays in this volume document the multiple texts and contexts of Heidegger's discussions of the holy, and they offer detailed readings and their own particular interpretations and applications. The essays, taken together, make a significant contribution not only to the Heidegger scholarship but also to our understanding of our essential human situation in relation to Being-as-the holy. For my part, I wish to make a few overarching observations regarding his motif of the holy.

It is evident that a "religious" or "spiritual" sensibility suffused the later Heidegger's thinking of Being. Too often, this salient feature of his later thought is overlooked or set aside, especially in recent times. There are no doubt several reasons for this, but we may leave such an inquiry for another time. What is more important is to attend to Heidegger's own experience of Being and, more specifically, of Being-as-the holy.

Consider, for example, his evocation of "the holy" in his 1943 elucidation of Hölderlin's poem "Homecoming" ("*Heimkunft*" in GA 4: 9-31). Just a few citations are needed. Heidegger invokes that which "grants" and "hails" the human being with a multitude of names inspired by Hölderlin's poem: "the holy"—but also "the gladsome," "the highest," "the most joyful," "the joyful one," "the most serene," "home," "homeland," and "the source" (*der Ursprung*). The names are manifold, but, as Heidegger tells us, "the holy" is the unitary and unifying "source" of human beings and of all things. This "joyful one" is "the gladsome," which "illuminates the hearts of human beings, so that they may open their hearts to what is genuine and noble in their fields, their towns, and their homes" (GA 4: 19).

"The holy" as "the joyful one" reaches human beings especially through the poet's words, but the poet's words can never exhaust the holy as "the source." The best that we human beings can do is draw near to the source and dwell in nearness to the source ("homecoming"), but we can never penetrate the ultimate mystery of the source: "we must preserve the mystery as mystery" (GA 4: 24). What is more, according to Heidegger, "the source" keeps itself in "reserve" no matter how it springs forth into beings and no matter how we address it and name it. The source keeps to itself and remains itself even as it flows forth out of itself, and this mystery, he admits, confounds "the principle of contradiction" (GA 4: 24; also GA 4: 146).

We may delve further into the details of the text, yet the key point is this: The religious and spiritual resonance of Heidegger's language is unmistakable. His language of "the holy" as "the source" and "the gladsome" that pours forth "light" and abiding "joy" for humans and for all beings is a religious and spiritual language—which certainly has metaphysical and theological implications.

Of course, here is where the matter gets tricky. It is true that Heidegger himself made no such explicit commitments and simply allowed his language to resonate freely. And we know, too, that he insisted that Being is not "a being" and therefore not to be construed in terms of a metaphysics or theology of *substance or subject.* Being-as-the holy is not the highest god or the highest being, if this is understood as the highest substance or subject.

Yet we must be careful. These considerations do not close the door on *all* metaphysical and theological speculation because metaphysics and theology, *even historically,* are not limited to considerations of substance, essence, subject. For example, Neoplatonic thinkers over many centuries made the metaphysical claim that the One is *beyond* (*epekeina*) such categories as substance; the One (that is not One) is the utterly unnameable "source" of all that is. Their thinking—and not theirs alone—certainly cannot be facilely criticized or dismissed as "onto-theological."[2]

Thus, we must acknowledge that the later Heidegger's language of Being (and of Being-as-the holy) calls forth the religious and spiritual, and we are left to consider the implications of his manifold expressions. To be sure, he was a harsh critic of a certain kind of metaphysics and theology, but it is also the case that his later thinking of Being leaned in the direction of a renewed and revised metaphysical and religious outlook. He allowed his poetic philosophical language to suggest—again and again—precisely these possibilities for thought. Consequently, the important lesson to be learned is that by no means did Heidegger "overcome" metaphysics as such. In other words, genuine thinking, by whatever name, is inevitably led to consider, in one way or another, all things and ultimate matters.

As thoughtful readers, we should be mindful of Heidegger's distinctive approach and style, but we are not obliged to follow his very same path. We are free to think along with Heidegger—but also beyond Heidegger. We are free to give form and shape to whatever creative metaphysical, spiritual, and religious speculations are suggested by his own resonant language of Being. This volume of essays is a superb guide to Heidegger's theme of "the holy," but it is also intended to help us pose the most fundamental questions that we human beings can ask, and to pursue answers to such questions for ourselves. This is the ongoing task for thinking that does not end with Heidegger or with any one thinker.[3]

*****

And, finally, may the reader of this collection of essays on "the holy" pause along the way and give careful consideration to some of Heidegger's many declarations such as:

The original essence of joy is becoming at home in nearness to the Source. (GA 4: 25)

This is not merely an elucidation of Hölderlin's poem. Is this not, after all, Heidegger's own profession in the form of commentary? Is this not, after all, his own testimony to the joyful secret at the heart of things? After all, is this not his own testimony to the truth and promise of the ultimate and unfathomable mystery of the Source?

NOTES

1. For further discussion of the development of Heidegger's thinking and of the other themes and terms mentioned here, see my books *Engaging Heidegger* (2010), *Heidegger's Way of Being* (2014), and *Heidegger's Being: The Shimmering Unfolding* (2022), all from the University of Toronto Press. See also William J. Richardson, *Heidegger: Through Phenomenology to Thought* (The Hague: Martinus Nijhoff, 1963/1974), and for "Being as the Holy," see especially, 426-27.

2. For more on this point and for considerations on Heidegger's relation to the Hermetic traditions of thinking, see my *Heidegger's Being: The Shimmering Unfolding* (cited above).

3. For more on Heidegger's critique of a metaphysics and theology of substance and for suggestions on the parallels between Heidegger's later thinking of Being and Alfred North Whitehead's "process" metaphysics, see my *Heidegger's Being: The Shimmering Unfolding* (cited above).

Chapter 1

The Holy in Heidegger

The Open Clearing as Excess and Abyss

John W.M. Krummel

In the last century and a half, many have lamented the loss of a sense of the holy (or the sacred)—*das Heilige* in German—that is, the condition of modernity that Friedrich Nietzsche called the "death of God" or what Friedrich Hölderlin poetized as the "flight of the gods." Martin Heidegger, even while speaking of the forgetting of Being (*Seinsvergessenheit*) in the history of Being, and even as he had discoursed on the nihilism of modernity, appropriated this term, *das Heilige*, as one of his many terms for Being (*Sein*) as distinct from, and yet granting, beings (*Seiende*). In what sense, then, is the holy for Heidegger tied to its apparent opposite in the modern world—the sense of desacralization or nihilism in modernity—while also being the Being of beings? And how are we to (co-)respond to the holy in an unholy (desacralized) world? In the following, I will attempt to unpack this paradox. Keys to solving this question may be found in the ancient Greek concepts of *chaos* and *chora* to which Heidegger's understanding of the holy is connected. Heidegger's own concepts of *Lichtung* (clearing) and *Gegend* (that-which-regions, regioning) can also be related to his view of the holy.

When thinking of the holy in phenomenology, some may be reminded of Rudolf Otto's famous analysis of the phenomenon (which Otto also called "the numinous") in his 1917 work *Das Heilige* (*The Idea of the Holy*).[1] Heidegger was asked by Edmund Husserl to review Otto's book soon after it had been published. Heidegger was unable to complete the review but allegedly regarded Otto's book as a major contribution to the emerging field of phenomenology of religion.[2] But following the publication of Otto's book, in his preparatory notes for writing the review, Heidegger criticizes Otto's phenomenology as a failure due to its confinement to a modern subjectivistic framework that takes consciousness as predetermining phenomena, and in the face of the overwhelming numinous, cowering in fear. At the same time,

Heidegger found Otto's book to ignore the historical genesis that gives rise to the experience of the holy. In the following years, in his lectures from 1920–1921, *Phänomenologie des religiösen Lebens* (*Phenomenology of Religious Life*), he goes on to emphasize the historical as the core phenomenon of religion instead.[3] Nevertheless in his post-1930 works, Heidegger develops his understanding of this concept of "the holy" (*das Heilige*), further, as another name for Being, but which in some aspects also is reminiscent of Otto's understanding. In some ways, it is a development of Otto's concept but also an improvement upon it in an ontological direction that subtracts the subjectivist Kantian trappings to give greater voice to its alterity and excess that overwhelms humanity and its environing aspect that clears room for our dwelling. In the following, I will focus on Heidegger's works after 1930 where he connects Being qua the holy with the clearing makes gives room for the world while exceeding it.

I. THE UNHOLY WORLD OF MODERNITY

Heidegger's discussions of the holy in his works after 1930 first appear in the context of his Being-historical thinking (*seinsgeschichtliches Denken*) concerning the destining or sending (*Geschick*) of Being. In the 1930s, most notably in his *Beiträge zur Philosophie* (*Contributions to Philosophy*), Heidegger speaks of "the holy" in association with "the passing of the last god" that marks an empty clearing or spacing whence all metaphysical absolutes or gods have withdrawn—an exhaustion of absolutes that characterizes the modern condition. This is what Nietzsche had called "the death of God" and Hölderlin poetized as "the flight of the gods" (*die Flucht der Götter*).[4] Nietzsche had proclaimed the "death of God" in his *Die Fröhliche Wissenschaft* (*Gay Science*) (§§ 125, 343)[5] to announce the advent of European nihilism, meaning that the normative values predicated upon belief in a higher transcendent world, having revealed their all-too-human origins, are no longer tenable and without valence. Thus discredited, "the belief in the Christian God has become unworthy of belief" (§343).[6] In the same century, the poet Hölderlin spoke of the "flight of the gods" in a similar vein. As is well known, Heidegger was very much interested in both thinkers. Certainly with the global pervasion of capitalism and scientism and technicity, we find ourselves today in a de-sacralized or unholy (*heillos*) world where quantification prevails, reducing reality to calculation and consumption. But for Heidegger, the resulting unholiness is ultimately not due to man's lack of belief or that we had somehow "killed God," but to Being itself in its unfolding of the constellations of concealment/unconcealment. And yet that does not mean that we are exempt from responsibility.

The question is how are we to respond to this unfolding of Being in its withdrawal of the divine? The withdrawal of absolute principles at modernity's end, dislodging us from the familiar but no longer viable—the fleeing of the gods—invites us to think-through the conditions of their possibility, the empty clearing that has been made manifest. Thus, while Nietzsche proposed to replace that dead god, God crucified that for him symbolizes life-negating values, with a dancing god, Dionysius, representing the very earth whereupon we dwell, Heidegger, on the other hand, looks to Hölderlin's sense of the holy as an open clearing that encompasses the gods who flee but also give room for the potential reappearance of gods. Precisely in that negativity of the renouncing of the old gods is to be found "godliness" (*Göttlichkeit*).[7] And yet that negativity—the open clearing that withdraws to make room—might also be connected to the Heideggerian sense of the earth in its relation to the world.

II. THE CLEARING AS UN/GROUND

What then is the clearing or the open? One sense of the open clearing for Heidegger is that wherein, or whereby, beings are given, hinting at the *Es* ("it") of *es gibt*... ("there is... (x)" or literally "it gives... (x)"). Heidegger designates this openness of the Being of beings, their unconcealing out of concealment, as "the holy" in Hölderlin's sense to convey the sense that it is an irreducible and overwhelming excess—the excess of Being over, and its irreducibility to—beings (entities), by always retaining a concealment accompanying the unconcealed, a chaos (χάος) in Hesiod's sense of a chasm that engulfs the ordering (*kosmos*) or world of beings.

In *Einführung in die Metaphysik* (*Introduction to Metaphysics*) of 1935, Heidegger asks whether Being as ground is the absence of ground or unground, an abyss (*Ab-grund*).[8] As "Being remains untraceable," it "is almost like the nothing [*das Nichts*], or in the end completely like it."[9] In *Contributions* of the same period, he writes that that unground is the clearing for beings. In this denial of ground, "originary emptiness [*ursprüngliche Leere*] opens up, and the originary clearing [*ursprüngliche Lichtung*] occurs ... the first clearing of the open [*Lichtung des Offenen*] as the 'empty' [*Leere*]" (§242),[10] wherein beings—man, gods, earth, world—all emerge in mutual strife, be-fitted, en-owned into their own (*er-eignet*) and to each other, gathered in mutual differentiation. This abyss that clears space is also the *not* of Beyng (*Seyn*) that gives, allows for, releases, beings into their own as what they are.[11] It is this abyssal element, the excess of Being as such, that the dominant metaphysics of modernity and global technology had concealed in their focus on rationality, utility, and objectification. In this the holy as such had been forgotten even prior to the disestablishment of supersensory absolutes of previous epochs, including the God of metaphysics and onto-theology under modernity's technological enframing (*Gestell*). In modernity, Beings have become objectified as nothing but "standing-reserve" or "stock" (*Bestand*) for representation and manipulation, decided in advance, while what stands to be questioned, their Being, becomes obscured. And yet, engulfing that desacralizing famework of the unholy (*heillos*) world is the clearing in its abyssal depths, a groundless ground or un/ground (*Ab-grund*). As ontologically irreducible, Heidegger describes the emptiness of this clearing as an all-pervading *not* (*Nichthfafte*). Yet this emptiness is also what permits the fullness of Being as that wherein everything, including our own being-(t)here (*Dasein*) stands.

Earlier in his *Kant und das Problem der Metaphysik* (*Kant and the Problem of Metaphysics*) of 1929 Heidegger spoke of the concept of *mana* (*Mana-Vorstellung*) as characterizing the Being of the mythical "world" and of the mythical "being-(t)here" (*Dasein*), the "how" of Being whereby the actual (*das Wirkliche*) assaults (*überfällt*) our human being-(t)here.[12] Its understanding of Being as *mana*[13]—"the basic feeling of the holy" (*Das "Grundgefühl des Heiligen"*)[14]—is "lived out" in the practices of the mythical being-(t)here, "a particular configuration of 'being-in-the-world,' pre-reflectively inhabiting a tacit understanding of meaning . . . expressed in thought and practice."[15] Here in 1929, Heidegger understands Being qua holy in terms of *mana* that is "overpowering" and deeper than the specific "worlds" constitutive of any particular religious tradition as a mode of being-in-the-world. This understanding of *mana* seems to approach Otto's position concerning the holy from his 1917 *Das Heilige*.[16] But also as a background opening to a particular world, including the framework of religions, as well as the desacralized modern world, and constitutive of man's being-in-the-world, it connects to this later sense of the open clearing, which is how Heidegger comes to explicitly understand the holy when he turns to Hölderlin's poetry in response to the crisis of late modernity. In his 1943 reading of Hölderlin's poem, *"Heimkunft/An die Verwandten"* ("The Homecoming/To Kindred Ones"), Heidegger takes the holy to signify the background for the horizon of meaning. He takes the poems' theme of "gaiety" (or "the serene," "the gladsome") (*die Heitere*) to be interchangeable with what Hölderlin also calls "the holy." For the "holy" (*Heilige*) etymologically connects to this sense of "gay" or "cheerful" (*heiter*), which in turn originally referred to the sky or "heavens above" in their awesomeness or majesty.[17]

But this also refers to the abyssal opening of Being behind the coming and going of beings. For he claims that "the joyous" (*die Heitere*) is what "first 'makes room,' that is, grants, the open to every 'space' and to every 'time-space' [*Zeitraum*]" and "it is the holy."[18] The holy as such is the background against which phenomena can meaningfully arise for man. In its awesomeness, overpowering us like *mana*, it allows things in general to show up but it can become concentrated or expressed in concrete sacred or holy objects and locales. And hence God or gods manifest on the basis of the holy. And the "death of God" and "flight of the gods," made manifest in modernity, also give voice to this engulfing abyss that is the holy. We thus need to turn to this topic of God and gods, their presence and absence, in their relation to the holy.

III. GOD/S, GODHOOD, AND THE PASSING OF THE LAST GOD

Heidegger interprets Nietzsche's diagnosis for the death of God as the end, not necessarily of God per se, but of metaphysics as such and of the supreme principle of onto-theology that attempts to provide the definitive answer to the question, "Why is there anything at all?" in terms of a grounding presence. God here is one being among others albeit the highest or supreme being. But such a god of philosophy is not awe-some. In his 1957 work, *Identität und Differenz* (*Identity and Difference*), Heidegger says that one can neither pray nor offer sacrifice to it.[19] But more importantly, it is still *a being* among others. What then does Heidegger mean by gods in the plural and how do both the monotheistic or metaphysical God and the plural polytheistic gods relate to the holy? Heidegger's understanding of the holy is inspired by Hölderlin's poetizing of the holy. While the thinker's task is to proclaim the truth of Being, Heidegger understands the poet's mission to name Being's mystery in its concealment that accompanies its giving of beings: "The thinker says Being. The poet names the holy."[20]

The poet responds to the address of Being in its mysterious self-concealing revealing of beings by putting it into words in poetry and naming it as the holy. But metaphysics can only think substantively or onto-theologically and fails to adequately conceive Being. In refusing the grasp of onto-theological categories, that is, metaphysics, Hölderlin's sense of the holy escapes modernity's desacralization (or de-holification). In 1957, Heidegger remarks that "the godless thinking which must abandon the god of philosophy, god as *causa sui*, is . . . perhaps closest to the divine god [*göttlichen Gott*]."[21] And in his 1966 *Der Spiegel* interview, after mentioning how "only a god can still save us," Heidegger adds that "the only possibility for salvation . . . is to prepare readiness, in thinking and poetry, for the appearance of god or for the absence of god during the decline, so that . . . when we decline, we decline in the face of the absent god."[22] Who or what then is the "divine god" or this "absent god"? Is it in any sense closer then to what Hölderlin calls the holy?

In his turn to Hölderlin, Heidegger treads a path that is neither theological nor purely ontological. This is exemplified by a phrase Heidegger, under Hölderlin's inspiration, repeats throughout his *Contributions to Philosophy* of the mid-1930s to mark the clearing that is made manifest by the fleeing of the gods: "the passing-by of the last god" (*der Vorbeigang des lezten Gottes; das Vorbeigehen des lezten Gottes*). What is this "last god" that passes? He proclaims that the "greatest nearness of the last god" is "self-refusal."[23] Distinct from the simple coming and going of previous gods, its passing is a self-refusal, a hinting from out of the withdrawal of Beyng (spelled as *Seyn*). A "god beyond god/s," utterly alien to human perspectives, escaping our projections and concerns, the "last god" (*der lezte Gott*) surpasses any determinate configuration of divinity: It is "wholly other [*ganz Andere*] than those that have been [*die Gewesenen*], especially over against the Christian [*den christlichen*]."[24]

Its passage instead points to the mystery of Being in its concealment that accompanies every unconcealment. In facing its silent refusal, we sense its overwhelming power. "Last" as such refers to "the highest form of denial," the originary no-thing of Beyng (*Seyn*),[25] which at the margins of modernity bring the incubation of further possibilities, a transition to an "other beginning" (*der andere Anfang*) of "immeasurable possibilities of our history" (*unermeßlicher Möglichkeiten unserer Geschichte*),[26] a hinting toward a future excess of surprise and refusal, the open-endedness or novelty of the future that cannot be predetermined. This "last god" gathers the manifold horizons of possibility— named "gods" (*Götter*) in the plural—an inner richness (*Reichtum*) of potential grounds and abysses (*Gründe und Abgründe*) to which plurality is subjected.[27] This gathering shapes, or *is*, the regional-epochal configuration or economy of concealing/unconcealing that discloses the meaning of the divine,[28] and to which both theism and atheism, as well as other -isms are relativized. Its ontological status is thus neither theistic nor atheistic[29] and it "stands outside the calculating determinations meant by terms such as 'mono-theism,' 'pan-theism,' and 'a-theism'"[30] for each such alternative assumes a metaphysic that thinks in terms of beings (entities). The last god, as thus originary, reducible neither to flight nor arrival nor both, is "the fullness of the granting of Beyng in refusal" (*die Fülle der Gewährung des Seyns in der Verweigerung*).[31] As *other* than any present being—including a god—it is *as* the abyssal "space" of Beyng itself (*dem abgründigen "Raum" des Seyns selbst*),[32] the very clearing wherein the question of god/s first arises, permitting its/their affirmation or denial—the momentary "time-space for decision concerning the flight and arrival of the gods" (*Zeit-Raum der Entscheidung über die Flucht und Ankunft der Götter*), their domain of decision (*Entscheidungsbereich*).[33]

The decisive takes its origin therein in a de-cision (*Ent-scheidung*), separating and differentiating beings, including gods and man (*Götter und*

Menschen), distinguishing each into its own while the open clearing in itself remains un-decided.[34] The "flight of the gods" that empties this space as the withdrawal of Beyng, "the highest form of withdrawal" (*die höchste Gestalt der Verweigerung*),[35] is this "stillness of the passing of the last god" (*die Stille des Vorbeigangs des lezten Gottes*).[36] Even while marking the absence of absolutes in the nihilism of modernity, it marks the clearing open wherein the wonder that asks "why?" can occur in its full power. And in that openness gods "come and go" and world-horizons are constellated for the meaning of Being (or Beyng). This "last god" that passes by, wholly other and abysally silent, then is another name for what Heidegger calls "the holy"—Being or Beyng in its excess that overwhelms but makes possible our world/s. Later after the 1930s, Heidegger no longer speaks of "the last god," but in 1945, he speaks of the "all unifying One" (*alles einigende Eine*), which is "the divine itself" (*das Göttliche selbst*)[37] and in 1963, he speaks of "the god of gods" (*der Götter Gott*) that may appear in the site of the locale that is the destiny of Hölderlin's poetry.[38] That site would be the holy.

In *Wozu Dichter?* ("What are Poets for?") and *Brief über den 'Humanismus'* ("Letter on Humanism"), both from 1946, Heidegger makes use of the threefold scheme of the gods (*die Götter*), godhood (*Gottheit*) (often translated as godhead), and the holy (*das Heilige*). Gods are understood only in light of the dimension of godhood. In the plural "gods" mark the horizonal delimitations of possibilities from the past and for the future, and the holy is the very expanse, wherein any god can appear or any claim to the absolute be made, the environing abyss wherein such horizons are constructed or deconstructed. Heidegger, as is known was fond of Meister Eckhart, and for Eckhart, godhood (*gottheit*) is the "region of the unspeakable," where God is none of the Persons of the Trinity—neither Father nor Son nor Holy Spirit—and is no longer "objectified" in opposition to the knower nor the Creator opposed to creation.[39]

It is the "naked formless essence [*das blose formlese wesen*] of divine unity, 'without name' (*namloz*), the potentiality of nothingness from out of which creation occurs."[40] But Heidegger here views godhood as essencing within the domain of the holy,[41] the "essential space of godhood" (*Wesensraum der Gottheit*) that, in turn, is the "dimension for gods and god" (*Dimension für die Götter und den Gott*),[42] the openness that calls forth mortals and divinities. In his 1951 essay, *Bauen Wohnen Denken* ("Building Dwelling Thinking"), Heidegger writes, "The divinities [*die Göttlichen*] are the hinting messengers of godhood [*die winkenden Boten der Gottheit*]. Out of the holy sway [*heiligen Walten*] of godhood, the god [*der Gott*] appears in his presence or withdraws into his concealment."[43] God appears only on the basis of godhood but only from the essence of the holy as such is "the essence of godhood to be thought."[44] But in turn to think the holy as such we need to think the "truth of Being,"[45] that is the open clearing making room for beings. As such the holy is connected to Heidegger's earlier notion of being-in-the-world and is what constitutes the background for the horizon allowing reality, including the ordinary or mundane—the profane in Mircea Eliade's dichotomous terms of the sacred and the profane—to show up. Only in the background of Being in its awesome otherness as the mysterious holy—a background that is an un/ground—can beings, including the gods, show up. The human encounter with divinities first becomes possible on the basis of the holy as what makes the constitution of their meaningfulness possible from an ontologically deeper layer.

The holy itself as the Being of beings enfolds and unfolds beings, mortals, and gods. In relation to mortals, divinities, and the order shaping the world on the basis of assumed rationalities and principles, the holy is an omni-presencing *chaos*, which Heidegger understood in its etymological ancient Greek sense, and with Hesiod in mind, as the initial gaping and abyssal chasm that swallows up everything while granting each its delimited presence in time and space.[46] Nothing real precedes it, everything emerges out of it. For Hesiod in his *Theogony*, *chaos* is the mother of the gods, simultaneously engulfing and giving birth to the world. Heidegger understands *chaos* as such, the holy, as providing the space both for our dwelling as mortals and for what we look up to as the divine.[47] In its overwhelming omnipresencing, gushing forth and exceeding the orders we attempt to establish, it overwhelms us and invokes awe (*Scheu*). Following Hesiod, Hölderlin himself in *Wie wenn am Feiertage* ("As on a holiday") referred to the "holy chaos" (*heiligem Chaos*), "from high aether down to the low abyss. . . . the recurring all-creative [*die Allerschaffende wieder*]."[48]

The mystery (*Geheimnis*) of the holy with its uncanniness, in the exhaustion of absolutes, is nevertheless our "home," where "the world's night is . . . the holy night [*heilige Nacht*]."[49] It displaces but summons us, overriding and exceeding our self-resolution or will. It frees us from our entanglements with the self-evident or familiar. Its alterity addresses us as it withdraws into silence, escaping our comprehension, even as it gives beings for our understanding and appropriation, while remaining in excess to our projections. Only on its basis can we project our projects and construct the world. But with its refusal of ground, forcing us to face its irreducible excess—the unsettling call (*Zuruf*) of "the last god" in its "passing-by"—we are freed into the open to wonder and question. This is the holy as the clearing of concealment/unconcealment, from whence the world arises, beings are given, gods come and go, and history commences. What the thinker thinks of as "Being," even as it withdraws from conceptualization, the poet—responding to it in wonder as it opens the very question of Being, the truth of Beyng—names "the holy."

IV. CHAOS, CHORA, AND REGIONING

If the holy is the space of godhood and realm wherein gods come and go, it is also that wherein mortals build their places of dwelling, the holy chaos encompassing worldly order. In Hesiod, as mentioned above, *chaos* is the pre-cosmic chasm or abyss that in its undifferentiatedness initiates cosmogony through differentiation. If the omni-presencing chaos in Hesiod is the holy, we can also link the holy to the Greek sense of *chora* (χώρα) that was etymologically related to *chaos*[50] and which Heidegger develops in terms of *region* or *that-which-regions* (*Gegend*). Suggestions have been made[51] that Hesiod's *chaos* was the source of Anaximander's idea of the *apeirōn* (the boundless), and in turn many[52] have noted the similarity of the latter to Plato's notion of *chora* in the *Timaeus*, the undifferentiated realm from out of which the world (*kosmos*) is to be formed. In Plato's *Timaeus*,[53] *chora* is the formless (*amorphon*) matrix (*ekmageion*) for all things (50b-51a), itself devoid of characters (50e, 51b). In its in-definition, *chora* provides the abode or situation (*hedra*) for *genesis*—the defining, differentiation, or formation of things (50b-c, 52b). In Plato's *Philebus*, this same idea is in fact called the *apeiron*, requiring *peras* (limit). The Greek *chaos* that gives birth to the world is also intertwined with the concept of *peras* as the difference or distinction necessary for plurality. Heidegger understood *peras* to mean "that from which something begins its essential unfolding."[54] *Peras* permits the differentiation that allows beings to unfold into what they are. This unfolding of beings out of concealment is truth as *a-letheia* and their emergence is nature as *physis* (φύσις). In the case of Hesiod's *chaos*, that differentiation of the cosmos—the emergence of the earth and from it the world—occurs within and from out of it.

In the dualistic scheme of Plato's *Timaeus*, however, that limitation is provided by the *demiourgos* imposing *ideas* (forms) upon it from "above" (whether taken as transcendent or as transcendental). Nevertheless as *chora*, in its formlessness and constant flux, resists the imposition of limits and determination, its depth (*bathos*), like *chaos*, seems bottomless and could be construed, contra-Plato, as a bottomless source of creation. On the one hand, Plato's dichotomization of the real into the absolute and the relative relegates *chora* to a subordinate position of subjection. But, on the other hand, at the same time, its very recklessness and amorphousnesss—as *amorphon* (50b-51a)—threatens to dismantle the demiourgos' designs—the metaphysical hierarchy that Plato seeks to install—even while providing a place for the formation of the *kosmos*. Its abyss or uncanniness is concealed even while permeating the world. As *anomos* or *apolis*, it is a deconstructive undertow beneath our *polis* and its *nomoi*. *Chora* as such also appeared in other ancient Greek texts as an initial emptiness or "a large and dark space existing prior to the emergence of things."⁵⁵ As the bosom of *genesis*, *chora* is the yawning wherein the *kosmos* arises, but that yawning is *chaos*, the depth (*bathos*) of which, like the boundless *apeiron*, may be bottomless, an abyss. *Chora*'s relationship to *kosmos* morphs in Heidegger's works of the 1930s into the earth in its dynamic pairing with the world.⁵⁶ Earth grounds the world, giving it room, while escaping or exceeding its horizons.

Heidegger articulates this idea in his 1935 lecture, *Der Ursprung des Kunswerkes* ("The Origin of the Work of Art") in terms of the primal strife (*Urstreit*) between the earth (*die Erde*) and the world (*die Welt*).⁵⁷ While supporting the world, the earth refuses itself, beyond the horizon constitutive of human meaning. While the world cannot subsist without the earth's support, the earth in exceeding the world will not guarantee its subsistence. The world's ground is abyssal, an un/ground, the concealment behind the unconcealed. For Heidegger that abyss is Being's withdrawal, and in a parenthetical remark to his *Introduction to Metaphysics* of the 1930s that he inserted in the 1950s, he reads Plato's *chora* to be that which withdraws to make room for the presencing of things.⁵⁸ Therein he also refers to human creativity that constructs a historical world—through the strife of "creators, poets, thinkers, and statesmen"—and its abode as where the sway of *physis* is made to stand.⁵⁹ Thus *chora*, related to *chaos*, connects with *physis*.

Chora's connection to earth and nature that grounds or surrounds man's dwelling was more explicit centuries before the exegetical history of Plato's text when the ancient Greeks understood *chora* in its pre-philosophical significance as the environing region or milieu inclusive of the land or country surrounding one's city or town, the concrete region providing one's habitat. On this basis contemporary French geographer and philosopher Augustin Berque, appropriating Heidegger's term, understands *chora* to designate the open shaping our concrete dwelling space upon the earth, as the environing field of human–nature interrelationships constituting and surrounding the *polis*, on the basis of which a thing is what it is—the process of which he also calls *choresis*.⁶⁰ This field, in the midst of which we dwell, nevertheless extends into nature, exceeding our grasp and all-too-human will, threatening the *polis* with its wilderness or wildness—an irreducible alterity. But under the inspiration of Hölderlin that excess was what Heidegger also called the holy.

Berque refers to Heidegger and was undoubtedly influenced by Heidegger's concept of the region (*Gegend*, *Gegnet*). "Region" was also a development of Heidegger's earlier world–earth dynamic from the 1930s. In the 1940s and 1950s, he expands the notion of the earth in its dynamic pairing with the world in this conception of "region"—"regioning" (*Gegend*) or "that-which-regions" (*die Gegnet*)—while also associating it with *chora* and *chaos*.⁶¹ The region is that which environs us while withdrawing to clear space for our dwelling, gathering, and holding together a plurality of places (*topoi, Orte*). In his summer 1944 lecture on Heraclitus, *Logik. Heraklits Lehre vom Logos* ("Logic: Heraclitus' Teaching of the *Logos*"), Heidegger renders its sense as that which "surrounds" or a "surrounding giving" or "surrounding region" (*Umgebung, umgebende Umgegend*) that makes room for the presencing of things through its absencing or withdrawing.[62]

And shortly after, in 1944–1945, Heidegger further develops the idea of region in *Zur Erörterung der Gelassenheit* ("Toward a Discussion of Releasement"), where he takes *Gegnet* in its "surrounding" aspect as the open, the free expanse (*Weite*), or lingering expanse (*verweilende Weite*), an "open that surrounds us" (*das uns umgebende Offene*) while withdrawing to make-room, wherein beings may "while" or "linger" (*verweilen*) as they come and go, presence and absence.[63] Here he takes what Husserlian phenomenology calls "horizon" (*Horizont*), with its subjectivistic connotation, as but the interior aspect (*Aussehen*) turned toward us of the region in its regioning,[64] extending beyond it from its *other* side, implying alterity and excess. Like *chora* that surrounds the *polis* for the ancient Greeks and the earth that grounds the world, region surrounds and grounds the place of our dwelling, but without guarantee, escaping our grasp. Then in the 1950s, for example in *Das Ding* ("The Thing") and *Bauen Wohnen Denken* ("Building Dwelling Thinking"), Heidegger refers to the four cardinal "regions" (*Gegenden*) of "the fourfold" (*das Geviert*), involving mortals and divinities, heaven and earth, gathered to constitute between them a primal spatiality for human dwelling.

In the 1953 parenthetical remark to his 1935 *Introduction to Metaphysics*, mentioned above, after having thus developed the notion of region, Heidegger once again refers to *chora* as that which withdraws to make-room for the presencing of things, "the self-separating from every particular, the withdrawing, which in such a way admits and 'makes place' [*Platz macht*] precisely for another."[65] His further 1950s discussions of "making-room" (*einraumen*) for a locality (*Ortschaft*) of places (*Orte*) in his *Das Wesen der Sprache* ("The Essence of Language")[66]—a clearing-away of the wilderness that brings forth an open space for dwelling—continues this same idea of the formless and indefinite *wild*-erness or *chaos*, as a regioning, allowing for forms and definitions, to found an inhabited space.[67] The withdrawing that clears room for dwelling, or the concealing that unconceals beings, is the yawning that ungrounds and yet allows grounding within its abyssal space. This un/ground that embraces while withdrawing in its excess—the awesome—is precisely what Heidegger means by the holy.

By why is that yawning open the holy? As *other* (*heteron*) than what any being is, the excess to what we can grasp, it evokes awe (*Scheu*). It is overwhelming and awe-some. Yet as the death of God or the fleeing of the gods makes explicit, the holy is not transcendent up there but down here in our midst, surrounding us, the region environing us, the abyssal chaos engulfing the world and creation.

V. DWELLING AND NATURE

The holy therefore makes possible our dwelling on earth. For Heidegger, what poets poetize in terms of the holy is that open clearing as the place of human dwelling, together with the things belonging there and the bonds between people, things, and landscape. Any genuine experience of the holy is to be accompanied by man's cultivation of that place (*Ort*) of dwelling. In a 1969 seminar, Heidegger reflects upon his own path of thinking as having traversed three stages: (1) The question of the meaning of Being as formulated in *Sein und Zeit* (*Being and Time*); (2) The question of the truth of Being initiated in the 1930s; and finally, (3) The question of the place or locality (*Ortschaft, Örtlichkeit*) of Being, or the topology of Beyng (*Topologie des Seyns*).[68] That place sinks into an abyss (*Abgrund*) while sustaining our dwelling and the presencing/absencing of things. In that abyssal excess that overwhelms our comprehension, it is the holy.

The place of dwelling is a major theme for Heidegger in the 1950s. In both "The Thing" and "Building Dwelling Thinking," Heidegger discusses how dwelling is possible only on the basis of the four regions (*Gegenden*) gathered to constitute a place of dwelling, grounding our world—"the fourfold" (*Geviert*), we mentioned above, as the originary but dynamic unity in mirror-play of earth and sky, divinities and mortals. Within this fourfold in their oneness, the earth surfaces and the skies open, mortals dwell on the earth and under the sky, look up to the gods, appearing out of its holy sway, await for their intimations, and heed the beckoning of the holy.[69] Through this gathering for the fourfold and their concentration in concrete things or sites, such as a temple or a bridge, a world is installed for human dwelling amidst the surroundings. Thus in "The Essence of Language," for example, Heidegger speaks of how space "makes-room [*einräumt*] for a locality or district [*Ortschaft*] and places [*Orte*], releasing them."[70] Later in 1969, in *Die Kunst und der Raum* ("Art and Space"), he speaks of the movement that "releases [*ist Freigabe*] places [*Orte*]" and "brings forth a locality [*Ortschaft*] preparing for dwelling."[71] The founding of an inhabited space, a *topos* as a gathering predicated upon an entire network of relations given room, takes place on the basis of the free expanse (*die freie Weite*) of "that which regions" (*die Gegnet*).[72] The elements gathered configure a settlement but by assuming what lies beyond the horizon, the overwhelming excess—the holy. The holy as this ontological opening wherein and whereby we receive the gift of Being and beings, in which we are both partakers and receptors, provides the space for our dwelling as mortals—a temporal configuration in the co-respondence between ontological excess and the finite responsiveness of man.

The place of our dwelling, cleared by the regioning and grounded upon the earth, is also amidst nature that Heidegger understood in terms of *physis*. The holiness of a land, as part of nature as *physis,* is what inspires awe. We dwell in the midst of this manifesting of nature that the ancient Greeks experienced as *physis*. Heidegger states in his *Introduction to Metaphysics* of 1935 that *physis* occurs everywhere, in the rising of the sun, the waves of the ocean, the growth of plants, the birth of animals and humans from the womb, and so on.[73] In his 1943–1944 Heraclitus lectures as well, everything emerges into the open from out of *physis* that exceeds—is "beyond" (*über*)—them.[74] In "As on a Holiday" of 1941, Heidegger connects the holy with Hölderlin's conception of "nature" as "the chaos," as the clearing wherein all beings can be present.[75] Nature is the holy for Hölderlin because she is "older" than all, even the gods.[76] Nature as the holy is thus "the originary" or "first" (*Anfängliche*), which "remains in itself unbroken and 'whole' [*heil*]. The originary 'wholeness' [*ursprünglich 'Heile'*] . . . through its omnipresence, confers to everything actual the grace [*das Heil*] of its own whiling [*Verweilung*]."[77] But nature as *physis* is thus the very unceasing and emergence, lingering, and passing into and out of Being, whereby all things come-to-presence in the dynamic of concealing/unconcealing. When nature is thus allowed to be itself, it is "divine" (*göttlich*).[78]

VI. AWE, WONDER, *ETHOS*

Authentic dwelling within the fourfold, upon the earth, amidst nature, in its regioning, thus in the face of the holy then calls for a certain *ethos*. The primal abyss is withdrawn from human grasp and yet gracious in the provision of our being-(t)here (*Dasein*) and living space and world of beings we can make sense of. But we need to remember our finitude as human vis-à-vis that graciousness that we are called to respect in the depths of our own being. The passing of the last god that moves within this gracious abyss calls our being-(t)here not to ground but to let-go of grounds vis-à-vis its awesomeness as the holy, its ontological excess that is extra-human in origin.

Kyoto School philosopher Ueda Shizuteru, who was also a reader of Heidegger, remarked that thought, in response to the call of the nothing that constitutes the very horizon of Being and thinking, would have to proceed not through any kind of ontology or attempt to ground metaphysics or return to its ground, but instead by listening to the words of poetry.[79] He has in mind here Heidegger's turning to Hölderlin's poetizing of Being in terms of the holy. For the holy, in invoking in us awe, is the domain of poetizing wonder—*thaumazein*—as the common source of both religious and philosophical experience. For Heidegger in the 1940s, the appropriate response to Being qua the holy seems to be joy. As noted above, in his 1943 reading of Hölderlin's poem, "The Homecoming/To Kindred Ones," Heidegger takes the poem's theme of *die Heitere* (the "gay," "cheerful," "serene," "gladsome," or "joyful") to be etymologically connected to *das Heilige*.[80] If Being unfolds in *Being and Time* through the mood of *Angst* in the face of death, for the later Heidegger in the 1940s, it is through joy in the face of the holy. In the face of the holy, our joy is really an amazement or wonder at the mystery of Being. So, as stated above, despite his earlier critique of Otto's phenomenology of religious experience for being limited by a Cartesian understanding of consciousness in its relation to the irrational numinous,[81] Heidegger's later understanding of the holy as an ontological excess that overwhelms us and invokes in us awe, is rather reminiscent of Otto's analysis but minus the Kantian limitations. Specific modes of being-in-the-world, including religion, are each made possible by our dwelling within this tacit relation to Being as the overwhelming source of being and meaning—poetized as the holy—and invoking, no longer anxiety as in the Heidegger of *Being and Time* but a joyful awe or wonder.

Awe and wonder also calls for a kind of respect and care for this abyssal opening wherein and whereby we dwell that is the holy as such, overwhelming us in its excess. Heidegger did not provide us with an explicit theory of ethics, but his notion of Being qua holy seems to imply a certain *ethos* or way of being on the part of human beings. The earth upon which a place for our dwelling has been cleared nevertheless suffers for our occupancy and hubris, a planetary disease that James Lovelock in his Gaia hypothesis calls a *disseminated primatemia*, a plague of people in their superabundance.[82]

In 1600, the population of *Homo sapiens* was approximately half a billion. In the 1990s, it increased by another half billion. Today in 2020, it is 7.8 billion. It is predicted to grow to 9.9 (almost 10) billion by 2050.[83] John Gray claims that little will remain on Earth but us human beings and our prosthetic environment.[84] Human beings have ravaged the planet with arrogance, ruining the habitat of countless species and leading many to extinction. Gray argues that the Earth can recover only when it is done with human beings and human civilization is forgotten.[85] Nature, *physis*, can and will go on without man. As the biosphere is older and stronger than the human species, Gray asserts that instead of man killing off life on this planet, it is more likely for man to wreck the environment sustaining human life so that large segments of humankind will end facing less hospitable climates to be trampled and tossed aside like straw dogs. The population will be reduced to pre-plague levels and sooner or later human beings will go extinct and Earth will forget the human species and "the play of life will go on."[86] The imposition of our will has led to the mechanization of life on Earth, covering it with human artifice—another aspect of the modern "the flight of the gods." But the human world is still surrounded by the natural milieu, supported by what Heidegger called "earth" in the 1930s.

Nature as such resists the (human) world's incursions but the world cannot be without it. As stated above, the earth grounds the world without guaranteeing that ground. The earth grounds the world while escaping its horizons as also articulated in Heidegger's notion of the regioning. If the heavenly God has died—revealed for Nietzsche as an all-too-human projection—and nihilism is what ensues in its death, leaving us with nothing but the earthly, but which we, nevertheless, have ravished, raped, and desacralized in our drive to produce and consume, ought we not to assume responsibility as shepherds to re-sacralize or re-holify our home, that which has provided us with our being-(t)here, to "lead . . . the flown-away virtue back to the earth . . . that it may give the earth its sense"?[87] Heidegger's prescription in the face of the alterity of nature was not to conquer it but to let-be, to let the holiness of *physis* be. An example may be the Standing Rock Sioux tribe of the Lakota people who acted (until the pipeline was ordered to shut down in July 2020) not only to prevent the water contamination that could come from the pipeline being constructed to pass through Lake Oahe in North Dakota but also to protect the holiness of the tribe's burial site through which the pipeline was set to run.[88] In Iceland, a conservation act was introduced in 1990 with a clause protecting sites traditionally deemed to have supernatural significance, such as jagged rocks of lava fields in the country taken to be the dwelling places of *huldufólk* or "little people" (elves). One must clear these laws, if one wants to build a road, house, or dam in these areas. As one Icelandic landscape architect put it, "the elves stand for living in harmony with nature."[89] These cases may serve as examples for what a Heideggerian ethics of awe vis-à-vis the holy might look like.

As Richard Capobianco points out, in *Zu den Inseln der Ägäis* ("On the Islands of the Aegean") of 1967, Heidegger prescribes a return to the ancient Greek experience of the "originary meaning of nature as *physis*" (*anfänglichen Sinn der Natur als φύσις*) as the "emerging-and-letting-come-to-presence of the presencing" (*Aufgehen- und Anwesenlassen des Anwesenden*).[90] And in his *Le Thor* seminar of 1969, he tells us how unencumbered by subjective mediation, the ancient Greeks experienced and dwelled in the midst of nature as the emerging of all things in its "overabundance, the excess of what presences" (*die Überfülle, das Übermaß des Anwesenden*) evoking the human response of astonishment (*thaumazein*) before the overflow or excess of presence (*das Übermaß der Anwesenheit*).[91] Overwhelmed by nature, one is forced out of the comfort zone of subjective projections and is unsettled (*unheimlich*), standing-out before the holy. Faced with overwhelming overflow, we are called to regard the earth that clears our dwelling space but also in the sublimity of its force always greater than man—a force repeatedly exemplified, among other things, in the 2011 Fukushima disaster as well as the devastating hurricanes that periodically attack the Caribbean and Atlantic coasts of North America—as holy. The reticence of nature in its withdrawing silence calls for us to cor-respond likewise in reticence with humble respect and awe, mindful of Being in its alterity and sublimity as the holy. The holy—after the death of God—is no longer simply "up there" in a transcendent world but rather revealed to be also down here as the concrete un/ground of our world. Ought we not then to respond mindfully with responsibility for the earth, nature, environing us?

CONCLUSION

Heidegger's "last god" refers neither to the god of the Christians nor of the philosophers but to the holy of the poet as this domain of poetizing wonder—*thaumazein*—which is the common origin of both religious and philosophical experience, a pre-Christian poetic dimension more originary than the God of theology. It marks the clearing space that permits both presence and absence of the divine, both theistic and atheistic interpretations, the space wherein the very question of God and subsequent conceptualizations are possible. For even in the disenchantment of modern times, Being as this bottomless clearing for the concealing/unconcealing of beings holds a mystery reawakening our sense of awe that beholds the holy.

Richard Capobianco has suggested that to recover that "Greek experience" would be "to recover the joyful wonder and astonishment" at that overwhelming awesome excess of Being *in*—or *as*—the giving-forth of beings and "to accept with humility the *limit* of all our saying, language, meaning concerning what is."[92] For the truth of Being is never exhausted in our being-(t)here,[93] there is always the concealment behind the unconcealed, the *lethe* of *aletheia*, the earth extending beyond the world, the regioning surrounding us but on the other side beyond the horizon. To recover the Greek experience of the astonishment or wonder at Being's inexhaustible giving in and as nature would require us to be humble—in what I have called elsewhere an ethics of humility[94]—and be aware of our own finitude vis-à-vis that ontological excess. If we take Nietzsche's death of God in modernity in a *kenotic*[95] sense as Being's self-withdrawal in the way Heidegger takes Hölderlin's flight of the gods, in contrast to the modern attunement of anxiety or despair under nihilism, the appropriate co-response on our part as we are faced in awe and wonder with the awesome holy, would *also* be *kenotic*, as a letting-be in response to Being's letting-be of beings. Awe (*die Scheu*) as such is thus the attunement of one—whether poet or thinker—toward Being, who has come home to one's source.[96] Awakening to the clearing of the economy of concealment/unconcealment, from whence the world arises and history begins, encountering it with amazement and awe, as we thus simultaneously face our own finite situatedness and earth-boundedness, we come home to the awe-someness of the holy and enter the calm of releasement (*Gelassenheit*).

Freed therein, we can no longer ask the metaphysical question of "what grounds beings?," but instead can only ask the fundamental question (*Grundfrage*) of the truth of Beyng, "How can there be beings without ground?":[97] the truth of Beyng as the abyssal clearing for beings. In such wonder, bewildered by the chaos of Being, which initiates our questioning but which can only let beings be, we affirm earth and life in their radical contingencies and come home to releasement—to the holy.

NOTES

1. Rudolf Otto, *The Idea of the Holy*, trans. John W. Harvey (New York: Oxford University Press, 1958).

2. Benjamin D. Crowe, *Heidegger's Phenomenology of Religion: Religion and Cultural Criticism* (Bloomington, IN: Indiana University Press, 2008), 105.n.11.

3. GA 60: 31, 76, 323, 333. In this and all references to Heidegger's works, I have either used my own translation or consulted and modified existing English translations. Gregory P. Floyd, "Proclamation of the Words: Heidegger's Retrieval of the Pauline Language of Factical Life," *Ad Fontes: Studien zur frühen Phänomenologie* (Nordhausen: Bautz), draft (https://www.academia.edu/34675075/Proclamation_of_the_Words_Heideggers_Retrieval_of_the_Pauline_Language_of_Factical_Life), 4–5; Dermot Moran, "Choosing a Hero: Heidegger's Conception of Authentic Life in Relation to Early Christianity," in Elementa, vol. 80: *A Companion to Heidegger's Phenomenology of Religious Life*, ed. S. J. McGrath and Andrzej Wierciński (Leiden: Brill: 2010), 349–75, 354.

4. GA 39: 80f.

5. Friedrich Nietzsche, *The Gay Science*, trans. Thomas Common (Mineola, NY: Dover Pub., 2006), 90–91, 155–56.

6. Nietzsche, *Gay Science*, 155.

7. GA 39: 95.

8. GA 40: 5.

9. GA 40: 39.

10. GA 65: 380.

11. In *Contributions*, Heidegger uses this archaic spelling of *Seyn* instead of *Sein* for "Being" in the attempt to de-hypostatize, de-reify, de-nominalize the sense of the term. But in other writings, he resorts to the regular spelling of *Sein* in distinction

from *Seiendes* (entity, being). He also tries putting an 'X' over *Sein* in some later works as well.

12. GA 3: 257–58, 267.

13. The term *mana* originally referred to the spiritual life force or energy pervading the universe in Melanesian and Polynesian culture, and was academically discussed by nineteenth-century anthropologists like Robert Henry Codrington.

14. GA 3: 258.

15. Crowe, 108–109.

16. On this see Crowe, 110.n.13.

17. Crowe, 112.

18. GA 4: 18.

19. Martin Heidegger, *Identity and Difference* [bilingual edition], trans. Joan Stambaugh (New York: Harper & Row, 1969), 140 (German), 72 (English).

20. GA 9: 312. On this and the following, also see Frank Schalow and Alfred Denker, *Historical Dictionary of Heidegger's Philosophy* (Lanham, MA: Scarecrow Press, 2010), 141, 143, 243, 288, 296.

21. Heidegger, *Identity and Difference*, 141 (German), 72 (English).

22. GA 16: 671.

23. GA 65: 411.

24. GA 65: 403.

25. GA 65: 416.

26. GA 65: 411.

27. GA 65: 411.

28. GA 65: 405.

29. GA 9: 352.

30. GA 65: 411.

31. GA 65: 405.

32. GA 65: 416.

33. GA 65: 405.

34. GA 65: 87.

35. GA 65: 416.

36. GA 65: 406, also 412.

37. GA 77: 224.

38. GA 4: 195. On this also see Bret Davis, "Heidegger and the *Gottesfrage*," 4–5. First accessed October 4, 2018 from Bret Davis' Academia page: https://www.academia.edu/37530171/Heidegger_and_the_Gottesfrage.

39. Reiner Schürmann, "The Loss of the Origin in Soto Zen and Meister Eckhart," *The Thomist* 42, no. 2 (1978): 281–312, 298; and Schürmann, *Wandering Joy: Meister Eckhart's Mystical Philosophy* (Great Barrington, MA: Lindisfarne Books, 2001), 69.

40. Meister Eckhart, *Die deutschen und lateinischen Werke: Die deutschen Werke dritter band* (Berlin: Kohlhammer, 1976), 437–38, 441; Eckhart, *The Complete Mystical Works of Meister Eckhart* (New York: Crossroad Pub., 2009), 462, 463, 571–72.

41. GA 5: 272.

42. GA 9: 338.
43. GA 7: 151.
44. GA 9: 351.
45. GA 9: 338.
46. GA 4: 63. "Chaos" (χάος) is derived from the Greek root *cha-* (χα–), which implies "yawning," "gaping," "opening," "hollow," and from the verb *chainō* (χαίνω) for "opening." It is also interesting to note here its etymological link to chōra (χώρα), which we will discuss below. See Max Jammer, *Concepts of Space* (Cambridge, MA: Harvard University Press, 1970), 9, and F. M. Cornford, *Principium Sapientiae* (New York: Harper & Row, 1965), 194 and n. 1. Also see Edward Casey, *The Fate of Place* (Berkeley, CA: University of California Press, 1997), 345 n. 13; and Cornelius Castoriadis, *Figures of the Thinkable*, trans. Helen Arnold (Stanford, CA: Stanford Unviersity Press, 2007), 239–40; and Augustin Berque *Fudogaku josetsu: bunka o futatabi shizen ni, shizen o futatabi bunka ni* (Tokyo: Chikuma shobō, 2002), 36. Aristotle took Hesiod's *chaos* to mean "place" and as the first and necessary condition for the being of all else. Physics IV, 208b 29–33 (in e.g., Aristotle, *The Basic Works of Aristotle*, ed. Richard McKeon (New York: Random House, 1941), 270.

47. This juxtaposition of the holy with chaos differs from how Mircea Eliade understands the holy (commonly translated as "sacred" in Eliade's works) vis-à-vis chaos. For Eliade, the irruption of a sacred (holy) space projects a fixed point into the chaos of profane space, making orientation possible. Through the fixing of limits and the establishment of order, this "founds the world." In other words, through the revelation of the sacred (the holy), chaos is organized into cosmos via structure, forms, norms. A world is thus established vis-à-vis the chaos threatening it from without. See Mircea Eliade, *The Sacred and the Profane: The Nature of Religion* (San Diego, CA: Harcourt Brace, 1987), 23, 30–31, 47, 63, 65. For Heidegger, on the other hand, the holy (or sacred), prior to its derivative differentiation from the profane, is chaos as the clearing that establishes a world.

48. Friedrich Hölderlin, *Poems and Fragments*, trans. Michael Hamburger (London: Anvil Press Poetry, 2004). See also Babette Babich, "Heidegger and Hölderlin on Aether and Life," *Études phénoménologiques—Phenomenological Studies* 2 (2018): 111–33, 123 & n.36. Indeed as Babich says, here Hesiod helps us to read Hölderlin, and certainly Heidegger would have noticed this.

49. GA 5: 272.

50. Max Jammer, *Concepts of Space* (Cambridge, MA: Harvard University Press, 1970), 9; F. M. Cornford, *Principium sapientiae* (New York: Harper & Row, 1965), 194.n.1; Edward Casey, *Fatee of Place* (Berkeley, CA: University of California Press, 1997), 9–10, 345.n.13. See Hesiod 2008: especially 6–7 and the translator's comment about the word on 64.n.116.

51. G. S. Kirk, J. E. Raven, and M. Schofield, ed., *The Presocratic Philosophers: A Critical History with a Selection of Texts* (Cambridge: Cambridge University Press, 1983), 41.n.1.

52. See, for example, Nader El-Bizri, "*'Qui ētes-vous, XΩPA?'*: Receiving Plato's Timaeus." *Existentia* 11 (2001): 473–90, 474.

53. Plato, *Timaeus* in *Plato: Complete Works*, ed. John M. Cooper (Indianapolis, IN: Hackett, 1997), 1224–91.

54. On this see Susanne Claxton, *Heidegger's Gods: An Ecofeminist Perspective* (London and New York: Rowman and Littlefield International, 2017), 35, also 34–36. Claxton is here referring to the reading of Drew Hyland, "First of All Came Chaos," in *Heidegger and the Greeks*, ed. Drew Hyland and John Panteleimon Manoussakis (Indianapolis, IN: 2006), 9–22.

55. Anatole Bailly, *Dictionnaire grec-français* (Paris: Hachette, 1950), 2122 cited in Berque, *Fudogaku josetsu*, 36, 37n.17.

56. Augustin Berque, "*Where* is Knowledge? (in the Mediate Data of the Unconscious)," paper presented at the *International Conference on Knowledge and Place*, Soka University, Dec 9–10, 2000, 9, accessed February 15, 2012, http://pweb.ens-lsh.fr/omilhaud/berque_knowledge.doc.

57. GA 5: 48–50.

58. GA 40: 71.

59. GA 40: 66.

60. Berque, *Fudogaku*, 42–43, 49, 53; Augustin Berque, "The Choretic Work of History," *Semiotica: Journal of the International Association of Semiotic Studies* 175, no. ¼ (2009): 163–76, 165, 166; Berque, "*Where* is Knowledge?," 6, 8–9, n.73. Berque (*Fudogaku*, 40, 41.n.22, 43.n.24; and "Overcoming Modernity, Yesterday and Today," *Journal of East Asian Studies* 1, no. 1 (2002): 89–102, 94, 101.nn .20–21) refers to Pradeau, Brisson, and Boutot, all of whom take chora as milieu or field of relations, e.g., Jean-François Pradeau, "Être quelque part, occupier une place. Topos et chora dans le Timée," *Les Études philosophiques* 3 (1995): 375–400, 396; Alain Boutot, *Heidegger et Platon. Le problème du nihilism* (Paris: Presses Universitaires de France, 1987), 131, 222; and Luc Brisson, *Le même el l'autre dans la structure ontologique du Timée. Un commentaire systématique due Timée de Platon* (Sankt Augustin: Akademia Verlag, 1994). In a variety of works Berque (such as in *Fudogaku*, 163–64) goes on to develop his understanding of *chora* in terms of our eco-techno-symbolic milieu. Milieu in this sense is both natural and cultural. And "[t]he whole of human milieux forms the ecumene [ecoumene], which is the relationship of humankind with the earth" (Berque, "Research Agenda on the History of Disurbanity—Hypotheses and First Data," *International Journal of Urban Studies* 5, no. 1 (2001): 1–13, 1). See also Berque, *Japan: Nature, Artifice and Japanese Culture*, trans. Ros Schwartz (Northamptonshire, UK: Pilkington Press, 1997), 9, 99, 116–17, 226.

61. GA 55: 335.

62. GA 55: 335.

63. GA 13: 46–47.

64. GA 13: 45, 55.

65. GA 40: 71.

66. GA 12: 202.

67. Martin Heidegger, *Die Kunst und der Raum, l'art et l'espace* (St. Gallen: Erker Verlag, 1969), 10; and Heidegger, "Art and Space," *Man and Worl* 6, no. 1: 3–8, 6.

68. GA 15: 335.

69. Denker, *Historical Dictionary*, 40.
70. GA 12: 202.
71. Heidegger, *Die Kunst und der Raum, l'art et l'espace*, 9; "Art and Space," 5.
72. Heidegger, *Kunst und Raum*, 10; "Art and Space," 6.
73. GA 40: 16–17.
74. GA 55: 172–73.
75. GA 4: 59.
76. GA 4: 59.
77. GA 4 63.
78. GA 75: 208.
79. Ueda Shizuteru, *Basho: nijū sekainaisonzai* [*Place: Being-in-the-Twofold-World*] (Tokyo: Kōbundō, 1992), 62–63.
80. GA 4: 18; also see Crowe, 112.
81. GA 60: 76, 333.
82. James Lovelock, *Gaia: The Practical Science of Planetary Medicine* (London: Oxford University Press, 2000), 155, 168.
83. 2020 World Population Data accessed November 14, 2020: https://www.prb.org/2020-world-population-data-sheet/.
84. John Gray, *Straw Dogs: Thoughts on Human and Other Animals* (New York: Farrar, Straus and Giroux, 2003), 8, 10.
85. *Straw Dogs*, 6ff, 17.
86. *Straw Dogs*, 8–9, 11, 12, 34, 151. For some of these claims Gray refers to Reg Morrison, *The Spirit in the Gene: Humanity's Proud Illusion and the Laws of Nature* (Ithaca, NY: Cornell University Press, 1999).
87. Friedrich Nietzsche, *Thus Spoke Zarathustra*, trans. Graham Parkes (New York: Oxford University Press, 2005), 66.
88. S. P. Bailey, "The Dakota access pipeline isn't just about the environment. It's about religion", *Washington Post* (December 5, 2016). Accessed December 26, 2016: https://www.washingtonpost.com/news/acts-of-faith/wp/2016/12/05/thedakota-access-pipeline-isnt-just-about-the-environment-its-about-religion/?utm_term=.25e2233382b0. And R. R. LaPier, "Why understanding Native American religion is key to resolving Dakota access pipeline crisis," *Religion News Service* (November 3, 2016). Accessed December 26, 2016: http://religionnews.com/2016/11/03/why-understanding-nativeamerican-religion-is-important-for-resolving-the-dakota-access-pipeline-crisis/.
89. O. WainwrightIn Iceland, "Respect the elves—or else," *The Guardian* (March 25, 2015). Accessed December 26, 2016. https://www.theguardian.com/artanddesign/2015/mar/25/iceland-construction-respect-elves-or-else.
90. GA 75: 260. Also see Richard Capobianco, *Heidegger's Way of Being* (Toronto: University of Toronto Press, 2014), 43.
91. GA 15: 331. See also Capobianco, *Heidegger's Way of Being*, 44–45.
92. Capobianco, *Heidegger's Way of Being*, 47.
93. GA 9: 373–74.
94. For example, in my *Nishida Kitarō's Chiasmatic Chorology: Place of Dialectic, Dialectic of Place* (Bloomington, IN: Indiana University Press, 2015).

95. The term *kenosis* (κένοσις) appears in Paul's *Letter to the Philippians* (2: 6–8): Christ "emptied himself, taking the form of a servant, being born in the likeness of men." The term comes from the verb *kenoo* (to empty), deriving from *kenon* (void).

96. GA 4: 131–32. Also see Richard Capobianco, *Engaging Heidegger* (Toronto: University of Toronto Press, 2010), 79.

97. GA 65: 75–77.

Chapter 2

The Unsayable Mystery of the Holy
Hölderlin's Late Poetry
Sazan Kryeziu

There is probably no other great philosopher who, like Heidegger, merged his thinking with the writing of a poet. Heidegger's reading of Hölderlin brings the essence of language into the center of his thought. In Heidegger's view, the poet's task is to name what is "holy" just as the thinker's task is to proclaim "Being." Yet it is the poets who, as guardians of the *Logos*, are closer than others to its source, the poets who can hear "the peal of stillness" in language and echo it. So for Heidegger, Hölderlin's poetry is the returning home to a nearness to the origin, that is, to the *Logos* itself, which is not due to concealment, but to the open space as "clearing."

Juxtaposing Heidegger's discussion of the "holy" with Wittgenstein's conception of language as "the inexpressible" as presented in his *Tractatus*, I maintain that the holy is *the immediate* that cannot be said, but which is the principle of all saying. Being as the holy refers to the poet who responds to the Saying by articulating this Saying in founding language, but what is made manifest thereby retains, nonetheless, a dimension of concealment.

I. HEIDEGGER'S DISCUSSION OF THE HOLY

According to Heidegger, Being is named in many ways in Hölderlin's poetry, yet the core matter remains the same. Being is called *Nature*, that is, nature not as opposed to art, but in the sense of the Greek word *physis*; nature as "the way" whereby all things come to presence, *physis* as "arising into the open"—as Richard Capobianco has highlighted this in Heidegger's work. In this sense, Nature is the poetic name for Being. Capobianco has elucidated one of Hölderlin's late and last poems that Heidegger very much favored titled "Autumn," which was composed "one year before Hölderlin's death."[1] The following is the poem in full as translated and discussed by Capobianco in his book *Heidegger's Way of Being*:

Nature's gleaming is higher revealing,
Where with many joys the day draws to an end,
It is the year that completes itself in resplendence,
Where fruit come together with beaming radiance.

Earth's orb is thus adorned, and rarely clamors
Sound through the open field, the sun warms
The day of autumn mildly, the fields lie
As a great wide view, the breezes blow

Through boughs and branches, rustling gladly,
When then already to emptiness the fields give way.
The whole meaning of this bright image lives
As an image, golden splendor hovering all about.[2]

The first line "Nature's gleaming is higher revealing" is the one the poem grants to the reader; it is indeed another saying of the ontological difference between Being and beings, as Capobianco discusses in detail. Heidegger's commentary on the poem as a whole[3] uncovers the poem's resonances according to his distinctive vision. Yet the philosophical language that Heidegger uses is also the language that Hölderlin tries to convey to us. Nature's gleaming is indeed a "higher kind of manifestation," that is, of divine essence as *spirit*. Nature as *spirit* gives life to all beings present, it be-spirits all beings into their Being. As such, nature's gathering of itself in its unconcealment is to be seen both as an endless origin and as a perpetual presence of existence. This kind of presencing of existence as *spirit* serves as mediation among beings. But this much Hölderlin's poem itself says. By drawing a contrast between "nature" and "landscape," Heidegger asserts that landscape "lets appear nature in an initial gleaming."[4] What makes "nature's gleaming" holy?

Nature safeguards and conserves beings (man and things alike) in the integrity of their being. For Hölderlin, nature is the holy because it is the *all-creative* and *all-alive* and is *older than the ages and above the gods*. The holy is that which comes before humans, gods, God or any divine entity; in other words, it is that by which they, too, are: "The holy is not holy because it is divine; rather the divine is divine because in its way it is 'holy.'"[5] Nature for Hölderlin is holiness itself. As a *law* that lies beyond human law or God, it is that which makes possible the integrity of all beings in their being. In this respect, the holy as the essence of nature (the divine One) gathers together All, that is, the multiplicity of all beings (men, landscape, seasons, trees.) This *gleaming* manifests itself as a "higher revealing" or appearing, hence a manifestation of the holy (the One) as the source of light by which all beings shine-forth and manifest themselves. In this sense, nature as "a golden splendor" imbues everything that is there, by "hovering all about."

We should note that the view and rendering of "One is All" is not a new one, since Being and the One have been conjoined since Parmenides. Nevertheless, Heidegger insists that the One that he is speaking about has nothing to do with any metaphysical entity and that "the gleaming of nature is not a state or condition (*Zustand*), but a happening (*Geschehen*)."[6] This gleaming as a self-revealing aspect of Being constantly makes itself felt in the multitude of beings and events through its variously articulated forms of nature. But since this multitude of beings is ultimately nothing other than an unveiling or self-revealing aspect of Being itself, one who approaches nature only through its variously articulated temporal forms would fail to perceive the unrevealed presence of All that passes from god(s) to man, without which nature as the holy would lose its essence; that is, "nature is Nature only after the naming it receives from the poet, since, if the speech that establishes comes from him, he is only answering the exigent call of the Sacred."[7]

The All is to be found in the poet's calling of the holy because only through his song will the gods find their truth among the living. The poet's task is to say this unsayable poem. We should, however, note the difference between saying and naming. According to W. S. Allen, the difference is that "while the holy unveils itself *in* the word it does not do so in a manner that would make it present *as* the *saying* of the word. This is because its essence is to be coming, so in becoming separated from its non-essence as what is present, poetic naming names what is *as* what is coming, that is, what is *not* present. Thus the essence of nature, the holy, unveils itself not by becoming apparent in the saying of its name but in unveiling itself *as* the inapparent of the word, its imminence."[8] In this regard, it might be said that, for Hölderlin, the holy is the All that is the concealed name of Being.

In the second stanza of Hölderlin's Pindaric hymn "As When on a Holiday" (1800), the emergence of the holy is conceived as a wonderfully "All-present" which embraces the poets:

So in favorable weather they stand
Whom no master alone, whom she, wonderfully
All-present, educates in a light embrace,
The powerful, divinely beautiful nature.
So when she seems to be sleeping at times of the year
Up in the heavens or among plants or the peoples,

The poets' faces also are mourning,
They seem to be alone, yet are always divining.
*For divining too she herself is resting.*⁹

Heidegger observes: "Only because there are those who divine, are there those who belong to nature and correspond to it. Those who correspond to the wonderfully all-present, to the powerful, divinely beautiful, are 'the poets'" (78). Poetry is in essence a relation between gods and the people; in addition, the very essence of the poet is drawn into this omnipresent embrace of the holy, and, thus, only an authentic poet is able to speak of the gods (experience the holy) and name the divine: "Because this light embrace [of the Holy] educates the future poets, they, as the initiated ones, know the holy" (85). As "[nature] seems to be sleeping at times" and "poets seem to be alone," they both share a common mourning. Why mourning? Heidegger explicates that "this mourning, however, is not merely an arbitrary darkness, but a divining rest. Night is the resting divination of the day" (80).

But now day breaks! I awaited and saw it come,
And what I saw, may the holy be my word.

The contrast between the passing of the night's darkness and the coming of daybreak may not be understood merely in the sense of Heidegger's explication, namely as "the coming of the divining nature that has been to rest" or "the pure calling of what those poets who are always divining wait and long for" (80). Rather, it may also refer to that particular realm of Being as the holy as it discloses itself to the poet at the stage when "*according to firm law, as once begotten out of holy Chaos/ Inspiration, the all-creative/ Again feels herself anew*"(69). The poet witnesses the *holy Chaos*, that is to say, he experiences the annihilation of all outward manifestations of nature. In my view, Hölderlin does not seem to say that this inspiration (in the sense of divine madness) is a falling into *abyss* where nothing could be discernible anymore, but rather that this abyss is also said to be bright insofar as Being in itself is essentially luminous, illuminating itself as well as the poet's self.

According to Heidegger, "the poem speaks of the poets and of the gift of the song only because the holy is the terror of universal shaking" (94), yet why must the final word of the poem return to the holy? For de Man, "it is not because he has seen Being that the poet is, therefore, capable naming it; his word prays for the *parousia*, it does not establish it. It cannot establish it for as soon as the word is uttered, it destroys the immediate and discovers that instead of stating Being, it can only state mediation."¹⁰ De Man rejects Heidegger's reading of Hölderlin arguing that Heidegger's interpretation of Hölderlin's poetry raises a question of the very possibility of naming Being.

For this theorist of Deconstruction, no event that is present in Hölderlin's poetry is about the coming-into-being of the holy, but instead it is about the rift between language and Being or the articulation of the difference and opposition between the immediate Being and a mediating language; that is to say, it is about the difference between the absolute Being and languaged being.

We might say that the holy is the trace of the unsayable mystery of the poet's speech that is made manifest in his words, yet cannot be said, except through this trace that it leaves behind in the language that cannot say it. The poet yearns to say it, but cannot, since the very calling of it would extinguish it. Yet, the holy as the unsayable mystery of speech is the very source of presence by which gods and men are present to each other and to Being; hence, Being functions as the immediate mediation between them. But the holy is not yet the poet's word, for the poet still needs the omnipresence to exist:

Like sleeping infants the gods
  breathe without any plan;
    the spirit flourishes
      continually in them,
        chastely kept,
          as in a small bud,
            and their holy eyes
              look out in still
                eternal clearness.

A place to rest
  isn't given to us.
    Suffering humans
      decline and blindly fall
        from one hour to the next,
          like water thrown
            from cliff to cliff,
              year after year, down
                into the Unknown.[11]

The holy is the trace of the departed gods. The poet must take a stand and speak of the gods, for his task as mediator is to connect the near to the far. Gods themselves determine what the poet is to the divine, and, therefore, the poet must be responsive or attune himself wherever the holy discloses itself to him. Such attuning will be possible if the poet expresses a word that only the holy, preserved within him, may utter. By preserving the holy, he becomes a seer who foresees the time of the thing created, of which he is the creator. "It is because," as Blanchot observes, "the poem is previous to the poet, and exactly this *ahnen* is the way for the poet to feel that he exists before himself and, *free as he may be, as free as the swallow,* in the dependence on this very freedom, his response may be free but it is a response to this freedom."[12]

For Hölderlin, the holy is the *immediate*. The *immediate* establishes a mutual relationship among beings; hence, it serves as mediation among them. Inspired by an early fragment of Pindar, Hölderlin writes:

> The immediate, strictly speaking, is as impossible for the mortals as for the immortals; the god must distinguish different worlds, in accordance with his nature, because heavenly goodness, for its own sake, must be holy, pure. Man, as the knowing one, must also distinguish different worlds, because knowledge is only possible through opposition. For this reason, the immediate, strictly speaking, is as impossible for the mortals as for the immortals. Strict mediatedness, however, is the law. (84)[13]

The holy as the immediate, however, is not directly approachable to the poet, for he cannot name it *in itself*; rather it discloses itself to him *mediately*, that is, in and through beings which it renders present. Human beings dwell in the vicinity of the holy in the same manner as the gods do. Mediation is first to be seen as an "openness of the open which comes into a connection with what we call a 'world'" (86). The openness is the dwelling place of the poet where he welcomes the gods in his poetry. But to unveil the mystery of language is to unveil the origin of Being. Instead, the poet's task as "half-god" or privileged mortal is to respond to Being and recognize the holy as mediated through beings, for he must accept and respect the inaccessibility of Being itself. As Heidegger puts it:

> The immediate is itself never something mediate; on the other hand, the immediate, strictly speaking, is the mediation, that is, the mediatedness of the mediated, because it renders the mediated possible in its essence. (84)

Mediation comes from what is superior or *above* the poet, that is, closer to some source of light of the holy, but not itself the holy, since it is only a being. Through the source of light, the poet may be enlightened by the holy, for the holy cannot be found by itself but rather in the beings that it illuminates. The poet is aware of the fall into *the Unknown*, since this was the destiny as determined by the gods; and whether the coming of gods will be the gods of ancient Greece or the Christian God is determined from and within the realm of Being. Hölderlin's god is *unknown*. The god that the poet refers to is not the religious God of the Christian faith, for Hölderlin is not a religious poet, but "a poet of Being," as Heidegger puts it.

In my view, the human drive to reach and grasp the concrete coordinates of individual existence is to be understood as a religious drive (religious, not necessarily according to the doctrines of religions, but in terms of the Transcendent itself.) This is particularly the case with Hölderlin's much interpreted line "poetically man dwells on this earth," about which Heidegger dedicated a whole essay. Following Jung's assertion that "man is naturally religious,"[14] we think that Hölderlin's line may also be understood in the same light; that is, humans are supposed to *dwell poetically on this earth* in the sense of a syncretism between conscious and unconscious dimensions. In this aspect, the reality of Dasein is mystified; that is, it is not (merely) a thingly existence, but fused with mysterious dimensions (God, gods, sky, plants). There is in the human being a feeling of affinity with all things that surround and fill him: animals, plants, sky, gods, and the eternal.

For Hölderlin, Christ is a divinely begotten hero.[15] Gadamer, on the other hand, observes that for Hölderlin, Christ is of different nature than a mere presence:

> *The poets, then, must be of this world, because they can sing only of the present in which they are imprisoned. It is part and parcel of Hölderlin's present that Christ is not accessible to poetic form. The Greek gods are the present time of legend that becomes reinterpreted for the poet in the light of "ever-present" nature. Christ, on the other hand, is he who lives in faith and whose worship is "in the spirit." For Christ still lives.*[16]

In the poem that bears the title "The Poet's Vocation," Hölderlin writes: "fearless/man stands, and lonely before God/no weapon he needs/till God's being not there helps him."[17] The poet's task is to remind his people not to give homage to false gods, but to await the signs of the approaching of a future god as a salvation for his people. It seems as if Hölderlin foresaw the godless world of the modern age characterized by the technological worldview of Western civilization in which the absence of a god holds sway. We are living in an epoch that lies between the absence of the past gods and the absence of a new one; therefore the poet, as long as this absence lasts, must teach his people how to live in the vicinity of "the essence of things" or *dwell poetically on this earth*. In his essay "What are Poets For?" Heidegger remarks:

> The default of God means that no god any longer gathers men and things unto himself, visibly and unequivocally, and by such gathering disposes the world's history and man's sojourn in it. The default of God forebodes something even grimmer, however. Not only have the gods and the god fled, but the divine

radiance has become extinguished in the world's history. The time of the world's night is the destitute time, because it becomes ever more destitute. It has already grown so destitute, it can no longer discern the default of God as a default.[18]

This is what Nietzsche would call "the death of God," insofar as we are living in an epoch that has forgotten Being. For the philosopher of nihilism, *the death of God* marks the death of metaphysics, or rather the forgetfulness of Being as a "mittence of Being."[19] For Hölderlin, the poet is given the understanding of Being as a necessity for the encounter with gods in the presence of the holy. By living in the presence of the holy, and therefore letting the truth appear, the poet will show his people how to *dwell* on this earth. The holy is revealed to him in the form of verbal expression, and it is by reason of this very essence that Being passes into a word. Yet, the final words of Hölderlin's hymn "As When on a Holiday..." read:

. . . I approached to see the Heavenly,
And they themselves cast me down, deep down,
Below the living, into the dark cast down
The false priest that I am, to sing,
For those who have ears to hear, the warning song.
There[20]

This last stanza of Hölderlin's hymn does not appear in every edition of his poetry collections nor does it appear in Heidegger's *Elucidations* (who surprisingly decides to leave the lines out); however, it can be found in the original manuscript of Hölderlin which shows that the poet crossed out a number of verses and words. The lines express the poet's recognition of the absence of an authentic language in the epiphany of his suffering self-negation. The poet can hear the voice of gods but is cast down to live on earth and sing to his fellow men in a real language. This authentic language is silence.

The poet realizes that he can enter into an appropriate relationship with the gods only through a grounding-attunement, which dwells in silence, after realizing that his poetic language could not reveal the Being of things. Yet the poet is "into the dark" that refers to the unreality of the world that he has been experiencing. In this aspect, the holy functions as an impenetrable dark veil obstructing the poet's sight to *see* or approach the self-revealing truth of Being. Thus, it is through silence as the unsayable of the holy that humanity can reach into the depths of God. Yet how can the holy, which is unsayable, become speech? Blanchot insists that it can insofar as "silence is marked by the same contradiction and the same tearing apart as language: If it is a way to approach the unapproachable, to belong to what is not said, it is 'sacred' only insofar as it makes communication of the incommunicable possible and arrives at language."[21]

The unsayable is a prerequisite for dwelling in the vicinity of the holy and must not be identified with the holy itself. The unsayable is to be understood as a mode of augmented receptivity to the word, but not constitutive of it. There must be silence for this word to make itself heard, or in other words, it is through silence that we can clearly hear and understand the spoken word.

It is important to further affirm the interrelationship between the unsayable beyond language and ordinary language in terms of Meister Eckhart's ontological distinction between *Beyond-Being* and *Being*: "God is a word, an unspoken word... Where God is, He utters this Word—where He is not, He does not speak. God is spoken and unspoken."[22] Speaking in accordance with Eckhart's distinction, one could say that unsayability may be found in the omnipresence of God's no-thingness, or as Kazemi observes: "At the plane of Being"—"where God is"—the Word is spoken, while on the plane of Beyond-Being—"where He is not"—there is silence, no-thing. This does not mean "nothing" in the sense of the negation of Being, but rather nothing as That which surpasses all "things" as well as Being itself. As Eckhart says: "God is spoken *and* unspoken" (135).

In this way, the poetic word becomes the concrete site of unconcealment, and thereby takes the poet in the vicinity of the holy, which allows otherness to spring forth as guarding the relation between mortals and divinities, man and God. This event of mutual bestowing and receiving in the manner of gathering what is unconcealed from out of concealment draws forth a mystery (*Geheimnis*) in our *Dasein*. We are drawn toward this *mystery*, we "ceaselessly 'reach out' (*ausholen*) unto Being and 'bring back' (*einholen*) in the *word* what is addressed to us by Being itself as the primordial *Logos*," as Capobianco observes.[23] We stand together with others on the ground of *Logos* in gathering in language, and that is our "dwelling."

Still more puzzling is the question of whether what *can* be experienced *cannot* be said into words. Alfred Schutz notes that "for 2,000 years, the problem of philosophy has been not "How do I know the things of the outer world?" but 'what is the relation of the concept to that which I have designated with and also apperceived in a word?'"[24] Our question would be: does the world of words exist only outside the world or is our cognition of it possible only through words? And will one's original experience be altered if one names the experience linguistically?

Does the mystic's view that the unsayable is beyond language make it non-linguistic? Or is the unsayable unrelated to language (Blanchot)? Or is it inseparable from language (Derrida)? Or is it the essence of language (*das Wesen der Sprache*), as Heidegger maintains? Paradoxically enough, it might be said that the unsayable is made possible only through language, as in the lines of Rumi: "When you say, "words are of no account," you negate your own assertion through your words. If words are of no account, why do we hear you say that words are of no account? After all, you are saying this in words."[25] In order to make some sense of these questions, we will attempt to discuss Wittgenstein's views on language, silence, and the mystical (*das Mystische*) as the "inexpressible," as he discussed these notions in the *Tractatus*.

II. WITTGENSTEIN AND THE LIMITS OF LANGUAGE

Ludwig Wittgenstein claims in the *Tractatus* that "what finds its reflection in language, language cannot represent" and that "what expresses *itself* in language, *we* cannot express by means of language" (4.121).[26] To achieve this representation we would have to place ourselves "somewhere outside logic, that is to say outside the world" (4.12), and if this logical form *is mirrored in propositions*, what could be *identified* in the unsayable (as the outside of the world), that the reflection is of the world? It seems that nothing that is *sayable* could *identify* what is *unsayable* as identically mirrored in language.

He further observes: "Language disguises thought. So much so, that from the outward form of the clothing it is impossible to infer the form of the thought beneath it, because the outward form of the clothing is not designed to reveal the form of the body, but for entirely different purposes" (4.002). On this view, then, language disguises its essential structure. According to Wittgenstein, a proposition can only say how a thing is and not what it is. Furthermore, "to view the world *sub specie aeterni* is to view it as a Whole—a limited whole" (6.45). This world as "a limited whole" (*begrenztes Ganzes*) is what Wittgenstein calls the "mystical." The infinity of language encounters a limit: The unsayable is checked by the silence or speechlessness of nature. There are, indeed, says Wittgenstein, things that cannot be put into words (6.522). Yet in the context of our argument, the following question must be posed: Can the logical limits of language be transcended by poetic language? William Franke observes:

> It seems that poetry excels only in the expression of inexpressibility and that this alone, paradoxically, becomes the mode in which the sense of alterity and singularity can be communicated. Not by being communicated but rather by being marked as evading all linguistic formulations, the inexpressible is made at least to show up in poetry. As in Wittgenstein's dictum, the inexpressible "*shows* itself, it is the mystical."[27] (85)

This inexpressible as the mystical *shows itself*; yet might this way of showing be something that cannot be said, or in other words, is there a *showing* of what cannot be said? According to Franke, "the linguistic trace of what cannot be said must precede—and in fact constitute—any presencing or evidencing of the unsayable, which is, to this extent, intrinsically linguistic, that is, an effect of language" (153). Taking his cue from Derrida's discussions of the trace, Franke maintains that "the trace is all that ever becomes real and effectual of the presence, which is never manifest as presence itself and as such but always only as some recognizable, specifiable trait, an instituted trace, which refers to what it is not and cannot represent but can only mark as vanished, absent, inaccessible." The unsayable is thus "a *trace* that cannot be traced back to any origin" (153).

We cannot trace the unsayable back to its origin because we cannot put ourselves "outside of the world." In these terms, "what *can* be shown, *cannot* be said," claims Wittgenstein insofar as language is just its in-the-world structure. Wittgenstein sees a unity between two kinds of showing: the showing of what lies outside the world and the showing that lies *in*-the-world. These two worlds are not separate but bounded by a mutual structure of consciousness that is transcendental that manifests itself both in the realm of logic and outside logic. Language and mind are the limits of the world which are separated by the transcending experience of the mystical. Russell Nieli remarks:

> One cannot *say* what does not exist in the world, because what does not exist *in* the world is the out-of-the-world mystic union, and for expressing this experience, the in-the-world structure of language and logic is not appropriate. Similarly, the out-of-the-world experience cannot be construed in thought, because "thought" (*Gedanke*), in the technical sense of the *Tractatus,* is closely tied to picture-propositions (3.01, 3.1) that is, to what can be said in language.[28]

In the mystical realm of experience there occurs a disembodiment of the self, for as Wittgenstein puts it: "the philosophical self is not the human being, not the human body, or the human soul, with which psychology deals, but rather the metaphysical subject, the limit of the world—not a part of it" (5.641). The disembodied self is therefore represented as the reduction of the metaphysical *I* from its body (the denial of the reality of the ego) to a point from which it views the whole world. In other words, only in a mystical "flight" does a "world" come into being. Likewise, it might be said that only insofar as the poet destroys himself and the language he has created will the "world" come into being. Only at the limit of this negation might the *unsayable* take place.

Whereas, for Wittgenstein, the limits of the language are the limits of the world, for Heidegger language is the house of Being, and in this house human beings dwell. He does not directly maintain, as Wittgenstein asserts, that beyond the philosophical language lies the "mystical." Heidegger attempts to create a new transformed language by demanding that language and grammar be freed from logic:

> The Greeks had no word for "language"; they understood this phenomenon "in the first instance" as discourse. But because the logos came into their philosophical ken primarily as assertion, *this* was the kind of *logos* which they took as their clue for working out the basic structures of the forms of discourse and its components. Grammar sought its foundations in the "logic" of this *logos*. But this logic was based upon the ontology of the present-at-hand.[29]

Yet for Heidegger, poetry is opposed to inauthentic discourse. Poetry (*poiesis*) is not a particular part of language; language originates in poetry. Poetry, he maintains, names Being and the essence of all things; it is poetry which makes language possible in the first place. In this sense, the essence of language itself is to be understood through the essence of poetry. However, Heidegger's suggestion that we should seek that essence in poetry, as Karsten Harries remarks, "is no more convincing than Wittgenstein's decision to accept our language as a ground beyond challenge. Logic, ordinary language, and poetry must not be understood as three stages, where each successive stage is taken to be more fundamental than the one which preceded it, but as three dimensions which have to be seen together."[30]

It is also important to direct our attention here, however briefly, to Wittgenstein's paralleling of ethics with aesthetics: "Ethics and aesthetics are one and the same" (6.421). What is the relation binding them given the fact that they are two different domains? According to B.R. Tilghman, "they are parallel in that both belong to the domain of *the unsayable*; just as there are no ethical propositions, so there are no propositions stating aesthetic judgments. Both values can only be shown. Both involve a way of looking at things that is contemplative."[31] Ethics and aesthetics, in Tilghman words, "are intimately related in that art is one of the most important ways in which ethical value can be shown and a solution to the problem of life made manifest" (65). This plausible idea, however, raises a number of dilemmas, for our question would be: what does Tilghman mean by ethics, if he does not speak about the ethical act, but refers to the ethical only in light of the individual quest for spiritual balance?

Wittgenstein's identification of "the mystical" with that which cannot be put into words is closer to Eckhart's mysticism than to Heidegger's thought.

Heidegger's thought is linguistic rather than mystical. Whereas for Meister Eckhart silence replaces language, for Heidegger silence is the condition and also an attribute of authentic language, but only insofar as it is a break off or cessation within language. Consider the lines of Stefan George's poem "The Word": "So I renounced and sadly see: Where word breaks off no thing may be" (73).[32]

The thing itself comes into being for us "only through language, and where there is no word, there is no thing either." As Heidegger remarks in his explication of the poem: "No thing is where the word is lacking. 'Thing' is here understood in the broad sense as meaning anything that in any way *is*. In this sense even a god is a thing. Only where the word for the thing has been found is the thing a thing. Only thus is it—*for us*. Accordingly we must stress as follows: *for us*, no thing *is* where the word, that is, the name is lacking" (61-2). But once the poet experiences the limitation of language, he writes a poem instead, and does not lapse into silence. Why? Heidegger answers: "because this renunciation is a genuine renunciation, not just a rejection of saying, not a mere lapse into silence. As self-denial, renunciation remains Saying. It thus preserves the relation to the word" (147).

The difference between what is sayable and what is "unsayable in what is said" is *rift* (*Riss*). As Bernasconi explains: "Rift is the withdrawal, the withholding, the unspoken that accompanies all language and resounds in *das Geläut der Stille*. The recognition-in remembrance-of the history of Being does not mark the withdrawal of Being's withdrawal. It means rather that the silence is to be heard as silence and that the silence comes to permeate all speaking. The rift would thereby be maintained as a rift between the 'inside' and 'outside' of metaphysics or, better, between the first and another beginning."[33]

Wittgenstein, on the other hand, is more restrained than Heidegger in this respect. Wittgenstein attempts to draw a limit to the expression of thought in language. Beyond this limit, there is nothing but silence. For Wittgenstein, silence is the only realm for the revelation of the mystical as the unsayable, which shows itself at the point or limit where language cannot reach. This realm where language cannot reach belongs to the sphere of aesthetics. To reach this aspect of the world in which the aesthetic and ethical resides, the metaphysical I, or the self, must transcend the specifics of rendering this world only by means of speech, babbling, and theorizing. It is for this reason, perhaps, that Wittgenstein ends his *Tractatus* in silence: "What we cannot speak about we must pass over in silence" (7). According to Dieter Mersch, "the mystical represents the place where every definition of the question of 'what' or 'how' ceases and only the pure presence in relation to absence *manifests* itself. That means: the world, as the *self-revealing* entity, '*is*' only *in the event*."[34] But the mystical is not just the world, or being, or existence. The limits of Being are non-being, nothingness, emptiness or the void, which are key concepts in mystical poetry as well. And if Being as *self-revealing* originates in an event, it might be argued that the event discloses the emptiness (void) or nothingness of the place whence the Being as truth originates. This is what Hölderlin told us:

[Gods] themselves cast me down/
Below the living/to sing,
For those who have ears to hear, the warning song.
There

The poet sings his song by naming the holy as *there*, *there* as the very being of the place as void (silence). Poetry as the essence of all things goes beyond logic and concepts and excels precisely in the expression of the inexpressible, becoming thus the only form in which the sense of singularity and otherness can be expressed. The inexpressible makes itself manifest in poetry, not by being expressed or articulated, but rather by avoiding linguistic formulations. The poet speaks, yet does not speak, and what is shown by him, is left unexpressed. But if *gods* ask him to speak to his audience through language, how is it possible for the audience or reader to hear and understand the poet? The idea of the audience in this respect might be related to Heidegger's conception of *keeping silent* "as another essential possibility of discourse."[35] By keeping silent at hearing the poet's word, the audience "can develop an understanding, and he can do so more authentically than the person who is never short of words" (208). As Heidegger puts it:

> Keeping silent authentically is possible only in genuine discoursing. To be able to keep silent, Dasein must have something to say—that is, it must have at its disposal an authentic and rich disclosedness of itself. In that case one's reticence [*Verschwiegenheit*] makes something manifest, and does away with "idle talk" [*Gerede*]. As a mode of discoursing, reticence Articulates the intelligibility of Dasein in so primordial a manner that it gives rise to a potentiality-for-hearing which is genuine, and to a Being-with-one-another which is transparent. (208)

CONCLUDING REFLECTION

We began this essay by highlighting passages from Hölderlin's late poetry that illuminate Being as Nature and as the Holy. We proceeded to analyze Hölderlin's idea of the holy principally according to the philosophical views of Heidegger and Wittgenstein, and attempted to make an analogy between Hölderlin's idea of the holy and Wittgenstein's conception of language as the "inexpressible." Following Heidegger's thought, we have observed that the essence of poetizing is to be understood through the essence of language.

In the second part, we juxtaposed Heidegger's view with Wittgenstein's and found that to trace the mystery of what cannot be said back to an origin means placing ourselves outside of the "world" (outside logic), passing into the realm of silence. We noted several passages that supported this interpretation. For Wittgenstein, it is through silence that the revelation of the mystical as the unsayable is made possible, the mystical which makes itself manifest at the point where language fails. Whatever the differences in their thinking, in the end, *both* Wittgenstein and Heidegger point to *silence* as the ultimate human response to mystery. As Heidegger reminds us, it is in "the peal of stillness" (*das Geläut der Stille*) that we are in the presence of the mystery of the unsayable. And in Meister Eckhart's words:

First we will take the words: "In the midst of silence there was spoken within me a secret word".... Yet in that ground [of the soul] is the silent "middle": here nothing but rest and celebration for this birth, this act, that God the Father may speak His word there, for *this* part is by nature receptive to nothing save only the divine essence, without mediation.[36]

We may sum up what we have found by saying that in Hölderlin's poetizing the holy describes *the immediate* that cannot be said but that is the principle of all saying. The holy bestows the originary word upon the poet who is able to speak only by heeding silence. Struck by the holy, the poet hears the withholding of language in a transformed way. Hölderlin writes: "Often we must keep silence; holy names are lacking/Hearts beat and yet does speech hold back?"[37]

Poetic language opens our world and guides our way; but silence before the Mystery remains for the poet—and for us all.

NOTES

1. Richard Capobianco, *Heidegger's Way of Being* (Toronto: University of Toronto Press, 2014), 29. For this present section, see especially Capobianco's Chapter 2 "On Hölderlin on 'Nature's Gleaming.'"
2. *Heidegger's Way of Being*, 28–29.
3. *Heidegger's Way of Being*, 28–37.
4. *Heidegger's Way of Being*, 30.
5. Martin Heidegger, *Elucidations of Hölderlin's Poetry,* trans. Keith Hoeller (New York: Humanity Books, 2000), 82.
6. *Heidegger's Way of Being*, 33.

7. Maurice Blanchot, *The Work of Fire* (Stanford University Press, 1995), 119–20.

8. William S. Allen, *Ellipsis: Of Poetry and the Experience of Language after Heidegger, Hölderlin, and Blanchot* (State University of New York Press, 2007), 101.

9. All page references are to *Elucidations of Hölderlin's Poetry,* trans. Keith Hoeller (New York: Humanity Books, 2000), 67–99.

10. Paul de Man, *Blindness and Insight: Essays in the Rhetoric of Contemporary Criticism,* Revised Second Edition (London: Routledge, 1983), 258–59.

11. See *Poems of Friedrich Hölderlin,* trans. James Mitchell (San Francisco, CA: Ithuriel's Spear, 2007), 35.

12. *The Work of Fire,* 118–19.

13. All page references are to *Elucidations of Hölderlin's Poetry,* trans. Keith Hoeller (New York: Humanity Books, 2000).

14. This assertion lies at the core of Jung's psychology/philosophy. For a detailed understanding of this thinking see, for example, C. G. Jung's "The Function of Religious Symbols" and "On Spiritualistic Phenomena," in *The Symbolic Life: Miscellaneous Writings: The Collected Works of C.G. Jung,* ed. W. McGuire (Princeton, NJ: Princeton University Press, 1997). See also Richard Capobianco's several discussions on the thematic similarities between Jung's understanding of *therapeia* and the later Heidegger's thinking.

15. Wilhelm Dilthey, *Poetry and Experience,* Volume V (Princeton University Press, 1985), 383.

16. Hans-Georg Gadamer, *Literature and Philosophy in Dialogue* (State University of New York Press, 1994), 79.

17. Trans. Christopher Middleton in *Friedrich Hölderlin: Hyperion and Selected Poems,* ed. Eric L. Santner (New York: Continuum, 1990), 157.

18. Martin Heidegger, *Poetry, Language, Thought* (New York: Harper & Row, 1971), 89.

19. William J. Richardson, *Heidegger: Through Phenomenology to Thought,* 4h edition (New York: Fordham University Press, 2003), 436.

20. Trans. Michael Hamburger in *Friedrich Hölderlin: Hyperion and Selected Poems,* ed. Eric L. Santner (New York: Continuum, 1990), 197.

21. *The Work of Fire,* 129.

22. Reza Shah-Kazemi, *Paths to Transcendence According to Shankara, Ibn Arabi, and Meister Eckhart* (Indiana: World Wisdom Inc., 2006), 135.

23. *Heidegger's Way of Being,* 94.

24. Alfred Schutz, *Literary Reality and Relationships,* Collected Papers VI (New York: Springer 2013), 127.

25. Steven T. Katz, *Mysticism and Language* (Oxford University Press, 1992), 3. On the other hand, for the similarity of the views of Rumi and Heidegger, see Richard Capobianco, *Heidegger's Being: The Shimmering Unfolding* (Toronto: University of Toronto Press, 2022).

26. All references of propositions and statements are to Ludwig Wittgenstein, *Tractatus Logico-Philosophicus* (London: Routledge, 1974).

27. All references below are to William Franke, *A Philosophy of the Unsayable* (Indiana: University of Notre Dame Press, 2014).

28. Russell Nieli, *Wittgenstein: From Mysticism to Ordinary Language* (State University of New York Press, 1987), 119–20.

29. Martin Heidegger, *Being and Time*, trans. John Macquarrie and Edward Robinson (New York: Harper & Row, 1962), 209.

30. Karsten Harries, "Wittgenstein and Heidegger: The Relationship of the Philosopher to Language," *The Journal of Value Inquiry*, no. 2 (1968): 291.

31. B. R. Tilghman, *Wittgenstein, Ethics and Aesthetics: The View from Eternity* (Hong Kong: Macmillan, 1991), 64.

32. All page references are to *Poetry, Language, Thought* (New York: Harper & Row, 1971).

33. Robert Bernasconi, *The Question of Language in Heidegger's History of Being* (Atlantic Highlands: Humanities Press, 1985), 63.

34. Dieter Mersch, "There are, indeed, things that cannot be put into words." [sic] in *In Search of Meaning: Ludwig Wittgenstein on Ethics, Mysticism and Religion*, ed. Ulrich Arnswald (Universitätsverlag Karlsruhe, 2009), 30. Mersch further explains (44) that "the expression 'event' or 'happening' (*Ereignis*) implies that the distinction between what can be said and not said is not accessible: it is not a constructive effect of a discourse: it *happens*. It is therefore also not, as Derrida and J. Butler meanwhile seem to infer, marked arbitrarily and, by that, not *transferable*."

35. All the following page references are to *Being and Time*, trans. John Macquarrie and Edward Robinson (New York: Harper & Row, 1962), 208.

36. Frank Schalow, *Heidegger and the Quest for the Sacred: From Thought to the Sanctuary of Faith* (Netherlands: Kluwer Publishing, 2001), 61.

37. See Hölderlin's poem *Heimkunft /An die Verwandten* (stanza 6): "*Schweigen müssen wir oft; es fehlen heilige Nahmen / Herzen schlagen und doch bleibet die Rede zurük?*" in Heidegger's *Elucidations of Hölderlin's Poetry* (New York: Humanity Books, 2000), 30 (slightly modified).

Chapter 3

The Divine as the Origin of the Work of Art

Lawrence Berger

Watch ye therefore: for ye know not when the master of the house cometh, at even, or at midnight, or at the cockcrowing, or in the morning: Lest coming suddenly he find you sleeping. And what I say unto you I say unto all, Watch.

Mark 13:35-37

One must come to the sight with a seeing power made akin and like to what is seen. No eye ever saw the sun without becoming sun-like, nor can a soul see beauty without becoming beautiful.

Plotinus, *Enneads*, I.6.9

He who with the entire force of his being "turns" to God, lifts at this his point of the universe the divine immanence out of its debasement, which he has caused.

Martin Buber, *The Way of Man*

I wish to show that for Heidegger, the divine makes itself manifest in great works of art. Such a work requires ontological effort on the part of mortals to preserve the truth that shows itself therein, but the impulse for such effort ultimately issues from the divine itself. I argue that this effort of the whole human being is best rendered as an acute and sustained attentiveness, a *staying-with*, a readiness, waiting, watchfulness, or mindfulness (*Achtsamkeit*). This puts Heidegger squarely within the contemplative traditions, both East and West, where such practices have been in place for thousands of years. And, after all, nothing less than an effort of one's whole being could be called for in a quest for the ultimate.

I review "The Origin of the Work of Art"[1] from this perspective, but I first look to *Contributions to Philosophy*[2] for more of the context in which the essay develops. *Achtsamkeit* does not appear in this work, rather appearing in the form of steadfastness (*Inständigkeit* and the associated *stehen* and *halten*, which appear in various forms), which is explicitly related to *Achtsamkeit* in the 1940s and beyond, as I have shown elsewhere.[3] After discussing the nature of ontological effort and how the divine may be made manifest in these earlier works, I show how the same themes appear in the later "Building Dwelling Thinking"[4] along with some citations from the 1940s, with *Achtsamkeit* now front and center as the essence of the required effort.

I. ONTOLOGICAL EFFORT IN *CONTRIBUTIONS TO PHILOSOPHY*

I first consider how ontological effort is called for in *Contributions*, where the question is how to sustain an effort of one's whole being. Heidegger is of course aware of the classic problem of will and grace, and opts for the primacy of Being, the appeal of which impels human beings to *Inständigkeit*.[5] He asks "How is this unique accomplishment to be brought about? There is no precedent for it and no foothold" (GA 65: 5/6). Hence, the need for a leap out of the ordinary into preparation for the event. This only appears to be something that can be carried out by humans; "actually, being human occurs as historical through the appropriation that summons Da-sein in one way or another" (235-36/186), as can be seen in the discussion of the call of Being as a "hesitant withholding."[6] For Heidegger, it is "not what *we* think up but what compels *us* . . . into a thinking . . . which grounds truth." (243/191). In this regard, he also discusses the *decision* which either leads to the pursuit of the path to the other beginning or to a continued decline into non-being. It comes about not through any act of the human being, but by way of the action of Being itself, which calls for us to stay with the beings of worldly engagement and thereby enable the divine to shine through and be preserved therein.

Being disposes us by way of the call of its withdrawal. In the opening section of *Contributions,* Heidegger discusses the complex of dispositions which are associated with the required effort. In particular, he discusses shock, restraint (both of which constitute presentiment), renunciation, and diffidence. In all of these cases, a response is demanded from the negative call that arises from the manifestation of Being as absent, withdrawn, and, in its full extent, as refusal. I focus largely on the disposition of restraint in what follows.

Restraint is a *cor-responding* (*Ent-sprechung*), which means that we respond and belong, thereby relating to the truth of Being that shows itself in the clearing to which Da-sein is assigned (i.e., essentially related). That responsiveness comes about by way of extraordinary attentiveness, by staying-with steadfastly. Restraint is the appropriate, corresponding disposition of Da-sein given the withdrawal of Being and the abandonment of the divine. That is what calls Da-sein to its task, the being disposed out of the event of appropriation. Disposition thus comes out of the event that essentially relates man and Being. The disposition is the basis for steadfastness in Da-sein: "Presentiment places inceptual steadfastness into Da-sein" (GA 65: 22/19), but there is always the historical contingency of the actual response of humanity to the call. The question is if we correspond, "Whether *this call* . . . still happens openly, or whether the plight becomes mute instead and all reigning is withheld, and whether the call is still taken up, provided it does happen at all . . . therein is decided the future of humans" (408/324). The problem is that we are not even aware of the plight. Much of Heidegger's discussion centers around that possible responsiveness.

The response to Being as refusal must consist in a corresponding decisive preparatory renunciation. The decisiveness here comes out of "the enthusiasm for the inconceivable donation of the refusal" (GA 65: 23/20), so the givenness of Being (the inconceivable donation) manifests in fundamental concealment and the called-for response of Da-sein. We are called to hold fast to the alienation, the negation that arises out of essentially self-concealing Being. This theme continues when Heidegger asks, can the refusal of Being "become in the extreme the most remote appropriation [*Ereignung*]" (8/9)? This seemingly negative refusal is in fact the most remote appropriation, meaning that it is the "highest gift" (241, 246/190, 194), in that it enables the movement toward transformation. It is the most essential manifestation of Being itself, in its most remote concealment, which is nevertheless accessible in this form—this is what we must steadfastly stay with by way of extraordinary and acute *Achtsamkeit*.[7]

Heidegger characterizes restraint as a predisposition, in that it enables one to be properly disposed to stay with the refusal as gift (GA 65: 15/14). What reigns in restraint is the staying-with the hesitant withholding. The refusal of the self-concealing to reveal itself is the plight we must bear, and it is essential to *stay-with* the plight as it presents itself so that true participation in that manifestation can occur: "Such creating must make ready for the stillness of Being but also must be decisively *against* every attempt . . . to confuse and weaken the unrelenting urgency in the plight of meditation" (95/75). The plight must be preserved (240/189), it must not weaken. We must let it be, stay with it as it manifests itself to us. This sort of participation is essential here, which Heidegger expresses in terms of experience when he says that the seeker must experience the plight of the abandonment by Being (16/15).

II. EFFORT FOR THE DIVINE

We now turn to the question of the relation to the divine, which Thomas Kalary sees as a co-dimension of Being.[8] Heidegger considers the relation between Da-sein and the divine in a discussion of appropriation and the encounter:

> Ap-propriation: i.e., in the indigence [Notschaft] out of which the gods need Being, Being compels Da-sein to the grounding of the truth of Being and thus lets the 'between', the appropriation of Da[-]sein by the gods and assignment of the gods to themselves, essentially occur as the appropriating event.... The appropriation, as de-cision, brings the separated ones into the *en-counter* [*Entgegnung*].... The en-counter is the origin of the strife, and the strife essentially occurs by unsettling beings from their lostness in mere beingness. (GA 65: 470/370)

Being thus calls Da-sein to its task of grounding a site for the sake of the divine manifestation. The encounter is a relation that holds between Da-sein and the divine which unsettles mortals from their immersion in beings and urges them higher. Heidegger sees history itself as the result of the call of the divine: "History: conceived as the playing out of the strife between earth and world, assumed and performed out of the belonging to the call of the event as the essential occurrence of the truth of Being in the form of the last god" (96/76). Heidegger lays out a path to the divine as enabled by restraint, whereby "Da-*sein* is disposed toward the *stillness* of the passing by of the last god," and "the human being becomes the *steward* [*Wächter*] of this stillness" (17/16). The acute and sustained watchfulness for the presence of the divine enables participation in the stillness which is essential for the divine manifestation.

The source of the dispositions discussed above which enable steadfastness in Da-sein can be traced back to the divine, given that the force of the divine is essential for the nature of Being and hence the corresponding dispositions.[9] We participate in the showing of the divine by providing a site for its manifestation: "At issue is the retrieval of humans from the intractability of nonbeings into the tractability of the restrained creation of the site destined for the passing by of the last god" (7-8/9). Note the *restrained* creation of the site of manifestation, which disposition is required for the appropriate effort: "This restraint alone can gather humans and human assemblies to themselves, i.e., into the destiny of their assignment: the enduring [*Beständnis*] of the last god" (34/29).

We are called to ground the opening of the *Da* as a concrete site for the divine manifestation. What appears in the clearing is the truth of Being, so in this case what is made manifest is the remoteness of the divine—that is the truth of Being, what is shown from that which is self-concealing. This truth calls us to respond to it, to withstand the pain of the remoteness, to bear it and hold open the clearing in staying-with the pain. The staying-with this clearing of self-concealment enables a more profound showing of the hidden dimension.

We are assigned, appropriated to the gods for this task. We are at their disposal in order to open up the "open realm of divinization [*das Offene der Gotterung*]" (GA 65: 18/16-17). He asks: "How remote from us is the god, the god that appoints us ones who ground and create because the god's essence needs these?" (23/20). The divine is the highest and thus most concealed, and due to that remoteness, the most sustained and acute effort is required to clear the divine presence. This remoteness is the manifestation and requires a strenuous effort of staying-with for that reason.

Heidegger goes on to discuss how we are called to experience the plight of abandonment:

> This plight does not first need help but instead must itself first become the help. Yet this plight must actually be experienced. . . . The awakening to this plight is the first dislodging of the human being into that *between* where confusion presses on and, in like measure, the god continues to abscond. (GA 65: 25-26/22)

Staying with the plight can help us move forward to an active letting, a letting pass by. The dislodging refers again to the need to wrest human being out of immersion in the common understanding (*das Man*) in order to make the leap to the way of transition and transformation. We need to dwell in confusion rather than complacent "knowing" in order to be on the way. And we let the god continue to abscond, for we must stay with its manifestation to enable the transition. Heidegger goes on to say "If, through this dislodging, humans come to stand [*stehen*] in the event and remain steadfast [*inständlich*] there in the truth of Being," that will determine in part "the remaining absent or the intrusion" of the divine (26/23).

III. PRESERVATION OF THE TRUTH OF BEING IN BEINGS

The constitution, configuration, and restoration of beings are essential for the full occurrence of *Ereignis*:

> The abandonment by Being happens to beings and indeed to beings as a whole and thereby also to that being which, as human, stands in the midst of beings

and, in so doing, forgets their being. Through a disclosure of the abandonment by Being, the resonating of Being seeks to bring back Being in its *full essential occurrence* as event. That bringing back will happen only if, through the grounding of Da-sein, beings are placed back into Being as opened up in the leap. (GA 65: 116/92)

Thus, the abandonment of Being affects beings themselves, including human beings who stand in the midst of beings but are absorbed in them, thereby forgetting the Being that has withdrawn. The very disclosure of that withdrawal, the resonance of the abandonment by Being, calls on Da-sein to ground the *Da*, which would enable Being to be brought back to full essential occurrence (*vollen Wesung*). The key point is that *beings must be placed back into Being* in order for Being to be brought back to *Ereignis*. That is, beings are needed in this quest in what is an example of reciprocal relatedness in Heidegger's holism, in this case between beings and Being: "Being essentially occurs only in the appropriating eventuation [*Er-eignung*], in virtue of which Da-sein achieves a grounding of the truth of Being in a sheltering through beings" (118/94). This grounding of the truth of Being is achieved by way of great effort and strife, which enables it to be made manifest and embedded in concrete beings: "Only through great breakdowns and upheavals of beings do the beings . . . come to give way before Being and thereby enter its truth" (241/190). A further citation shows restraint as enabling such development of beings in the clearing of Being:

[Restraint] establishes . . . the opening of the simplicity and greatness of beings and the originally compelled necessity of securing in beings the truth of Being so as to give the historical human being a goal once again, namely, *to become the one who grounds and preserves the truth of Being,* to be [*sein*] the "there" as the ground required by the very essence of Being. . . . (16/15)

Restraint is a correspondence to the withdrawal which disposes Da-sein to *be* the *Da*, which means to provide the constancy that is required for *Ereignis*. This enables human beings to ground and preserve the truth of Being *in beings*—this is essential for it to be experienced (322/255), to be "read off" as it were from the concrete beings in which it is preserved.[10] Heidegger says that this preservation is required by the very essence of Being, where Da-sein becomes "steadfast in order to transform the plight of the abandonment by Being into the necessity of creating [e.g., works of art] as the restoring [*Wiederbringung*] of beings" (18/16). That is, a transformation in beings comes about by way of Da-sein discharging its task of preservation. This is Heidegger's version of world constitution, or re-constitution. Only then can "beings again be beings, i.e., can be for the sake of the preservation of Being"

(243/191). Thus the very steadfastness that is required for the constancy of the *Da* is also the basis for grounding the truth of Being in concrete beings for its preservation; that is, in constituting a world that is founded on that truth.

This process requires concrete sites for the manifestation of such beings, in order to carry out the re-creation of beings, where future "single ones" (GA 65: 96/76) ground the sites in advance of a more general transformation that is to be achieved by a critical mass of humanity. Works of art play an essential role in the process: "Because many of these preservations, and indeed exceptional ones, are required to let beings arise in themselves at all, there must be art, in whose *work* the truth is set" (243/191). Heidegger speaks of this process with Platonic overtones when he discusses the work of Da-sein here as a "downgoing (*Untergang*)": "Beings are brought into their *constancy* [*Beständigkeit*] through the *downgoing* of those who ground the truth of Being" (7/8). He refers to the "sheltering the truth of Being in beings as a restoration of beings" (27/23), which would indicate a return of sorts to a prior condition. The restoration can be viewed as a *resacralization* given the role that is played by the divine in the form of the last god, which would imply an earlier age where the presence of the divine was more palpable to humanity.

IV. THE PRESENCING OF THE DIVINE

The truth of Being must be sheltered in concrete beings, and ultimately the truth of Being is the divine (GA 65: 96, 331, 382/76, 262, 302). This means that the divine presencing itself is preserved in beings: "Da-sein, as the sustaining of this strife [*Bestreitung dieses Streites*], has its essence in the sheltering of the truth of Being, i.e., in sheltering, within *beings*, the last god" (34/29).[11] Da-sein must stand steadfast in the midst of the strife of beings (of earth and world) in order to provide the constancy that is required for the divine presence. This is the essential decision that historical humanity faces, whether or not the last god will be made manifest. Heidegger discusses the "last human being" who "denies to the historical human being the last god" (28/24), which refers to the fallen humanity that has failed to open to the sacred, in contrast to the human being of the future who belongs to the truth of Being. The decision calls for ontological effort to hold open and belong to the truth, thereby enabling the manifestation of the last god and its sheltering in beings.

Heidegger explains that this decision is necessary for the last god to be honored and preserved, which is required "by the god himself":

> The passing by of the last god requires a constancy of beings and thus of the human being in the midst of beings. In this constancy, beings in the simplicity

of their respectively regained essence (as work, tool, thing, deed, look, word) first withstand the passing by and so do not still it, but let it run its course. (GA 65: 413/327)

The contrast is interesting between the stillness that is required of Da-sein for the withstanding, while at the same time, the divine passing by is *not* stilled, but rather must be let be. The divine requires the constancy of Da-sein which enables the constancy of beings, which are thus able to *withstand* the passing by, to let it run its course. Human exertion is called for "to bring Being itself to its truth in beings" (85/68), and thus for the divine as the most concealed truth of Being to be made manifest in beings. This effort is simple watching [*wachen*] and waiting [*warten*] in the clearing for the intimations of the divine to arrive, in preparation for that event. Watchfulness enables and maintains the presencing of the divine in things. "Such preparedness above all requires that this truth itself already create . . . the basic traits of its site (Da-sein). The human subject must be transformed into the builder and steward [*Wächter*] of that site" (242/191). The creative efforts of human being are called for to build beings that enable the great stillness which can greet the coming of the divine.

The called-for attending can only be a waiting, a cor-responsiveness by way of acute steadfast staying-with the beings in which we are immersed. Such staying-with enables the truth of Being to be preserved (*wahren*) in those beings. This is world transformative, in that beings are themselves transformed when the truth of Being is preserved in them. Given that the manifestation of the divine is the most concealed phenomenon of Being, the essence of the truth of Being, this means that the divine enters the world in this transformation, and the dehumanization of humanity comes to an end as we are restored to our proper being.

V. THE ORIGIN OF THE WORK OF ART

I now consider "The Origin of the Work of Art," which was written at the same time as *Contributions* and referenced eight times in that text. As discussed above, Heidegger says in *Contributions* that for beings to arise at all "there must be art, in whose *work* the truth is set" (GA 65: 243/191). This theme of setting the truth into work is spelled out in more detail in "Origin." In this text, Heidegger discusses the nature of Being in the context of the work of art, where work is taken in the verbal/ontological sense of effort and strife. Setting means bringing to a stand, a standing that is enabled by the work, where the being of Da-sein and its effort of preservation is essential for such standing to occur. He also considers the question of the presencing of the divine, here in the context of a temple that serves to found a world of human relations.

Heidegger provides the example of a Van Gogh painting where the being of a pair of peasant shoes "comes into the steadiness of its shining" (GA 5: 36/35), and the constancy of the being of the shoes is enabled by being set in the work of art. He concludes, "The nature of art would then be this: the truth of beings setting itself to work" (36/35). Heidegger then considers a Greek temple as an example of non-representational art in order to get at the happening of truth in the work. The building encloses a statue of a god, the concealment of which is the basis for its presencing (*Anwesen*) in the temple, which in turn is the basis for the holiness of the holy precinct. Heidegger's insistence on the reality of the divine presence is consistent with the discussion in *Contributions*, where the truth of Being that happens there is that of the last god. The temple and its precinct is the basis for the open relational context which is the world of this historical people (28/41), which means that the presencing of the divine attunes, or sets the tone for that world.

Heidegger argues that the work of art must be understood within the context of the world that it creates, and that the world in turn depends on the work-being of the work. A world is not a collection of pre-existing entities to which is added the work of art, but rather the opposite: "The temple, in its standing there, first gives to things their look and to men their outlook on themselves. This view remains open as long as the work is a work, as long as the god has not fled from it" (GA 5: 29/42). The entities which are made manifest in that world are not pre-given, but rather their very manifestation depends upon the temple and its presencing god. Moreover, the presencing of the god sets the tone for the whole world of this historical people. Crucially, the look, the view that emerges here *depends on the work-being of this work of art*, and the presencing of the god must be sustained for that work-being to remain what it is. This is the work of preservation performed by historical humanity, which a key theme in the text.

The work of art is not a representation, but is rather a vehicle for the presencing of the divine. "The sculpture of the god . . . is not a portrait whose purpose is to make it easier to realize how the god looks; rather, it is a work that lets the god himself be present and thus *is* the god himself" (GA 5: 29/42). The sculpture enables the presencing of the divine, and the same is true for linguistic works. The theme of decision which is important in *Contributions* also appears here, and while Heidegger notes that this is not an act of the human subject, we participate in it to the extent to which our whole being is engaged in these works.

To further the point regarding the presencing of the divine, Heidegger discusses how the setting up of the art work differs from the ordinary erecting, or "bare placing" of a building, in that it is "erecting in the sense of dedication and praise":

> To dedicate means to consecrate, in the sense that in setting up the work the holy is opened up as holy and the god is invoked into the openness of his presence. Praise belongs to dedication as doing honor to the dignity and splendor of the god. Dignity and splendor are not properties beside and behind which the god, too, stands as something distinct, but it is rather in the dignity, in the splendor that the god is present. In the reflected glory of this splendor there glows, i.e., there lightens itself, what we called the world. (GA 5: 30/42-43)

The presence of the divine shows itself in the dignity and splendor that is to be experienced. These are not representations in a private mental sphere, but are rather in the world which glows in reflected glory. Thus the world of paths, relations, and decisions resides in the reflected glory of the splendor of the divine. The work keeps the world "abidingly in force," which means that ontological effort of preservation maintains the worlding of that world in the divine presencing.

Heidegger discusses how the being of the work sets up a world, and what that world is in relation to the earth. We saw above that the effort of preservation is required for the restoration of beings, for the production of constancy of entities in the strife of earth and world. He pursues this theme in the context of the work-being of the work of art, noting that the work holds open "the Open of the world" (GA 5: 31/44). World as essentially self-disclosing openness (35/47) needs these efforts of opening to be sustained in its worlding: "In a world's worlding is gathered that spaciousness out of which the protective grace of the gods is granted or withheld. Even this doom of the god remaining absent is a way in which world worlds. A work, by being a work, makes space for that spaciousness" (31/44). The presence or absence of the divine grace depends on the open spaciousness of world, which depends in turn on human efforts of opening and preserving the work-being of the work. The work makes a space; that is, ontological effort opens up a space that is an opening to the sacred in whatever manner it shows itself.

Heidegger also considers the strife (*Streit*) of the world–earth opposition, where earth is a self-secluding sheltering and concealing (GA 5: 34/47) which consists of materials that are set forth in setting up the work and its world. That is, these worldly materials "come forth for the very first time and to come into the Open of the work's world" (32/45). This interaction between the opening of world and the self-secluding grounding of the earth is the essence of the work-being of the work, in that it forms the basis for the standing self-subsistence of the work in a "closed, unitary repose of self-support" (34/47). That is, given that the work is the happening of truth, any repose has within it intense underlying activity, and is thus a rest that includes motion. "Where rest includes motion, there can exist a repose which is an inner concentration [*Sammlung*] of motion, hence a highest state of agitation, assuming that the mode of motion requires such a rest. Now the repose of the work that rests in itself is of this sort" (35-36/47). Thus, the work of art is an ongoing activity that has its state of repose, which comes about by way of a force that includes the work of preservation by human beings.

While the world as self-opening cannot bear anything that is closed, earth on the other hand is the "spontaneous forthcoming of that which is continually self-secluding" (GA 5: 36/47). In such opposition, they transcend themselves, going beyond what they would be in the absence of such opposition. "The fighting of the battle is the continually self-overreaching gathering of the work's agitation" (36/48). The unifying resting repose that arises out of such conflict is the work-being of the work, which depends in turn on the stabilizing influence of the preservers who "respond to the truth happening in the work" (54/64). Heidegger also says that the being of the work, the thrust and "the steadfastness of the work's self-subsistence" [*Beständigkeit des Insichruhens am Werk*] is expressed the more that the work opens itself and shows itself as created (53/63), which comes about by way of relatedness to the happening of truth in the clearing of Being.

The work itself instigates the striving between earth and world, so that the strife remains a strife (GA 5: 36/48). The key point, however, is that we participate in this work, as will be discussed below. This theme is also present in *Contributions*, in that we must stay with the truth of Being as it shows itself in order for transformation to occur. In *Contributions*, the indigence of the divine leads Being to call Da-sein to its appointed task (GA 65: 470/370, as discussed above), which is also the basis for the strife. Sustaining the strife brings each entity into its own as reconfigured, holding the work in its being and the associated underlying struggle between earth and world, which enables the being of the work to endure. This is the preservation of the being of the work, together with the presencing of the divine within the work and the associated beings in the reflected glory of the divine.

Ontological effort of standing and holding also appears at this point in "Origin": "Truth happens in the temple's standing where it is. . . . What is as a whole is brought into unconcealedness and held therein. To hold [*halten*] originally means to tend, keep, take care [*hüten*]" (GA 5: 42-43/54). Heidegger emphasizes beings as a whole, appearing in the clearing (unconcealedness) even though what is evident is the particularity of entities that are made manifest; but the very context for all that is forms the basis for their meaningful emergence. We also see the relation here between ontological effort of standing and holding, and care or preservation.

What is held in the work of art is the truth that is happening in the work. This is the actual created reality of the work, in the conflict between world and earth (GA 5: 45/56). Heidegger explains further why the truth needs to be established in beings:

> The openness of this Open, that is, truth, can be what it is, namely, *this* openness, only if and as long as it establishes itself within its Open. Hence there must always be some being in this Open, something that is, in which the openness takes its stand and attains its constancy [*Ständigkeit*]. In taking possession thus of the Open, the openness holds open the Open and sustains it [*hält sie dieses offen und aus*]. (GA 5: 48/59)

The nature of truth is to occur in the midst of beings because this enables the happening of truth to be sustained. There is a reciprocal relation in the manifestation and formation of beings and the opening of Da-sein, in that the opening of Da-sein enables the emergence of beings which in turn enables that opening to be sustained.

The point now comes "to take the step toward which everything thus far said tends" (GA 5: 54/64), as Heidegger discusses the preservation of the work of art which is essential for the being of the work. We are called on to preserve the work in a particular manner as we respond to the truth that is happening therein and are transported out of our ordinary ways of being:

> To submit to this displacement means: to transform our accustomed ties to world and to earth and henceforth to restrain [*ansichhalten*] all usual doing and prizing, knowing and looking, in order to stay within [*zu verweilen* (stay, linger, dwell)] the truth that is happening in the work. Only the restraint [*Verhaltenheit*] of this staying lets what is created be the work that it is. This letting the work be a work we call the preserving of the work. It is only for such preserving that the work yields itself in its createdness as actual; i.e., now: present in the manner of a work. (GA 5: 54/64)[12]

A *staying-within* the truth that is happening in the work is called for, which is the essence of *Achtsamkeit*. This staying is a letting, and Heidegger says in the Addendum that "this letting is nothing passive but a doing in the highest degree" (71/82), which evidences the activity that is called for in acute and sustained attentiveness. Related to this is the letting and preserving which is essential for the actuality of the work which shows itself in its createdness.

Preserving is a staying-with and a standing-within that is a *knowing* and a willing:

> Preserving the work means: standing within [*Innestehen*] the openness of Being that happens in the work. This "standing-within" of preservation, however,

is a knowing. . . . Knowing that remains a willing . . . is the existing human being's entrance into and compliance with the unconcealedness of Being. (GA 5: 54-55/65)

This is not the deliberate action of a subject, but is rather a freeing out of captivity to that which is (*das Man*); that is, from being immersed in beings to being present to the very event of their manifestation in the clearing of Being. Heidegger goes further and insists that this is not the private experience of an enjoyable work of art, but is rather a joining in our very being with the truth that is happening in the work: "Preserving the work does not reduce people to their private experiences, but brings them into affiliation with the truth happening in the work" (55/66). We are affiliated with the truth of the work and with our fellow historical beings by preserving the work of art in this manner. In addition, Heidegger links the knowing that comes about by participating in the happening of truth with a being resolved, and says "It is standing within the conflict that the work has fitted into the rift" (56/66), where the rift is the basis for the Gestalt of the work of art which comes about by way of the confluence of earth and world. The text (excluding epilogue and addendum) concludes with a statement linking this knowing and attending: "Are we in our existence historically at the origin? Do we know, which means do we give heed to [*achten*], the nature of the origin?" (66/75).[13]

For Heidegger, *Achtsamkeit*, or acute and sustained human presencing, enables our participation in the happening of truth and is thus a knowing that is not a representing, but rather a belonging to the very being of what is at stake in the matter. Compare the following citation from the 1942 *Parmenides* (GA 54: 4/3):[14]

> Everything depends on our paying heed [*achten*] to the claim arising out of the thoughtful word. Only in this way, paying heed to the claim, do we come to know the dictum. What man heeds [*achtet*], what respect [*Achtung*] he gives to the heeded, how original and how constant [*stetig*] he is in his heedfulness [*achtsam*], that is what is decisive as regards the dignity allotted to man out of history.
>
> To think is to heed the essential. In such heedfulness essential knowing resides.

VI. "BUILDING DWELLING THINKING"

Similar themes appear in "Building Dwelling Thinking," which originated from a 1951 lecture on "Man and Space" and published in 1952. Heidegger begins this inquiry into the nature of dwelling and its relation to building by noting that *Bauen* has roots in the High German word *buan*, which means to dwell, to remain, or stay in a place (GA 7: 148/144). This is related to *ich bin*, which refers to the way we *are* as humans on this earth (149/145), which in turn is a caring that only watches or tends to the growth that emanates out of its own source, not a making of anything. Heidegger will go on to say that dwelling is the basic character of human being, which I have argued elsewhere is the staying-with of *Achtsamkeit*.[15] Dwelling is related to a staying-with things that rest within themselves (in their own concealment) within the freeing clearing of Being.

Heidegger now discusses the fourfold, which consists of a "primal oneness" where "earth and sky, divinities and mortals—belong together in one" (151/147): "Mortals *are* in the fourfold by *dwelling*. But the basic character of dwelling is to spare, to preserve. Mortals dwell in the way they preserve the fourfold in its essential being, its presencing" (152/148). Thus the very being of human beings is dwelling in the fourfold, which is a preserving. But what they preserve is the presencing of the fourfold, which importantly includes the divine presencing: "They dwell in that they await [*erwarten*] the divinities as divinities. . . . They wait for intimations of their coming and do not mistake the signs of their absence. . . . In the very depth of misfortune they wait for the weal that has been withdrawn" (GA 7: 152/148). Thus in another reference to the doom of "Origin," we see the misfortune that is associated with the withdrawal of the divine. The "awaiting the divinities" recalls the waiting of the 1944–1945 *Country Path Conversations*, for instance, which in this text is associated with *Achtsamkeit*: "In waiting [*warten*], the human-being becomes gathered in attentiveness [*Achtsamkeit*] to that in which he belongs, yet without letting himself get carried away into and absorbed in it" (GA 77: 226/147).[16] The tendency to fall must be withstood, as we stay with the essentials that present themselves to us.

Heidegger continues to discuss preservation, which means that we care for the fourfold in its presencing (GA 7: 153/149). He concludes: "Dwelling itself is always a staying with things [*Aufenthalt*]. Dwelling, as preserving, keeps the fourfold in that with which mortals stay: in things" (153/149). Thus, staying with the things of everyday engagement (namely, the beings of *Contributions*) enables the fulfilled presencing of the things as constituted by the fourfold.

He goes on to inquire into the nature of a built thing, and considers the example of a bridge which gathers the earth as landscape around a stream, and grants their way to mortals (GA 7: 154/150):

> Now in a high arch, now in a low, the bridge vaults over glen and stream—whether mortals keep in attention [*in der Acht behalten*] this vaulting of the bridge's course or forget that they, always themselves on their way to the last

bridge, are actually striving to surmount all that is common and unsound in them in order to bring themselves before the haleness of the divinities [*das Heile des Göttlichen*]. The bridge *gathers*, as a passage that crosses, before the divinities—whether we explicitly think of, and visibly *give thanks for*, their presence, as in the figure of the saint of the bridge, or whether that divine presence is obstructed or even pushed wholly aside. (155/150-51, trans. mod.)

The bridge lies before us whether we attend to it or not; this refers to the primal *legein* that enables *homologein*. We must explicitly think of and give thanks for that presence, or risk obstruction or pushing aside the divine presence. When we do attend (*in der Acht behalten*) to the vaulting of the bridge and thus to the greater context in which we dwell, we remember our ultimate quest to transcend the "common and unsound" and relate to the divine, to bring ourselves "before the haleness of the divinities." Thus in this later work, we see explicitly the relation between *Achtsamkeit* and the divine which is so important in the world's spiritual traditions.

CONCLUSION

The indigence [*Notschaft*] of the divine is the origin of the work of art, and its manifestation shows itself in the fate of humankind and its relation to the divine.[17] For the presence or absence of the divine sets the tone for the world, which includes the disposition of the preservers of the site where the manifestation occurs, which is essential for that very presencing and the associated mortal disposition. This is Heidegger's hermeneutical and phenomenological take on the question of the relation of art and the divine and on the perennial notion of the spiritual quest. He comes to the astonishing notion of world re-sacralization, which means that the glory of the divine can reappear in the life of the people if they work to preserve that presencing in the things of this world, in which they themselves are included. Perhaps this means that we can aspire for our lives to be works of art which manifest the divine presence—as long as we persist in the effort to stay present to It ourselves.

NOTES

1. "The Origin of the Work of Art." In *Poetry, Language, Thought*. Trans. Albert Hofstadter (New York: Harper Perennial Modern Thought, 2013), 15–86. GA 5.
2. *Contributions to Philosophy (Of the Event)*. Trans. Richard Rojcewicz and Daniela Vallega-Neu (Bloomington, IN: Indiana University Press, 2012). GA 65.

3. L. Berger, "Attention as the Way to Being," *Gatherings: The Heidegger Circle Annual* 10 (2020): 111–56. The important cognate *Hören* appears much earlier, but in contexts that are typically limited to discussions of language.

4. "Building Dwelling Thinking." In *Poetry, Language, Thought*. Trans. Albert Hofstadter (New York: Harper Perennial Modern Thought, 2013, 143–59). GA 7.

5. See Richard Capobianco, *Heidegger's Way of Being* (Toronto: University of Toronto Press, 2014), especially Ch. 1 for a discussion of the primacy of Being. Also see Capobianco, *Engaging Heidegger* (Toronto: University of Toronto Press, 2010), especially Ch. 1.

6. E.g., "The hesitant [*zögernde*] withholding is the intimation that beckons Da-*sein*, and this latter is precisely the constancy [*Beständnis*] of clearing concealment" (GA 65: 380/300). See Berger, "Attention as the Way to Being," for further discussion.

7. I note again that although Heidegger does not employ *Achtsamkeit* in this text, he soon makes the connection in the early 1940s and beyond.

8. Kalary argues that the God question is a co-dimension of the essential occurrence of Being as *Ereignis*, which is the center of Being-historical thinking. "The divine . . . shows itself in an always already prevalent relationship that calls for and calls forth a continuous response. It is the type of human response that would decide whether the divine "passes by" or "stays away," whether man remains god-less and thus dis-humanized or god-filled and thus genuinely humanized." T. Kalary, "Heidegger's Thinking of Difference and the God-Question," in *Heidegger, Translation, and the Task of Thinking: Essays in Honor of Parvis Emad*, ed. F. Schalow, Contributions To Phenomenology 65, (Springer, 2011), 132.

9. E.g., "Being is the trembling [*Erzitterung*, quaking, silent power] of divinization" (239/189), and "disposition is the diffusion of the trembling of Being" (21/19).

10. "The grounding of Da-*sein* transforms every relation to beings, and the truth of Being is first experienced" (322/255).

11. See also "The essence of Da-sein . . . is the sheltering of the truth of Being, of the last god, in beings" (308/244).

12. See also "A work is in actual effect as a work only when we remove ourselves from our commonplace routine and move into what is disclosed by the work, so as to bring our own nature itself to take a stand [*Stehen zu bringen*] in the truth of what is" (62/72). Heidegger adds a marginal note to the Reclam edition of 1960: *im Sinne der Inständigkeit im Brauch*, so we see the appearance of *Inständigkeit* which is so important in *Contributions*, together with the notion of the usage of human being by Being.

13. "The Origin of the Work of Art" was delivered in a series of lectures in 1936, and we have seen that *Achtsamkeit* does not emerge as a theme for Heidegger until 1940. However, it was not published until 1950, and it was Heidegger's habit to often revise his works, even those that had already been published. In this regard, Heidegger says at the end of his notes in *Holzwege*, where "Origin" was originally published, that "In the intervening time these pieces have been repeatedly revised and, in some places, clarified." I have not been able to find evidence that this particular

statement was revised after 1940, but given that (to my knowledge) *achten* does not appear in a meaningful manner in this or any other text prior to that time, I believe that this sentence was modified to reflect his new appreciation for attention well after the lectures were delivered.

14. *Parmenides*. Trans. André Schuwer and Richard Rojcewicz (Bloomington, IN: Indiana University Press, 1992). GA 54.

15. Berger, "Attention as the Way to Being."

16. *Country Path Conversations*. Trans. Bret W. Davis (Bloomington, IN: Indiana University Press, 2010). GA 77.

17. See R. Polt, *The Emergency of Being: On Heidegger's Contributions to Philosophy* (Ithaca, NY: Cornell University Press, 2006) for a discussion of *die Not* in this context.

Chapter 4

Poetic Colors of the Holy

Heidegger on Pindar and Trakl

Ian Alexander Moore

In the epigraph to one of the most formative books for Heidegger's education, *Vom Sein: Abriß zur Ontologie (On Being: An Outline of Ontology)*, Carl Braig cites the medieval Franciscan St. Bonaventure:

> Strange, then, is the blindness of the intellect which does not consider that which it sees before all others and without which it can recognize nothing. But just as the eye, intent on the various differences of color, does not see the light through which it sees other things, or if it does see, does not notice it, so our mind's eye, intent on particular and universal beings, does not notice that being which is beyond all categories, even though it comes first to the mind, and through it, all other things.[1]

Bonaventure's analogy is clear enough. Color is to light as beings are to Being. Just as we do not pay attention to the light that makes the perception of color possible, so too do we not pay attention to Being, despite presupposing it in all our thoughts and actions. Yet how are we to understand the analogy when the terms are switched and Being itself is compared, not just to light, but to color, thus to what would seem to be merely *a* being or, at best, a finite set of beings? What, moreover, is going on when Being is not just *compared* to particular colors, but *equated* with them?

In this essay, I will examine the work of two poets who, on Heidegger's interpretation, use particular colors to characterize Being and the related concept of the Holy. Although separated by two-and-a-half millennia, Heidegger finds that the victory odes of the Ancient Greek lyricist Pindar and the melancholic poetry of the twentieth-century Austrian expressionist Georg Trakl were both written under a sort of "holy compulsion" (*heilige Zwang*) (GA 78: 67). Through them, Being spoke itself—synesthetically—in colors: gold in the case of Pindar, blue (along with gold) in the case of Trakl. I first look at Heidegger's extensive excursus on Pindar's 5th *Isthmian* in the undelivered lecture course *Der Spruch des Anaximander* (*Anaximander's Verdict*) (§1). Then I turn to Heidegger's discussion of Trakl's poems "*Ein Winterabend*" ("A Winter Evening"), "*Abendländisches Lied*" ("Occidental Song"), and "*Sommersneige*" ("Summer's Decline") in the first two chapters of *Unterwegs zur Sprache* (*On the Way to Language*) (§2). While it might seem that, at the ontological level, golden shining is proper exclusively to the ancients and bluish twilight to the post-Hölderlinian moderns, I argue that, in his respective analyses, Heidegger is drawing out different *aspects* of Being and the Holy that belong to all epochs, even if they cannot always be seen as such, and even if different gods show up in them. I conclude with some reflections on what might be called, following Goethe, a Heideggerian *Farbenlehre* ("color theory") (§3).

Before I begin, three caveats. First, I focus on material from Heidegger's late thought, starting in the 1940s. In the late 1910s and early 1920s, Heidegger, like many of his contemporaries (Ernst Troeltsch, Wilhelm Windelband), was quite interested in the significance of the Holy, especially in the wake of Rudolf Otto's pathbreaking quasi-phenomenological study *Das Heilige* (*The Holy*) (1917), where Otto famously coins the term "the numinous" to characterize the incomprehensible, mysterious, simultaneously threatening and enticing aspects of the Holy.[2] Husserl, on whom Otto's analysis had, in the words of the founder of phenomenology, "a stronger effect [. . .] than almost any other book in years," once expressed disappointment that Heidegger did "not have time to write a (thoroughgoing) critique" of it.[3] While it might be worthwhile to compare what Heidegger did manage to write on Otto in this time period (GA 60: 332–334) with his later treatment of Being and the Holy in Pindar and Trakl, for reasons of space I cannot do so here, especially since neither Otto nor the early Heidegger examines the Holy's chromatic manifestations.

Second, after Heidegger's interest shifted away from medieval mysticism and primal Christianity to phenomenological ontology in the mid-1920s, comments on the Holy nearly disappeared from his writings (the word is absent in *Being and Time*, for example), only to resurface in 1934–1935 with his first lecture course on Hölderlin. However, despite Hölderlin's overwhelming importance for the topic in Heidegger and for Heidegger's general appreciation of Pindar, the only times, of which I am aware, when Heidegger links the Holy to color (in this case, gold) in his writings on Hölderlin are when he is drawing on Pindar, whose work accordingly remains the primary source for Heidegger's appreciation of the colored aspects of the Holy.[4] Third, I will bracket the question of whether and to what extent Heidegger's articulation of the Holy overlaps with, or can assist in the understanding of, holiness in Biblical faith. In the "*Brief über den Humanismus*" ("Letter on Humanism"), Heidegger states that Being is that on the basis of which the Holy, the Godhead (*Gottheit*), and God (*Gott*) may be understood (GA 9:

351). And yet, in a later discussion with a group of philosophers and theologians, Heidegger clarifies that, in the "Letter," "God" is meant to refer "only to the god of the poet, not to the god of revelation."[5] This clarification would, presumably, also hold for the Holy, although that need not concern us here.

I. CHRUSOLOGY, ONTOLOGY, HIEROLOGY

Heidegger's most extensive engagement with Pindar's *5th Isthmian*—indeed his most extensive engagement with Pindar as such—can be found in a long introduction he wrote for a lecture course (never delivered) on Anaximander, which would later serve as the basis for the final chapter of *Holzwege* (*Logging Paths*). Although the manuscript is undated, it appears to have been written in 1942, thus as the first in a series of lecture courses on the pre-Socratics, followed by the treatment of Parmenides in 1942–1943 and that of Heraclitus in 1943–1944 (GA 78: 340–344; GA 54; GA 55). In this important manuscript, which has yet to be translated into English or discussed *in extenso* in the secondary literature, Heidegger turns to Pindar in order to elucidate the Greek experience of Being, which he then uses to interpret *ta onta* ("beings") in Anaximander's only extant fragment.[6] The manuscript contains two versions of Heidegger's commentary on Pindar: a first, shorter version, which draws heavily on the gold of the poet's earlier 1st Olympian (GA 78: 284–296), and a later, more elaborate version, which focuses almost exclusively on the 5th *Isthmian* (GA 78: 65–98). My remarks will center on the second version.

Heidegger's translation and interpretation of the first eighteen verses of Pindar's victory ode are as remarkable and creative as his translation and interpretation of the first stasimon of Sophocles's *Antigone* (in, for example, GA 40 and GA 53)—and they are just as liable to draw criticism from classicists the world over. Like his rendering of Sophocles's choral ode, Heidegger returned to and revised his rendering of Pindar on numerous occasions later in his career, including, as we will see, in his first essay on Trakl. In order to gain a sense for the radicality of Heidegger's reading of Pindar's poem, let us begin by comparing his translation of just its opening three verses with a couple conventional approaches. Here, first, is Pindar's Greek, along with my attempt at a literal, lexicological rendering:

Μᾶτερ Ἀελίου πολυώνυμε Θεία,
σέο ἕκατι καὶ μεγασθενῆ νόμισαν
χρυσὸν ἄνθρωποι περιώσιον ἄλλων.[7]

*

Mother of Sun, many-named Theia,
on your account humans judge gold
mighty far beyond other things.

Next, a translation into German that Heidegger consults—and criticizes—in his excursus on Pindar:

Mutter des Helios, vielnamige Theia,
deinetwillen glauben die Menschen
großmächtig das Gold, überschwänglich vor allem andern.[8]

Compare, finally, Heidegger's version:

Mutter des Helios, reichnamige, (die) Gottheit (selber den Göttern),
dich in der Acht, denn auch weitwaltend erachten
das Gold die Menschen, (das) anwesender rings um anderes alles. (GA 78: 65–66; Heidegger's parentheses)

*

Mother of Helios, richly named, (the) Godhead (even to the gods),
you, in consideration, because humans also consider gold
far-prevailing, (which) [is] more present around everything else.

At the grammatical-lexical level, Heidegger reads the last phrase of Pindar's invocation, *periōsion allōn*, independently from *megasthenē* ("mighty"), he takes *allōn* together with *peri-* ("around [all] others"), and he exploits the derivation of *-ōsion* from *einai* ("to be [present]"). Gold is not just *exceedingly* mighty in comparison with everything else (*periōsion* as adverb, *allōn* as genitive of comparison). Gold is *more in being, more present*, amid all else (*periōsion* as adjective, *allōn* as object of an implied prepositional phrase). How might Heidegger justify these idiosyncratic linguistic decisions, beyond simply claiming that all genuine translation first requires that *we* be translated, carried across, into the realm in which a poet or thinker speaks (GA 78: 55; GA 54: 17–18)?

On Heidegger's interpretation, Pindar's poem is not simply *about* the heroes it names, whether it be Phylakidas of Aegina, who won the all-in boxing and wrestling contest at the Isthmian Games, probably in 478 BCE (verses 17–19); the Greek sailors who had recently defeated the Persians at the battle of Salamis (verses 48–50); or Achilles, son of the local Aiakidai (verses 39–42). The poem is, accordingly, not simply an encomium or "the fitting boast, mixed with song, about toils" (κόμπον τὸν ἐοικότ' ἀοιδᾷ /

κιρνάμεν ἀντὶ πόνων), as Pindar himself sings in the second strophe (verses 24–25).[9] The 5th *Isthmian* also—and more fundamentally—names the Holy and lets Being appear. To cite Heidegger's conclusion right away (before working our way up to it):

> because the poetizing saying, in itself, brings the Being of beings to shine [*zum Scheinen*], everything that is said in the truly saying song "is" "more in being" [*"seiender"*], which is to say, however, more shining, more gleaming [*glänzender*]. For, the saying of the songs names the holiness [*das Heilige*] of Theia. They are therefore called *hierai aodai*, "holy songs." [. . . The] "ground," on the basis of which the poet says [such things], can [. . .] be called the "ground" of the pure gleaming forth [*Erglänzens*], the "gold-ground." (GA 78: 96–97, in reference to Pindar-Fragment no. 194[10])

In order to appreciate the foundational role that gold plays in Heidegger's analysis of Pindar, we must first shift our commonplace impressions of it, whether it be as (1) a color, (2) an element, or (3) currency. (1) Gold is not, fundamentally, the property of an object that causes ocular sensation through the reflection or emission of light. It is not the perception of a particular wavelength within the visible spectrum. If it were, gold would not shine most among the colors, and we would have to wonder whether, as the product of perception, it would even be a being at all, let alone Being itself. (2) Might Pindar be referring to the metal, then, which, unlike color, has chemical properties that explain its existence independently of human sensation? This brings us closer, but even the polished element is not the brightest of all. (3) Should we therefore return to the subjective standpoint and consider how people and the ancient Greeks, in particular, have tended to view it, namely, as valuable and thus as useful for exchange? Since, from this standpoint, gold has a greater purchasing power than other things—since it is greater in acquiring wealth (*ousia*) than they are—it is "mighty far beyond [*periōsion*] other things" (verses 2–3). Yet Heidegger does not, primarily, hear *ousia* in this sense. He is instead thinking about the word and its ontological roots (*einai, on*) before it becomes the guiding concept of substance metaphysics and before gold becomes little else than a quantifiable medium of exchange (see, however, GA 78: 60, 62, 93).

On Heidegger's reading, *einai*, "to be," has the sense of "to be present"—"present," not as an object among others or as a resource to be exploited, but as a being that rises up into unconcealment, shining in its finite splendor. We might think of the Athenian sculptor Phidias's chryselephantine statues of Athena in the Parthenon and of Zeus in the sanctuary of Olympia, which, surely, were *periōsios* in relation to everything around them; surely, these statues "out-gleamed and gleamed around and gleamed through" everything around them (GA 78: 73). Heidegger does not mention these works of art specifically, but, with their references to Victory and the most famous of the Panhellenic Games, they seem especially fitting as material counterparts to the epinician ode.

But even these artistic wonders do not do justice to Pindar's gold. We have to imagine something other than individual beings or even all beings as a whole, however glorious they may be. For, the gold of the *5th Isthmian* is such that its mightiness first lets all beings gleam forth. We therefore cannot understand its own gleam solely in terms of that which it makes possible. Exceeding each and every being, gold is of Being. In Heidegger's words:

> Gold is thus in no way named only as one gleaming thing among others, a thing that would, gradually by degrees, exceed these others in the intensity of its gleam. Rather, gold is named because, thought in Greek terms, the essence of Being consists in shining, so that this being that we call "gold" is in a certain way the Being of beings. In gold, the essence of Being has gathered itself in such a peculiar way that, in the Being of this being, Being can appear [*erscheinen*] as itself. (GA 78: 73–74)

We are accordingly beyond the realm of bodily sensation, despite the seemingly fundamental ocular terminology (appearing, shining, gleaming). Indeed, we cannot even take these terms as metaphors or analogically, since the shining of particular things is possible only on the basis of the prior, prevalent shining of golden Being itself, and there is no way from the former to the latter. We are not subjectively *deeming* gold great (*nomizein* [verse 2] in one of its derivative senses); we are letting it show itself as it is in itself and accordingly giving it its due: "letting what belongs to it belong to it," "heeding it in such a way that it comes into its own [*Er-achten*]" (*nomizein* in the more primordial sense Heidegger identifies in the word) (GA 78: 75, 292–293).[11] In order to have such a regard for gold—a regard that, notably, Heidegger contends is proper to our very essence (GA 78: 80–82, 86, 91–92, 94, 291, 295)—we must not interpret the shining of golden Being in traditional causal terms. It is neither mechanistic nor teleological. It is, instead, more like the blooming of Silesius's rose, *ohn warumb*, "without a reason why."[12] Its strength (*sthenos*, verse 2) is not the exercise of violence (*Gewalt*), but a gathered and gathering (*Ge-*) radiance that gently holds sway (*waltet*) over all things, *letting* them appear and thereby letting them *be* (GA 78: 73–74).[13] If gold, at this level, is holy—and, judging from some later commentaries on the poem (GA 12: 21; GA 80.2: 994, 1016), it is—then, for all its uncanniness, it has lost one of the key characteristics that Otto located in the numinous: fearsomeness. By this point in his career, Heidegger is much closer, not just temporally but also philosophically, to the releasement of the first "Country

Path Conversation" (GA 77) than to the violence of *Einführung in die Metaphysik* (*Introduction to Metaphysics*), where, incidentally, Pindar also appears as one of the great representatives of Greek poetry (GA 40: 108, 121).

We must, furthermore, not interpret the middle-voiced letting of ontological gold as the activity of yet another being, such as Helios, Selene, or any of the other Greek gods (to say nothing of God as *causa prima* or the maker god of metaphysics and monotheism). The gods, *theoi*, on Heidegger's interpretation, are so many ways of looking, *theasthai*, into beings, which is to say, bringing them to light, something along the lines of the formative imagination, *Ein-Bildung*, of the German theosophists. In the other direction, these gods are also so many names for and perspectives on Theia (GA 78: 77–79).

But isn't Theia also a goddess? Doesn't Pindar, following Hesiod (*Theog.* 371), describe her as the *mother* of Helios, the sun-god (verse 1)? And—we could imagine Socrates asking here—aren't the parents of gods also gods? Heidegger, who takes the Greek suffix -*ia* literally, as forming an abstract noun, interprets Theia as the essence of *theos*; "she"—if gender is even appropriate here—is, in Heidegger's rendering, *(die) Gottheit (selber den Göttern)*, "(the) divinity or Godhead (even to the gods)" (GA 78: 65; cf. 76).[14] Theia is, therefore, not *a* god or *a* being. We now need to consider whether she would then, in a certain way, be the same as Being and, if so, how she would relate to gold as, in a certain way, the same as Being.

It makes sense that Heidegger would identify Helios, god of the sun, as "pure shining." But, interestingly, he also describes the god's mother, who "shelters [*birgt*] pure shining in her womb," as "even more shining" than the sun. Shining, at its deepest level, is not what shows up to the animal eye; it is what "first bestows the luminous [*das Lichte*] and open" (GA 78: 77). In this respect, as the most shining, Theia most makes room for other things—nay, for all things—to shine. Heidegger therefore equates her with one of his most important ontological *terms d'art*: Theia is the *Lichtung*, the "clearing" for the manifestation of beings:

> The mother of light is the one who is invoked, insofar as she is *Theia*. As the latter, she grants, looking ahead to the brightness [*Helle*] of shining—before the brightness and always—the widely resounding [*weithallende*] open of the clearing. In this clearing, what comes to light is capable of first appearing and, as what is present, of shining. (GA 78: 78)

Although this is not his main focus, which lies, rather, on the shining of Being, Heidegger also uses the language of sheltering to describe Theia's essence, thereby anticipating the more nocturnal, "bluer" dimension of the Holy in the Trakl-lectures. (This, in spite of her different lineage from that of Night in the *Theogony* [123–124, 132–135].) "The maternal essence of the Godhead," Heidegger writes, "consists *im hütenden Hervorgehenlassen*"; rendered periphrastically: "in a letting emerge that, at the same time, tends and keeps watch over that which emerges" (GA 78: 79). Theia is the "womb and protection of what pertains to the gods [*des Gotthaften*]" (GA 78: 77). More than a god, she is also more abyssal than any god. She is like—or perhaps she just *is*—the *Geborgenheit* ("sheltering") and *lēthē* ("concealment") that lie at the heart of all truth, manifestation, and unconcealment (*alētheia*, *Unverborgenheit*).

In his commentary on Pindar, Heidegger does not delineate the fourfold order of implication *Sein–das Heilige–Gottheit–Götter* as clearly as he does in the "Letter on 'Humanism.'" It is obvious that the gods come last in both cases. But, in the Pindar-material, it is not so easy to distinguish Being, the Holy, and the Godhead from one another. On the one hand, Heidegger implicitly links Being and the Godhead (Theia) by describing the latter as shining, clearing, sheltering, and, through its/her connection to gold, gathering. He also explicitly associates them in an overview of verses 2–17, which he calls "the pure poem of the Godhead of the gods, and nothing else besides": "in the poetizing of the Godhead of the gods, the essence of Being is thought. For this reason, and only for this reason, is gold named" (GA 78: 78).

On the other hand, toward the end of his commentary, Heidegger situates the Godhead *within* what seems to be the deeper dimension of Being: "The Unifying One, which brings what appears to shine, is, as the gathering, as *ho Logos*, Being itself, wherein the Godhead of the gods [. . .] rests" (GA 78: 96). To resolve this tension, I am inclined to interpret Theia and gold as poetic articulations of different *aspects* of Being, rather than as lower members in a hierarchy. In Pindar's ode, which, Heidegger clearly states, "poetizes the essence of Being" (GA 78: 290; see also 64, 286), Theia stands for a more chthonic, lethic, even *choro*-logical aspect of Being, whereas gold is more ouranic, a-lethetic, *phainomeno*-logical— despite Theia's own oxymoronically obscure shining. Through the mouth of the poet, Being approaches us in the gleam of gold and in the *musterion* of Mother Theia.

There is, furthermore, something holy about this golden mystery. Pindar's poetry is not, on Heidegger's interpretation, about making things last longer by preserving them for posterity with compelling and beautiful words. Pindar's poetry is compelling, but this is because he, like few others, *assented* to "the holy compulsion" to sing of gold and "forge the 'gold-ground'" into a language in which things are "'more in being,' which is to say, however, more shining, more gleaming" (GA 78: 67, 96–97). To name this shining and all it involves is to name the "holiness of *Theia*." Pindar's chrusology is, at the same time, a hierology. His theology is—*sit venia verbo*—a theialogy. And his poetry, like any work deserving of the name, is an unspoken ontology.

II. *SACRÉ BLEU*

In the early 1950s, Heidegger returns to many of the ideas he had developed in his commentary on Pindar, including the synesthetic etymological link between *Helle* ("brightness") and *hallend* ("resounding") (GA 78: 78, 86, 88; GA 12: 40); the ability of poetry "to let the unspoken [dimension of Being] be in all its fullness and, in such letting, to bring it 'to' language and thereby bring it close to us" (GA 78: 283; cf. GA 12: 33–35); and, most importantly for the present study, the way in which holy Being manifests itself in particular colors. In his 1950 lecture *"Die Sprache"* ("Language"), which examines Trakl's poem "A Winter Evening" in order to let language speak (itself) beyond or before human expression, Heidegger even returns explicitly to the gold of Pindar's *5th Isthmian*. Here, it is a matter of understanding a peculiar couplet from the second stanza of Trakl's poem:

Golden blüht der Baum der Gnaden
Aus der Erde kühlem Saft. (GA 12: 20)

*

Golden blooms the tree of graces
Rising from the earth's cool sap.

Disregarding the Christian connotations of the couplet and of the poem in general (connotations which Heidegger would in any case see as derivative, at best), Heidegger glosses these verses in terms of what he had recently called the fourfold (GA 79: 12):

> The tree is rooted solidly in the earth. Thus, it thrives to the point of blooming, which opens itself to the blessing of the sky. [. . .] The poem names the tree of graces. Its solid blooming shelters the fruit that falls unearned: the salvific holiness [*das rettend Heilige*] that is propitious to mortals. In the golden, blooming tree, earth and sky, divinities and mortals prevail. Their united fourfold is the world. (GA 12: 21)

As in his reading of Pindar, Heidegger here associates gold with the Holy; only, this time, the Holy (*das Heilige*) is tied more explicitly to salvation (*Rettung, Heil*). Not, to be sure, the salvation of the soul and its promise of eternal bliss in the Beyond, but the salvation that comes with accepting "death" as "the highest concealment of Being" (GA 12: 20) or "of Beyng" (GA 80.2: 1016); salvation, not from the earth, but from the fantasy of everlasting life on the far side of it. Holy gold enables us to dwell authentically on the earth, accepting the gifts of Being even as we accept Being's insuperable concealment.

To develop the connection between the golden Holy and Being—a word (i.e., Being/Beyng) that Heidegger names, as such, only once in his lecture, but to which, by this point in its trajectory, he has already alluded with his reference to the fourfold of the world (see GA 79: 74)—Heidegger now invokes Pindar. In the recently published first version of "Language," Heidegger claims that, if we are to hear the color of Trakl's "A Winter Evening" "rightly," that is to say, the color of a poem penned by a drug-addled twentieth-century Austrian, then it is necessary to draw on, of all things, the Ancient Greek of a Theban lyricist (GA 80.2: 994). The second and final versions of the lecture (1951, 1959) are hardly less abrupt, although they not quite as assertive: the turn to Pindar seems more an issue of expediency, helping the audience to hear Trakl's gold "more clearly" (GA 80.2: 1017, GA 12: 21). In any case, it is plain that Heidegger simply imports his earlier analysis of the *5th Isthmian* into his interpretation of Trakl. Here, I am interested less in the legitimacy of this approach as a reading of Trakl than in what it reveals about Heidegger's own color theory when it comes to the Holy. In the first, more overtly ontological version of the lecture, Heidegger writes:

> At the beginning of this poem [*Isthmian* 5], Pindar names gold[,] *chruson*[,] [...] *periōsion allōn*, that which gleams above all and through all: all *ousia*, every instance of presencing, every shining forth [*Erscheinen*] into unconcealment. The word "golden" summons the luminous letting-gleam-forth, which brings everything forth into serene cheerfulness and shelters it therein. (GA 80.2: 994; Heidegger's ellipsis)

The final version, with its development of the prefix *peri-*, is even more reminiscent of the 1942 analysis:

> At the beginning of this ode, the poet names gold *periōsion pantōn*, that which, like a ring around everything that is present, gleams above all through all, *panta*. The gleam of the gold harbors everything present, bringing it into the unconcealment of its appearing [*birgt alles Anwesende in das Unverborgene seines Erscheinens*]. (GA 12: 21)[15]

These quotations suggest that Pindar's gold pertains as much to Trakl's world— and thus to our world—as it did to that of the pre-Platonic Greek world, even if we might need a different language for becoming attuned to it (German rather than Greek) or even a different attunement altogether (Hölderlin's holy mourning rather than wonder) (GA 78: 85; GA 39: §8). For, to modify a famous term for humans in Pindar's *8th Pythian*, daylight may well have past in the interim, making us *Nachtwesen*, "creatures of the night."[16]

In any event, the suggestion of subterranean continuity between Pindar's and Trakl's gold finds support in another reference to the invocation of Pindar's ode, this time in notes for a 1955 lecture on two poems by the nineteenth-century pastor Eduard Mörike. Regarding the latter's "September-Morgen," and in particular its final verse, which sings of "warm gold," Heidegger writes that one should compare it with the *5th Isthmian*, whose first three verses Heidegger cites and translates anew (GA 74: 177). Moreover, in a famous exchange from 1950–1951 with the literary scholar Emil Staiger, Heidegger argues that the word *scheint* in the final verse of Mörike's *"Auf eine Lampe"* ("On a Lamp") does not mean "seems," *videtur*, but rather "shines," *lucet*, in the precise ontological sense he finds in Pindar's ode.[17] Thus, if Trakl's and Mörike's concerns line up with those of Pindar, then the Greek *chrusos* and all it entails do not belong solely to the Greek experience of Being, as one might be led to expect from a study of the earlier treatment in the Pindar-commentary alone. They also belong—or more accurately, could and ought to belong, if only we were to pay heed to them—to our experience as well.

What, however, should we make of the fact that, in Heidegger's second lecture on Trakl, *"Die Sprache im Gedicht"* ("Language in the Poem"), it is, not gold, but blue that characterizes the Holy? Has Heidegger's position changed? Might this, moreover, mark a shift in his primary matter for thought? Has he, as Vincent Blanchet argues, moved beyond or before, not only the Greek understanding of Being—even in its most primordial form—but also beyond or before Being altogether? Has *alētheia* become irrelevant? Does, *horribile dictu*, even Hölderlin no longer have anything to say?

Blanchet, the only scholar I know of to bring Heidegger together with Pindar and Trakl, sets up what I believe is a false dichotomy:

> if Trakl surveyed the same dimension as Pindar, why did the holy [*le sacré*] open up around him in blue rather than through the radiance of gold? Does this ultimately mean that, in Pindar, gold was not itself the holy? Or is it, rather, a sign that the Pindaric Occident is not yet, or no longer, that of Trakl? The alternative, therefore, is as follows: either gold—thought in the most Greek way possible—is not the holy, or blue itself is no longer Greek at all. In this sense, what blue and gold fundamentally expose to us is the question of the difference between the site of *Ereignis* and that of *alētheia*.[18]

As I see it, and as I will attempt to demonstrate in the following, Heidegger is not suspending gold, Being, Hölderlin, and Grecian unconcealment in favor of blue, the appropriative event, Trakl, and Germanic *Wahr-heit*. It is, rather, a matter of emphasis, of highlighting different aspects of Being or, better, of letting Being show its true colors, which we can take literally as *both* gold and blue.[19] Heidegger does, admittedly, associate *polemos* with *alētheia* in the *Beiträge* and elsewhere (GA 65: §233; GA 54: passim), and, in a 1969 seminar, he claims that, with *Ereignis*, he is "no longer thinking in a Greek fashion" (GA 15: 366). But this does not necessarily mean that he is thinking in a Greek fashion when he is rethinking Pindar's gold, that *Ereignis* is incompatible with Being (or, more properly, with ~~Being~~ or Beyng), or that, just because Trakl sings of a gentle twofold (*Zwiefalt*) beyond all polemical discord (*Zwietracht*) (GA 12: 41, 46, 63, 74), *alētheia* and the Greek language would have fallen to the wayside. To cite just one example among many: one of the last things Heidegger ever wrote, he wrote *in Greek*, in a manuscript for a never-completed introduction to the *Gesamtausgabe* titled "*Vermächtnis der Seinsfrage*" ("Legacy of the Being-Question"). Here, it is precisely a question of how to think *alētheia* and therefore of *how to think as such*:

> When you attempt to think, heed beforehand and incessantly the state of affairs that the following word ventures to name: *en tēi archēi ēn kai menei hē Lēthē— tēs A-lētheiēs pēgē* "*In* the beginning concealment [*Verbergung*] (the sheltering [*die bergende*]) was and remains the source of unconcealment."[20]

Furthermore, the Pindar-material, which Blanchet references only in passing—he ignores the pivotal role of Theia, for instance—anticipates the very treatment of the Holy in Heidegger's second Trakl-lecture.

In this 1952 lecture on the *poète maudit*, Heidegger, unlike many commentators, concentrates not just on the pain and putrefaction, the agony and lamentation that pervade Trakl's poetry but also on the rarer moments in which the poet seems to prophesy redemption for the West and the possibility of what Trakl in his poem "Occidental Song" calls, following Böhme and Novalis, "*One Geschlecht*"—a gentle unification, without necessarily abolishing difference, of race, sex, generation, species, and even, if we take the dependence on Novalis seriously, color.[21] (Novalis: "Humans, animals, plants, stones and stars, elements, tones, colors, come together like One Family, act and speak like One *Geschlecht*.")[22] In the meantime, Trakl, like his poetic precursor Rimbaud and his painter friend Oskar Kokoschka, uses colors in oddest of ways. At times, these colors border on—or, as some commentators see it, even cross over into—meaninglessness. Trakl lifts color-adjectives from their corresponding nouns and places them beside words to which they otherwise don't belong ("red stillness of the mouth"). There are syntagms impossible to perceive ("black minutes of madness") and *contradictiones in adiecto* ("black snow"). Colors become adverbs ("The sun will shine blackly") or transform into substantives with radically distinct senses ("Out of derelict blueness steps something deceased," "Spiritually, / Blueness dawns over the thrashed forest").[23]

Heidegger, for his part, acknowledges the ambiguity of Trakl's discourse, which is essentially on the way to a new language and locale, or rather to a language and locale that have always been held in store for it, if only in the pauses between everyday chatter and in the cracks of metaphysical-Christian architechtonics. One the one hand, Trakl's poetry must draw on the language from which it is detaching itself. On the other hand, it speaks, full of intimation, of what is to come, namely, the "holiness of blueness" or "the blueness of the Holy" (GA 12: 61, 70). "The language of [Trakl's] poetic work," Heidegger explains, "is essentially polysemous, and this in its own way. We will hear nothing of the saying of the poetry so long as we bring to our encounter with it some dull sense of a univocal meaning" (GA 12: 70–71). Heidegger proceeds to adduce examples for such ambiguity, with particular emphasis on Trakl's colors:

> Twilight and night, downgoing and death, madness and wild game, pond and stone, bird-flight and rowboat, stranger and brother, spirit and God, likewise the words for color: blue and green, white and black, red and silver, golden and dark, in each case say something manifold. / "Green" is decaying and blossoming, "white" is pale and pure, "black" is gloomily closing off and darkly sheltering, "red" is crimsonly fleshy and rosily gentle. "Silver" is the pallor of death and the sparkle of the stars. "Gold" is the gleam of the true and the "hideous laughter of gold." (GA 12: 71)

Heidegger is quick to clarify, however, that the ubiquitous, supposedly dissonant ambiguity of Trakl's vocabulary is not the result of "lax impression." Rather, ambiguity is itself ambiguous, and Trakl's comes from the "rigor" of "letting" language and Being speak as they give themselves to be spoken. Trakl, like Pindar before him, is hearkening unto a sort of consonance whose intervals are not, as such, specified, but which—if only we had ears to hear it—has already gathered all the disparate tones into an *Einklang*, not exactly a "unison" in the literal sense of the word, but more like the state of being of a "single accord" (GA 12: 71). We might expect Heidegger to shift registers here and speak of a color—imperceivable by the senses, of course, but also incapable of depiction in the present state of the world or perhaps even as such—in which all colors are gathered together into a sort of *Einfarbigkeit*, not, for example, white as the totality of wavelengths of visible light or black as the absence of light, but a sort of gathering of color (*Farbe*) into the One (*Ein*). Instead, and despite his overt acknowledgment of its ambiguity,

Heidegger seems to except the color blue, along with blue's "darkness," and make it an *essential* aspect of holy Being and of the authentic human response to it. It is noteworthy that, of all the colors Heidegger mentions, he does not provide examples for the bivalent usage of blue in Trakl's oeuvre, although this would not have been hard to do;[24] "dark," for its part, appears only on the gentler, purer, side of "black."

In the poem "Summer's Decline," Trakl sings of a "blue deer" or "wild blue game" that, he hopes, will "commemorate the path of the stranger" and "the consonance of his spiritual years":

Der grüne Sommer ist so leise
Geworden und es läutet der Schritt
Des Fremdlings durch die silberne Nacht.
Gedächte ein blaues Wild seines Pfads,

Des Wohllauts seiner geistlichen Jahre![25]

On Heidegger's interpretation, the stranger is the one who treads the path away from the corrupt race of contemporary humanity and toward a new, more proper way of dwelling upon the earth. "Stranger," *Fremdling*, comes from Old High German *fram*, meaning, among other things, "on the way toward." Thus, Heidegger reads Trakl's sentence from "Springtime of the Soul," *Es ist die Seele ein Fremdes auf Erden*, not as, "The soul is something *strange on* the earth," but as, "The soul is *on the way toward* the earth" (GA 12: 36–37). The wild blue game represents those humans who are willing to follow the stranger thoughtfully into this new homeland. To this end, they must heed (related to the German *hüten*, "tend," thus as "shepherds of Being" [GA 9: 331, 342]) the holy blue. Glossing a verse from Trakl's "Occidental Song," which refers to "the gentle cornflower-cluster of night" (*das sanfte Zyanenbündel der Nacht*)[26]—interestingly, unlike the English, the German *Zyane*, from Ancient Greek *kuanos*, "cyan," bears a reference to the color of the flower's petals, although the English recalls the golden fields of wheat in which cornflowers grow as a weeds (see Van Gogh's *Wheat Field with Cornflowers*)—Heidegger writes, in words nearly impossible to translate:

> The night is a cluster of corn flowers, something gentle. [. . .] The cluster of blueness gathers, in the ground of its spray, the depth of the Holy. From out of the blueness, the Holy glows [*leuchtet*], even as it veils itself through the blueness's own darkness. The Holy holds together [*verhält*] while it withdraws. It confers its arrival by preserving itself in its holding withdrawal. The brightness that is sheltered in darkness is blueness. Bright [*Helle*], i.e., resounding [*hallend*], is originally the tone that calls from out of the sheltering

domain of stillness and thus lights up [*sich lichtet*]. Blueness resounds in its brightness by ringing. In its resounding brightness, the darkness of blueness glows. [. . .] Blue is not an image for the sense of the Holy. Blueness itself is the Holy, on account of blueness's gathering depth, which only first shines in its veiling. (GA 12: 40; see also 61)

There are numerous parallels between this passage and what we saw Heidegger develop in his Pindar-commentary. Blue, like Pindaric gold, is not a mere sign for the Holy; it *is* the Holy in one of its essential moments. In the Pindar-material, Heidegger emphasizes the luminous side of holy Being, without, however, ignoring its sheltering concealment (poetized as Theia). Here, he emphasizes withdrawal, even darkness, without, however, ignoring the brightness that it safeguards (poetized, in the spirit of Novalis's hymns, as night). At the ontological, hieratic level—or, in the language of the Trakl-essay, at the level of *Geist*—words indexed to sight intermix with those indexed to sound: we hear the brightness of blueness and see its paradoxically glowing darkness. Furthermore, just as it was crucial for Greek existence, in order to have the requisite regard for gold, to be "caught sight of [*erblickt*], i.e., shined on [*beschienen*] in the pure shining of the Godhead" (GA 78: 82), so do modern humans require a certain kind of colorful illumination in order to "become," to reference Pindar once again, "who they are":[27]

> In the poetic name "wild blue game," Trakl calls upon that human essence whose countenance, i.e., counter-gaze, is, in thinking of the steps of the stranger, caught sight of by [*er-blickt*, perhaps: 'brought into being through the glimpse of'; cf. GA 49: 125–129] the blueness of night and thus is shined on by the Holy. The name "wild blue game" names mortals who commemoratively think of the stranger and would like, with him, to wander out to attain the native element of the human essence. (GA 12: 42)

The poet, above all, is receptive to the resonant illumination of holy blueness, just as the poets of Greece were especially receptive to the shining peal of holy gold: "The lunar coolness of the spiritual night's holy blueness rings and shines throughout all gazing and saying. The language of the latter thus becomes something that speaks after and in accordance with this [*nachsagenden*], it becomes: *poetry*" (GA 12: 67; see also 70).

Heidegger cites numerous poems in support of his interpretation, none perhaps more beautiful than Trakl's "*Gesang des Abgeschiedenen*" ("Song of the Departed One"), with its blending of sight and sound, light and darkness; its palette of blue and crimson, green and black; its call for Hölderlinian measure and for the *Heiligung*, the "hallowing" or "sanctification," of bread and wine. Heidegger's entire interpretation of Trakl, one could say, is an effort to understand, to sanctify, and to safeguard the ontological import of what this poem refers to as "the blueness of night" and its sheltering "embrace." Only with efforts of this sort might we, in our current situation of global calamity (*Unheil*), find healing (*Heilung*) and salvation (*Heil*). Only then might we develop a genuine regard for the Holy (*das Heilige*). (Cf. GA 5: 319; GA 9: 352, 359–360; GA 78: 305–307). Here, in full, is Trakl's poem, which I have translated in accordance with the way in which Heidegger interprets Trakl's corpus in toto:

The flight of birds is full of harmonies. The green woods have
Gathered at evening to form lodges of greater stillness;
The crystalline pastures of the deer.
Dark makes gentle the splashing of the brook, the moist shadows

And the flowers of summer, which ring out beautifully in the wind.
Already the brow of the meditative man enters into twilight.

And a little lamp, the good, shines in his heart
And the peace of the meal; for hallowed are bread and wine
By the hands of God, and from night-like eyes
In stillness the brother beholds you, that he may find rest from thorny wandering.
Oh, dwelling in the ensouled blueness of night.

Silence in the room also lovingly embraces the shades of the elderly,
The crimson torments, lament of a great lineage,
Which now piously passes on in the solitary grandson.

For ever more radiantly does the tolerant one awaken
From black minutes of madness on a petrified threshold
And embracing him mightily is the cool blueness and the luminous decline of
    autumn,

The still house and the sayings of the forest,
Measure and law and the lunar paths of the departed ones.[28]

III. A HEIDEGGERIAN *FARBENLEHRE*?

To the many well-known words for Being in Heidegger's oeuvre—*Ereignis, Lichtung, alētheia*, and so forth.[29]—we must now, after our consideration of Heidegger's interpretation of the Holy in Pindar and Trakl, add the colors gold and blue. These colors, to be sure, are not reflections or emissions of light. Nor are they what we perceive, howsoever we perceive it, on the surface of beings. We are far from optics or even Goethe's alternative to Newton. Rather, gold and blue *are* Being insofar as it shines in truth and shelters in withdrawal. Colors, on Heidegger's theory, are ontological before they are aesthetic.

What, however, would happen to this theory, or at least to the ontological results it arrives at, if we were to consider other poets and other colors, or even if we were to take seriously the *unholiness* of blue in some of Trakl's own poems? Perhaps Hölderlin's "yellow pears" and the gentle law of Stifter's *Katzensilber* would be compatible, but what of Sappho's "more greenish-yellow than grass," Dickinson's "slash of Blue," or Celan's suppurating "gorselight" and yellow-starred arnica? What would Heidegger do with the post-Holocaust poet's appeal for a "'grayer' language, a language that, among other things, wants to know that even its "musicality" is situated in a place where it no longer has anything in common with that "euphony" which, in a more or less carefree manner, continued to resound in the midst of "the most terrible"?[30] Putting Celan's later poetry to the side, what would the *Meister des Denkens* do with the "ashen hair of Shulamite"? Are there colors for the Unholy?

Heidegger's poetics of the Holy perhaps calls for a poetics of sacrilege, but I must leave that for consideration on another occasion.

NOTES

1. Bonaventure, *Itinerarium mentis in deum*, trans. Philotheus Boehner (Saint Bonaventure, NY: The Franciscan Institute, Saint Bonaventure University, 1956), §5.4. Carl Braig, *Vom Sein: Abriß der Ontologie* (Freiburg: Herder, 1896), v. For an extensive treatment of Heidegger on "light" and on the possible influence of the medieval metaphysics of light on Heidegger's thinking, see Richard Capobianco, *Engaging Heidegger* (Toronto: University of Toronto Press, 2010), Chapters 5 and 6, especially, 108.

2. Otto, *Das Heilige: Über das Irrationale in der Idee des Göttlichen und sein Verhältnis zum Rationalen* (Breslau: Trewendt und Granier, 1917).

3. In Theodore Kisiel and Thomas Sheehan, eds., *Becoming Heidegger: On the Trail of his Early Occasional Writings, 1910–1927*, 2nd ed. (London: Routledge, 2009), 362, 367.

4. See Heidegger's elucidation of the verse "*Von goldenen Träumen schwer*," from Hölderlin's "*Andenken*" ("Remembrance"), in GA 52: §§35–43 (especially p. 130), where Heidegger draws on Pindar's 8th Pythian. On p. 121 of this Winter Semester 1941–1942 lecture course, Heidegger characterizes the golden dreams of Hölderlin's poem as "heavy from the solidity of the essential," "gleaming from the

preciousness of the approaching gift," and "noble from the purity of what is decided here." In the parallel passage of Heidegger's 1953 essay on "Remembrance," he inserts the language of the Holy, which had been peripheral in the discussion of gold in the lecture course: "The golden dreams are, like gold, heavy from the solidity of the essential character of their poem. They are, like gold, gleaming from the luminous glow of the Holy. They are, like gold, noble from the purity of what is decided and sent [*Geschickten*] from the Holy" (GA 4: 114). Heidegger's intervening commentary, from 1942, on the gold of Pindar's "holy songs" (GA 78: 97) is, I believe, responsible for the shift in emphasis. Heidegger's later analysis (composed sometime after July 1970) of the words "*goldne Pracht*" ("golden splendor") from one of Hölderlin's last poems, "*Der Herbst*" ("Autumn"), is also clearly indebted to Pindar (GA 75: 205–209).

5. Reported in Hermann Noack, "Gespräch mit Martin Heidegger," *Anstöße: Berichte aus der Arbeit der Evangelischen Akademie Hofgeismar* 1, no. 2 (1954): 33.

6. Discussions of the Pindar-material are available in Vincent Blanchet, "De bleu et d'or: *Das Heilige* et Heidegger," *Les Études philosophiques* 161, no. 1 (2016): 74, 82–83, 86–87; Richard Capobianco has discussed Heidegger's 1942 undelivered lecture course on Anaximander and his understanding of Pindar's "gold" as another name for Being in his "Heidegger on Heraclitus: *Kosmos*/World as Being Itself," *Epoché* 20, no. 2 (Spring 2016): 466–67; in his *Heidegger's Way of Being* (Toronto: University of Toronto Press, 2014), Chapter 2 (also 108, note7); and in Chapter 1 of his forthcoming book *Heidegger's Being: The Shimmering Unfolding* (Toronto: Univeristy of Toronto Press, 2022). Little has been written on Heidegger's relation to Pindar more broadly. In addition, see Adéline Froidecourt, "La poésie de Pindar à l'aube de la métaphysique," *Heidegger Studies* 28 (2012): 67–100, who focuses mainly on GA 40. Michael Theunissen, in his massive study *Pindar: Menschenlos und Wende der Zeit* (Munich: Beck, 2000), refers extensively (and critically) to Heidegger's treatment of time, but not to the latter's direct engagement with the Greek lyricist.

7. *Pindari carmina cum fragmentis*, ed. Hervicus Maehler, 2 vols. (Leipzig: Teubner, 1971), 1:175.

8. *Pindar*, trans. Franz Dornseiff (Leipzig: Insel, 1921), 56. GA 78: 291–92.

9. For background to the poem and various interpretations of it, see Anne Pippin Burnett, *Pindar's Songs for Young Athletes of Aigina* (Oxford: Oxford University Press, 2005), Chapter 6 ("*Isthmian 5*: Achilles and Telephos"); J. B. Bury, ed., *The Isthmian Odes of Pindar* (Amsterdam: Hakkert, 1965), 85–103; and M. M. Willcock, "On First Reading Pindar: 'The Fifth Isthmian,'" *Greece & Rome* 25, no. 1 (1978): 37–45. The last-named commentator recommends that one *start* one's study of Pindar with the *5th Isthmian*. Heidegger, it seems, would agree, but for radically different reasons. According to the philosopher, the *5th Isthmian* is the "most magnificent [*herrlichste*] of Pindar's odes": "The first three verses [. . .] gleam over and beyond [*überglänzen*] the entire opening of the song, gleam over and beyond the entire ode, gleam over and beyond the entire poetic work [*Dichtung*] of Pindar, clear [*lichten*] the relation of Being to the word and language"; verses 2–17 are "the pure poem of the Godhead of the gods, and nothing else besides" (GA 78: 76, 78, 97). Heidegger's

interpretation, unsurprisingly, differs from that of traditional scholarship. Although Heidegger is correct to link Theia with gold—Bury, for example, relates that Theia was also referred to as *Chryse*, 'golden goddess' (85)—other commentators have argued for a contrast between the invocation of Theia and the courage (*alka*) displayed in contest or battle. Burnett (94–95), for example, interprets *alka* and the *daimones* of verse 11 as marking a shift to the unseen and thus to what is independent from Theia and from the gold the goddess makes visible. Or, in Bury's pithy summary (85n3): "Gold is chased for the sake of Theia σέο Ϝέκατι l. 2; glory for the sake of Zeus, Διὸς ἕκατι, l. 29, in the same position in the same verse of the strophe. This is as much as to say that Theia is merely introduced in order to be shown her place."

10. *Pindari carmina cum fragmentis*, 2:131, verse 1: κεκρότηται χρυσέα κρηπὶς ἱεραῖσιν ἀοιδαῖς. Heidegger translates (GA 78: 97): "*Geschmiedet ist der goldene Grund / den heiligen Gesängen*," "Forged is the golden ground / unto the holy songs."

11. Although the language of *Ereignis*, intimated here, is largely absent from the Pindar-interpretation (see, however, GA 78: 68), Heidegger could have brought it into connection with *periōsion* by considering the Greek word's Biblical trajectory, which might present an alternative to his narrative about of the word's lapse into substance metaphysics. In Titus 2:14, it refers to a people who, through the sacrifice of Jesus, will come to belong to, and be cherished by, God, thereby, we might add, coming into their own: "[Christ Jesus] gave himself for us in order that he might redeem us from all lawlessness and purify for himself [for his own possession] a select people [*heautōi laon periousion*] who are zealous to do fine works." A *hapax legomenon* in the New Testament, the word is also found in the Septuagint, *Exodus* 19:5 et passim. For details, see Hermann Cremer, *Biblico-Theological Lexicon of New Testament Greek*, 4th ed., trans. William Urwick (New York: Scribner, 1895), sv. Περιούσιος.

12. Silesius, *Cherubinischer Wandersmann*, ed. Louise Gnädinger (Stuttgart: Reclam, 1984), Erstes Buch, #289, p. 69. See GA 10 for Heidegger's commentary on Silesius. See also GA 40: 16 (on the opening up of a rose as an example of originary *physis*) and Pindar's 7th Olympian, which plays on the anthetic birth of the island of Rhodes, the Greek *rhodon* ("rose"), and the nymph Rhode, wife of Helios. In this victory song, Pindar sings of the time when Zeus "inundated" one of the Rhodes's cities "with snowy gold" (βρέχε θεῶν βασιλεὺς ὁ μέγας χρυσέαις νιφάδεσσι πόλιν) after the birth of Athena (*Pindari carmina cum fragmentis*, 1:28, verse 34). Pindar's ode ended up dedicated in letters of gold in the Temple of Athena Lindia on the island.

13. For *legein* qua gathering, see GA 78: 93, 96. In the Pindar-commentary, Heidegger does not specifically use the word *sanft*, "gentle," which will play a crucial role in his reading of the spirit of Trakl's poetry; however, it is implied by the "exotic superlative" (Burnett, *Pindar's Songs for Young Athletes of Aigina*, 94–95) of verse 12, *alpniston*, "gentlest" or "smoothest," which Heidegger renders as *lieblich*, "lovely," "charming" (GA 78: 66). Note, moreover, Pindar's floral metaphor in verses 12–13.

14. One might wonder: if Theia is simply the Godhead, why, beyond the fact that the Greek suffix makes any noun to which it is attached feminine, retain the gender? Heidegger might reply that he is simply thinking through Pindar's poetry, which,

after all, refers to Theia as a mother. And yet, Heidegger continues to use feminine and maternal tropes for Being and language in his commentary, tropes that will reappear in his later interpretation of Trakl. Despite Heidegger's early claims about the non-gendered status of Dasein, perhaps what he is seeking is something along the lines of a maternity that is more motherly than all mothers, a femininity that is more womanly than all women. (Compare Heidegger's claim that *"Theia*, spoken from the perspective of later representations, is more spiritual [*geistiger*] than the 'spirits' that are otherwise known, and yet at the same time more sensuous [*sinnlicher*, sensual?] than any 'sensuousness' has ever been capable of" [GA 78: 88].) What this would mean, and whether it is even remotely plausible, I cannot address here.

15. I have been unable to determine, at the philological level, why Heidegger has *pantōn* rather than *allōn* here, especially since the earlier versions of his lecture both have *allōn* (GA 80.2: 994, 1017), as do his citations of the verse in GA 78: passim; GA 74: 177; and GA 81: 249. As a matter of interpretation, however, *pantōn* makes sense.

16. *Pindari carmina cum fragmentis*, 1:105, verse 95: *epameroi*, Tagwesen, "creatures of the day." GA 78: 79, 86–87, 326; GA 52: 111–12.

17. Martin Heidegger and Emil Staiger, *"Der Briefwechsel,"* ed. Werner Wögerbauer, *Geschichte der Germanistik* 25/26 (2004): 53–67.

18. Blanchet, "De bleu et d'or," 78.

19. Cf. ibid., 75.

20. Martin Heidegger, *Auszüge zur Phänomenologie aus dem Manuskript "Vermächtnis der Seinsfrage"* (*Jahresgabe der Martin-Heidegger-Gesellschaft* 2011–2012), 94. For more on this "last word of phenomenology" and its connection to the "saying of Being," see William McNeill, *The Fate of Phenomenology: Heidegger's Legacy* (Lanham, MD: Rowman & Littlefield, 2020), Chapter 7.

21. Trakl, *Dichtungen und Briefe: Historisch-kritische Ausgabe*, ed. Walther Killy and Hans Szklenar, vol. 1, 3rd ed. (Salzburg: Otto Müller, 1974), 66.

22. Novalis, *Heinrich von Ofterdingen*, in *Schriften*, Part One, ed. Ludwig Tieck and Fr. Schlegel, 5th ed. (Berlin: Reimer, 1837), 252.

23. Trakl, *Dichtungen und Briefe*, 37, 46, 59, 78, 79. For more examples and a helpful overview of Trakl's use of colors, see Christoph Grube's study on Paul Celan's relation to Trakl: *"so oder so, es bleibt blau oder braun, das Gedicht": Aspekte der Trakl-Rezeption Paul Celans* (Würzburg: Königshausen & Neumann, 2014), especially Chapter 5. Celan, like Heidegger, was fascinated by Trakl's colors, although, unlike Heidegger, he saw them as subversive "counter-words" rather than, as we will see, aspects of the Holy (at least regarding blue and gold). Walther Killy, on whom Celan is drawing, was the first to interpret Trakl's colors as void of symbolic value. See Walter Killy, *"Gedichte im Gedicht: Beschäftigung mit Trakl-Handschriften." Merkur* 12, no. 12 (130) (December 1958): 1108–21, and *Wandlungen des lyrischen Bildes*, 5th ed. (Göttingen: Vandenhoeck & Ruprecht, 1967), 116–35.

24. Perhaps most conspicuously, for our purposes, is Trakl's poem *"Vorhölle"* ("Limbo"): *"Bläue, die Todesklagen der Mütter. [...] Mit knöchernen Händen / Tastet im Blau nach Märchen / Unheilige Kindheitt"* ("Blueness, the dirges of the mothers.

[. . .] With bony hands / Unholy childhood / Gropes for fairy tales in the blue"). *Dichtungen und Briefe*, 73. For a critique of Heidegger's and other commentators' overemphasis on blue, see Robert Rovini, *La fonction poétique de l'image dans l'œuvre de Georg Trakl* (Paris: Les Belles Lettres, 1971), 101–102, 104–105.

25. Trakl, *Dichtungen und Briefe*, 75.

26. *Dichtungen und Briefe*, 66.

27. Cf. *Pindari carmina cum fragmentis*, 1:69, verse 72 (2nd Pythian): γένοι', οἷος ἐσσὶ μαθών.

28. Trakl, *Dichtungen und Briefe*, 78–79.

29. See Richard Capobianco, *Engaging Heidegger* (Toronto: Toronto University Press, 2010), 8, 142.

30. Paul Celan, *Gesammelte Werke*, vol. 3 (Frankfurt: Suhrkamp, 1986), 167.

Chapter 5

Tracing the Holy in Heidegger's *Hölderlin's Hymns "Germania" and "The Rhine"*

Elias Schwieler

In his *Aesthetics*, in the course of discussing architecture, Hegel defers to Goethe for a definition of the holy:

> "What is holy?" Goethe asks once in a distich, and answers: "What links many souls together."[1] In this sense we may say that the holy with the aim of this concord, and as this concord, has been the first content of independent architecture. The readiest example of this is provided by the story of the Tower of Babylonia. In the wide plains of the Euphrates an enormous architectural work was erected; it was built in common, and the aim and content of the work was at the same time the community of those who constructed it. [. . .] The ensemble of all the peoples at that period worked at this task and since they all came together to complete an immense work like this, the product of their labour was to be a bond which was to link them together. [. . .] In that case, such a building is symbolic at the same time since the bond, which it is, it can only hint at; this is because in its form and shape it is only in an external way that it can express the holy, the absolute unifier of men.[2] (638)

The tower of Babel, Hegel suggests, is the exterior, physical manifestation of the holy. The representation of the holy in architectural form is the sign of unity and community—that which binds people and peoples together. Building the tower was made possible, moreover, by the unity and community created by speaking one language, more precisely the Adamic language, the *Ursprache*, which all peoples of the earth shared. In *Genesis* 11: 1-9, the building of the tower of Babel was the attempt to build a tower reaching up to heaven, an endeavor which did not go unpunished by God, who condemned the peoples of the earth to speak different languages. In this sense, the holy bond between peoples was based on building as well as language. With the confusion of tongues, building such a tower would no longer be possible, since the community between people had been broken up.

We could say, then, following the myth of Babel and the subsequent fragmentation of language, that the holy as, according to Hegel, "the absolute unifier of men" withdraws or abandons the peoples of the earth. With no common language, people are condemned to live with misunderstanding, arbitrariness, and ambiguity, leading to polarization and conflict. With the dissemination of language, there is, in other words, discord instead of Hegel's concord. This is, we must infer, the situation we continue to live in, ever since the breaking of the bond of the holy—the unifying community created by building and the use of a common language. Accordingly, ours is a world where the holy has withdrawn. To recover the sense of the word, or to put it differently, its *Stimmung*, so as to be able to explore Heidegger's application of the holy, we must first return to its origins (there are arguably more than one) in language.

Hence, this essay sets out to trace Heidegger's reading of the holy in Hölderlin in the lecture course *Hölderlin's Hymns "Germania" and "The Rhine"* and also explores, more generally, how and in what ways the linguistic, the poetic, and the philosophic notions of the holy coincide and how they differ from one another. Still, the main focus remains on Heidegger's reading of the holy in the poetry of Hölderlin, a poet that he highly valued, no doubt, and considered to be the poet of poets. In what follows, I will begin by addressing the holy from the perspective of the science of language, or linguistics, and in so doing examine Emile Benveniste's theory of signification and referent in order to understand his approach to language in his work *Dictionary of Indo-European Concepts and Society*. This, I suggest, opens up a path to compare and contrast Heidegger's reading of the holy in Hölderlin with Benveniste's exegesis of the holy in Indo-European languages.

In my closing remarks, I sum up my preceding reflections on the holy in linguistics, poetry, and philosophy, with a particular eye toward Heidegger's thinking and the holy. Prominence will also be given to Goethe and his two distiches 68 and 69 in *The Four Seasons*, which can be said to bind my reflections together and also serve as an example of how the holy can be conceived of in what Heidegger calls poetizing, which translates the German *Dichtung*.

I. BENVENISTE: LANGUAGE, LINGUISTICS, AND THE HOLY

When we attempt to close in on the significance of the word "holy" we soon run up against the difficulty of disentangling the word's etymology as well as its history. As a point of departure, therefore, I will turn to Emile Benveniste's seminal work *Dictionary of Indo-European Concepts and Society*, a work published in French in 1969, and which has become widely considered as, in the words of Giorgio Agamben, a "masterpiece of the human sciences of the twentieth century."[3] To begin, it is first necessary to address Benveniste's method in the *Dictionary*, since it has ramifications for what we understand to be the "meaning" of a word; more precisely, we must clarify the distinction Benveniste makes between *désignation* and *signification*, that is, between reference and meaning. Thus, in the essay "The Semiology of Language" from 1959, Benveniste makes a distinction between semiotics and semantics, taking his cue from Saussure's theory of the sign. In the essay, Benveniste claims that there are two distinct but complementing systems of meaning or signification working simultaneously in language, namely the semiotic and the semantic. Benveniste's differentiation between these two systems, or orders of signification, runs as follows:

> Semiotics designates the mode of signification proper to the linguistic *sign* that establishes it as a unit. [. . .] Taken in itself, the sign is pure identity itself, totally foreign to all other signs, the signifying foundation of language, the material necessity for statement. It exists when it is recognized as signifier by all members of a linguistic community, and when it calls forth for each individual roughly the same associations and oppositions. Such is the province and the criterion of semiotics.[4]

In contrast, the semantic system of signification is concerned with discourse and enunciation:

> With the semantic, we enter into the specific mode of meaning which is generated by discourse. The problems raised here are a function of language as producer of messages. However, the message is not reduced to a series of separately identifiable units; it is not the sum of many signs that produces meaning; on the contrary, it is meaning (*l'intenté*), globally conceived, that is actualized and divided into specific signs, the words. In the second place, semantics takes over the majority of referents, while semiotics is in principle cut off and independent of all reference. Semantic order becomes identified with the world of enunciation and with the universe of discourse.[5]

This, then, is the difference Benveniste identifies between designation or reference and meaning or signification in the *Dictionary*. In the Preface, he gives the example of the Greek word *hegeomai* to illustrate his intention, when it comes to his study of Indo-European concepts, which lies on signification rather than designation:

> If we deal with the Greek verb *hegeomai* and its derivative *hegemon*, this is in order to see how the notion of "hegemony" was established, but without regard to the fact that Greek *hegmonia* came to mean successively the supremacy of an individual, or a nation, or the equivalent of a Roman imperium, etc. What concerns us is the connection, difficult to account for, between an expression of authority such as *hegemon* and the verb *hegeomai* which means "to think, to judge." In so doing, we explain the signification, leaving to others the problem of designation.[6]

The issue of designation, which Benveniste leaves out of his study, would consist in exploring the historical and sociological aspects of the word. Now, what is under scrutiny in the present essay is the word holy. Hence, under the heading "The Sacred," in Benveniste's *Dictionary*, we come across the word "holy," and, importantly, the German "*Heilig*," and its relation to the word pair *hagios-hieros* in Greek, and *sacer-sanctus* in Latin. Benveniste specifically highlights the fact that there are two terms for the scared, and besides the word pairs, just mentioned, in Latin and Greek, this is also true of the Germanic languages, so that we have the Gothic *weihs*, meaning consecrated, and the word *hailag* in Runic and *heilig* in Germanic, meaning holy.

Of the German word *Heilig*, Benvenste states: "The starting point for the notion represented today by German *heilig* 'holy' is the Gothic adjective *hails*, which expresses a quite different idea, that of 'safety, health, physical and corporal integrity'."[7] Moreover, in Old Icelandic we have the word *heil*, which means good omen, giving us the Icelandic verb *heilsa*, meaning to salute someone and to wish someone good health.[8] In addition, we have the meaning whole, to be intact, of the word *heil*, as in the German *heil* and *heilung*, to be whole, without injury, and healing, respectively, which according to Grimm's dictionary, derives from spiritual healing and salvation. As Benveniste also notes: "By its very nature divinity possesses this gift which is integrity, well-being, good fortune, and it can bestow this on men in the form of physical health and by omens of good fortune. The notion of *heilig*, though not present in Gothic, was latent in that language even though the nature of our texts do [*sic*] not bring it to light. In the course of time the primitive Gothic term *weihs* was replaced by *hails, hailigs*."[9]

Given this etymological analysis of the holy, and the double nature of the term that Benveniste insists on (consecrated and holy), what is the semiotic signification of the word? As Benveniste maintains,

> we are not in a position to construct a single model on the basis of these coupled terms. They function only within a given language, and the relations established

between the members of the pairs are not on the same plane; or else the notions expressed are the same but the terms are different. In Av. *spənta* and Gr. *hieros*, under etymologically different expressions we can discern the same idea, that of a power which is full of ardor and swollen with fecundity. To this there corresponds in Gothic *hails*, the notion of integrity, of perfect accomplishment: a force which protects the object or being from all diminution and makes it invulnerable. Latin *sacer*, on the contrary, conveys simply a sense of something set apart and hedged round, an august and awful quality of divine origin, which separates it from all human relations.[10]

And he concludes by saying:

Finally *hieros* and *hagios* show clearly the positive and negative aspects of the notion: on the one hand, what is animated by a sacred power and force; on the other hand, what is forbidden and placed out of bounds to human beings.

This is how these two qualities are distributed in the vocabulary of each language and illustrate the two aspects of the same notion: what is filled with divine power and what is forbidden to human contact.[11]

What we end up with is a double signification of the sacred, singular to each different language, but which follows the same pattern of meaning. From the perspective of semiotics, the holy belongs to one of these two significations, which is to say it signifies, in Benveniste's words, "what is forbidden and placed out of bounds to human beings." How does this meaning of the holy correspond to the notion proposed by Hegel-Goethe of the holy as bringing the souls of people together—the holy as a gathering force? On Hegel's view, the binding together of souls is the act of building, and to be able to build, a shared language is needed. The holy could thus be described as an activity characterized by its disinterestedness, by the collaborative effort demanded by building and which requires each soul to tend to itself as much as to other souls, bound together by a common activity and a shared endeavor. However, the building of the tower of Babel resulted in forgetfulness; the people, closely connected by language and culture, forgot the divine and in their hubris reached for the heavens. The conclusion of the story of the tower of Babel is well known. The holy and the sacred lost its meaning as well as its significance for the people, so that their building, guided by empty ambition and greed, turned into an effort that God punished by the dissemination of language—the confusion of tongues, the free play of the signifier. As we will see, this loss of the holy and of divine language, where Being, beings, and saying coincide is, what Heidegger calls, the *Grundstimmung*, the fundamental attunement, as holy mourning in Hölderlin's poetry.

Holy mourning is Hölderlin's manner of addressing the loss of the gods and of the language of the gods, while for Benveniste and the science of language, linguistics, it means the scientific recuperation of order and systematicity to language as, in Benveniste's case, reference and meaning or signification within semiology and semantics. In what follows, I will attend to an altogether other way of reading the holy, while keeping Hegel-Goethe and Benveniste in mind, namely Heidegger's remarks on the holy in his lecture course on Hölderlin's hymns "Germania" and "The Rhine."

II. HEIDEGGER AND HÖLDERLIN ON THE HOLY

We are now ready to enter, in Benveniste's words, "the world of enunciation and [...] the universe of discourse." However, we are entering two particular discourses and worlds of enunciation that by their very nature constitute a critique of and confrontation with the foundations of enunciation and discourse, namely philosophy and poetry. This brings us to Heidegger's readings of Hölderlin, which constitute one of the best examples of the intimate relationship and dialogue between thinking and poetry, and the way in which each sets out to express, but also question, the ground for and nature of human Dasein. The importance of philosophy for poetry, and of poetry for philosophy, is a salient feature of German idealism, which is also something that Heidegger points out in his reading of Hölderlin. In the lecture course, just mentioned, given in Freiburg in the winter semester of 1934–1935 on Hölderlin's hymns "Germania" and "The Rhine," Heidegger refers to Hölderlin's essay "On the Operations of the Poetic Spirit,"[12] about which he states: "The essay remains incomprehensible without a genuine understanding of the innermost core and of the fundamental questions of the philosophy of Kant and above all of German Idealism."[13] At the same time, he states that we should be careful not to simply "trace Hölderlin back"[14] to Kant and German Idealism generally, since when it comes to original thinking, Heidegger maintains, one cannot translate or transform one philosophy, or poetry for that matter, into or as an explanation of another.

Now, to get to the heart of the matter, what Heidegger's reading of Hölderlin's essay primarily considers is Hölderlin's reference to the holy. In doing so, Heidegger provides an account of what characterizes the holy in Hölderlin's understanding of it, after which he cites a number of passages from Hölderlin's poetry where the word holy can be found, in order to show its importance to Hölderlin. Heidegger states that "Hölderlin clarifies his own understanding of the holy precisely with reference to what we are naming a 'fundamental attunement'."[15] A fundamental attunement—*Grundstimmung*—Heidegger defines as an "originary mourning [*ursprüngliche Trauer*]" which is characterized by the *"lucid superiority of the simple goodness of a grave pain."*[16] What characterizes the holy is thus that it belongs to the fundamental attunement of mourning; in fact, "the entire fundamental attunement," Heidegger says, "is holy."[17] But, what exactly does the holy mean? Heidegger asks. To Hölderlin, the holy is "something disinterested [*uneignnützig*]" Heidegger points out, and disinterestedness means being without self-interest and self-limitation, it is neither useless nor involved in an economy of utility. Instead, Hölderlin's notion of the holy as something disinterested refers to the holy as, precisely, a *Grundstimmung*, a fundamental attunement. But what, exactly, we must ask, is a fundamental attunement?

It is at this point in his reading of Hölderlin's idea of the holy that Heidegger invokes the essay "On the Operations of the Poetic Spirit," which, Heidegger warns, "requires a supreme mustering of thoughtful energy and the longest endurance of a dialectical and metaphysical comprehension in order to follow the thinker-poet in his essay."[18] One cannot but agree with Heidegger when it comes to reading Hölderlin's essay, with its long winding sentences and internal contradictions. This difficulty becomes evident when Heidegger quotes a long passage from the end of the essay where Hölderlin mentions the holy. There, Hölderlin argues that the human being is a unity of opposites and that such unity can only come to pass through the divine. In Hölderlin's words:

> *For this is possible only in beautiful, holy, divine sentiment* [*Empfindung*], in a sentiment that is beautiful because it is neither merely pleasant and happy, nor merely sublime and powerful, nor merely unified and peaceful, but that is all at once, and can be such only in a sentiment, one that is holy because it is neither disinterestedly [*uneigennützig*] given over to its object, nor merely disinterestedly resting on its own inner ground, nor merely disinterestedly hovering between its inner ground and its object, but is all at once.[19]

These different sides that make up disinterestedness, Hölderlin insists, must be taken "all at once," bound together as a wreath as Goethe has it in distich 68 of *The Four Seasons*, for the sentiment, or as Heidegger prefers, attunement, to be considered "pure disinterestedness [*reine Un-eigennützikeit*]." Similarly, mourning, says Heidegger "is holy in this manner," that is, its fundamental attunement is pure disinterestedness. The holy, then, is the foundation of mourning and disinterestedness conceived of in this manner, and together they form the fundamental attunement of holy mourning. This is the point of departure for Heidegger's reflections on the holy and its fundamental attunement in Hölderlin's hymn "Germania."

However, we should keep in mind that when Hölderlin, as well as Heidegger, speaks of the holy they do so from the perspective of poetry, or rather, as the title of Hölderlin's essay makes clear, of the poetic spirit. It is through poetry that the holy is expressed, rather than explained; and poetry, in turn, is expressed through language. This is why Heidegger, in the lecture course, before starting out on his analysis of Hölderlin's notion of the holy, takes time to talk about language, poetic language in particular, and most importantly of *Dichtung*, poetizing. He does this in the Introduction and in chapter 1 of Part 1 of the published lecture course titled "Preparatory Reflection: Poetry and Language." There, Heidegger outlines what looks like a different approach to language, poetry, meaning, and signification than the one Benveniste proposes based on his notions of language, meaning, and significance, in general, and of the holy, in particular. (One consequence of this is that it will be necessary, as we will see, to recognize and invoke what Benveniste identifies as the two significations of the sacred, which relate to the holy in Heidegger's reading of Hölderlin. That is, Benveniste's conclusion that the Greek *hieros* and *hagios* relate to two different conceptions of the sacred, namely "what is filled with divine power [*hieros*] and what is forbidden to human contact [*hagios*]."[20]). But, first, it is crucial to outline Heidegger's thoughts on language and poetry as they are presented in the lecture course on Hölderlin's "Germania" and "The Rhine."

III. *DICHTUNG*: LANGUAGE, POETRY, AND COMMUNITY

Speaking of his approach to Hölderlin's poetry, Heidegger is careful to point out that he is not contemplating poetry in general, but specifically the poetry of Hölderlin. To do so is necessary, Heidegger maintains, because poetry is a situated and unique expression of language—each poet has his or her own way of engaging with language, which cannot be generalized into a poetics outside of the poet's own work. This is particularly true of Hölderlin, since he is, on Heidegger's view, arguably the most important poet writing in the German language.[21] Thus, to begin to approach Hölderlin's poetry, Heidegger first outlines how to understand language and poetry as expressions peculiar to the human being. Language, says Heidegger, is the most dangerous but also the most essential to human Dasein. It is dangerous because it has the possibility to make us forget what is worthy of speaking about, so that we only engage in prattle about everything and nothing. Language is the most essential, since it provides the means for human Dasein to found and ground itself in the world. In a significant passage, Heidegger states:

> Only where there is language does world prevail. Only where there is world— that is, where there is language—is there supreme danger: altogether *the* danger,

which is the threatening of Being as such by non-being. Language is dangerous not only because it brings the human being into a particular danger, but is *what is most dangerous*—the danger of dangers—because it first creates, and alone keeps open, the possibility of a threatening of Beyng in general. Because the human being *is* in language, he creates this danger and brings the destruction that lurks within it. As what is most dangerous, language is what is most double-edged and most ambiguous. It places the human being into the zone of supreme achievement, yet at the same time holds him within the realm of abyssal decline [*Verfall*].[22]

The essence of language, says Heidegger, is thus its dangerousness, a danger— *Gefahr*—which both presents human beings with the possibility to reveal Being as such and to degenerate into pointless and superficial chatter. Furthermore, it is from out of the essence of language, that is, its dangerousness, that poetizing [*Dichtung*] springs. Poetizing, Heidegger asserts, is the "originary language of a people [*Ursprache eines Volkes*]."[23] It is what founds and grounds the Being of human Dasein, and this is why Heidegger frequently returns to Hölderlin's lines in the poem which begins "In beautiful blue": "Full of merit, yet poetically / Human dwell upon this Earth [*Voll Verdienst, doch dichterisch wohnet / Der Mench auf dieser Erde*]."[24] This does not mean, however, that poetizing is free of the danger of language; on the contrary, as Heidegger points out, poetizing too can be watered down, turned into idle talk, and shallow prose, which has lost its relation to the divine, and so also lost its power to reveal Being; and so, has lost its relation to the holy.

Specifically, Heidegger explains how originary poetizing expressed as poetry declines into superficial prose in his reading of Hölderlin's "The Rhine": "Yet viewed with respect to its essence, language is in itself the most originary poetizing, and that which is poetized in language, in the narrower sense—that which we specifically call "poetry"—is the originary language of a people, which then disseminates itself as prose and becomes leveled out in such dissemination, so that poetry appears to be a deviation and exception."[25] As Heidegger reads Hölderlin, Hölderlin's mission is to restore the *Ursprache* of the (German) people in his poetry. This is why it often centers on the loss and mourning of the divine.

Heidegger's mission is similar in his attempt to restore the ability of the human Dasein to reveal Being as such, an ability which humans have let fall into oblivion. For both Heidegger and Hölderlin, then, the only way we can come to terms with the withdrawal of Being and the divine is to revive our sense of and sensitivity to language, so as to reach that state of mind in which we can thoughtfully think through what language is in its essence, that is, as *Dichtung*, poetizing: "Poetry [*Dichtung*] is," Heidegger states, "the awakening and delineation of an individual's ownmost essence, through which he reaches back into the ground of his Dasein. If each individual proceeds from there, then a true gathering [*Sammlung*] of individuals into an original community [*Gemeinschaft*] has already occurred in advance."[26] What is noticeable in this passage is how close Heidegger is to Hegel's and Goethe's idea of the holy as a binding together of souls, spirits, and people, which we started out with by quoting Hegel's reference to Goethe in his *Aesthetics*, and in reading Goethe's distiches 68 and 69 in *The Four Seasons*.

What is more, the notion of community and its relation to poetizing as the original language of a people makes it possible to read the story of the tower of Babel, which Hegel mentions, in an alternative, perhaps unorthodox, way. The loss of the holy is the loss of the original language (poetizing) and so also the loss of community. The dissemination of language is perhaps not so much its division into many languages, as it is a decline into prattle and idle talk, making poetry into superficial prose, which, as such, causes a loss of significance and understanding. After the fall of Babel, its *Verfall*, people became unbound and no longer recognized what language is in its essence, and so also lost the sense of unity, or *Gemeinschaft*. This situation corresponds, I suggest, to the forgetting of Being in Heidegger and the loss of the gods in Hölderlin; in both cases, it gives rise to Heidegger's ultimate formulation of the holy, which runs as follows: "The fundamental attunement of holy mourning, yet in readied distress [*Die Grunstimmung der heilig trauernden, aber bereiten Bedrängnis*]."

I will return to this formulation of the holy, but before I do so, I want to come back to the question of language with the aim of comparing some comments on language by Heidegger with Benveniste's linguistic project. Perhaps, after all, there are some affinities between these two thinkers that deserve to be highlighted. As already noted, the semantic for Benveniste is the world of enunciation and the universe of discourse, in which human subjectivity is constituted as such. It is within enunciation and discourse that human beings enter the world, or rather, how the world becomes meaningful. This is what Benveniste means by *significance*. Each enunciation is an event of language that generates significance, but for that matter not always meaning. And, with enunciation, we enter into a discourse which gives context and reference to the event of language that constitutes the enunciation. Enunciation becomes an experience, an exploration, in and of language, stretching the limits of discourse; for language, Benveniste holds, has no origin, but is always in development. Hence, the different meanings and significations of, for example, the word "holy," "*heilig*," "sacer," "sanctus," "*hieros*," and "*hagios*." These words can be traced to similar etymologies, but they differ in significance, precisely because of the work of enunciation and discourse.

Similarly, in speaking of "the essence and origin of language as poetizing,"[27] Heidegger states: "We humans are always already thrown into a spoken and enunciated discourse [*eine gesprochene und gesagte Rede hineingeworfen*], and can then be silent only in drawing back from such discourse, and even this seldom succeeds. Insofar as we stand within existence [*Dasein*], we ourselves are only a dialogue, and in such dialogue experience something like world."[28] Just as Heidegger here, Benveniste emphasizes the human being's contextualized experience with language as an ongoing dialogue, the significance of which Benveniste sets out to analyze by focusing on salient keywords in Indo-European culture and society.

Yet it must be said that while Benveniste is content with uncovering the linguistic significance of these words, such as the holy, Heidegger's project is to uncover, so as to prepare for the recovery of Being as such. Someone who has noted the similarity between Heidegger's and Beveniste's notions of language is Julia Kristeva, who in the Preface to the English translation of Benveniste's last lectures at the Collège de France in 1968 and 1969, addresses the similarity between Heidegger and Benveniste. She writes: "Indeed, according to *Being and Time* (1927), language is discourse (*Rede*) or speech, words having no signification outside the *Mitsein* of dialogue. It is the responsibility of *Dasein* to *interpret*: its localisation in the existential analytic is taken into consideration, to the detriment of language as such."[29] However, despite what she calls the "detriment of language," that is, what she finds being a limitation haunting the analysis of language in *Being and Time*, she suggests that with the later Heidegger of *On the Way to Language*, Benveniste and Heidegger "cross paths," even though their notions of language never come to complete agreement:

> For Benveniste, writing as graphism and as poetic experience—from Baudelaire to surrealism—seems to cross Heidegger's definition of "language that speaks only and solitarily with itself," and makes sonority possible. But to distance itself from it immediately, since the allusive remarks of the *Last Lectures* and the manuscript notes on Baudelaire place this "letting go" which would be the essence of language, deafly threatened with becoming "meaningless" in the later Heidegger, in apposition (more than opposition) to the vigilance of the linguist, for whom 'discourse includes both the limit and the unlimited', 'unity and diversity' (Thirteenth Lecture).[30]

Kristeva is certainly right in claiming that while there might be no clear opposition between Heidegger's and Benveniste's thinking concerning language, neither is there complete agreement. Rather, a more fitting stance is to view them as apposite philosophies, which might shed some light both on Benveniste's linguistics and Heidegger's thinking. However, it should be pointed out that in the lecture course of 1934–1935, which we are concerned with in this essay, namely *Hölderlin's Hymns "Germania" and "The Rhine,"* Heidegger insists on dialogue as being essential to human language, and so for the grounding of human Dasein. As he clearly states:

> Our beyng occurs as dialogue [*Gespräch*], in the happening of the gods' addressing us, placing us under their claim, bringing us to language with respect to whether and how we are, how we respond, by committing our beyng to them or by way of a telling refusal. Our beyng therefore occurs as a dialogue in so far as we, speaking as thus addressed, bring beings as such beings to language, open up beings in what and how they are, yet at the same time also cover over and dissemble them. Only where language occurs do Being and non-being open up. We ourselves are this opening up and veiling.[31]

It is in the unity of dialogue that we as human beings come together to discover who and in what way we are, that is, in what we show and do not show in and through language. And it is in this dialogue that the danger of language makes itself known, says Heidegger, a danger that we must pay heed to: "[W]e must fathom the entire dangerousness of language in order to experience what the event of language, the dialogue, is as the dialogue that we are. We are a dialogue in commencing and thus in ending history, as the supremely violent word, as poetizing, as keeping silent, and—as idle talk."[32] It is the silence, specifically, that speaks to us as the loss of the gods, which is what concerns Hölderlin in his poetry, a silence, moreover, that makes itself heard to the human Dasein as holy mourning in readied distress.

IV. SILENCE AND THE HOLY

Thus, engaging in dialogue can also be a response to the sign or the hint—*Wink*— which the gods' silence provides in their withdrawal and abandonment. This is what Heidegger calls a beckoning silence, so that what has left us and is denied us still speaks to us in silence. Indeed, silence speaks, but cannot be presented to us as such, it can only be represented as that which it is not. Silence is holy precisely because it is that which is forbidden and unavailable to human beings, as Benveniste reminds us. The holy thus comes to speak in the unspoken, in what Hölderlin calls the caesura, the pause, in his Sophocles translations, and it also speaks in the unspoken of poetry, meaning that which is not represented, but only presented as silence. We noticed this silence in how Goethe's distich 68 is enacted, where the holy is expressed in the silent gesture of the language of poetry—the poetizing binding together in language of what is not said, but still remains an essential part of the poem.

The holy *is* in this silence as the unity which binds the poem together and in poetizing binds souls and people together.

Just as with silence, the fundamental attunement of holy mourning in readied distress, says Heidegger, "does not represent something or set it before us"[33] but is rather an event [*Ereignis*], that is, "not a fixed attribute but a happening."[34] The fundamental attunement is a "transporting," more precisely, a "transporting out [ent*rückend*] toward the gods and a transporting into [ein*rückend*] the Earth[35] at the same time."[36] This transporting out and into is what first opens up the possibility of something being represented. But, it is active listening to the silence of what comes before any representation that gives rise to poetizing and, specifically, Hölderlin's poetizing as the fundamental attunement of holy mourning in readied distress. The silence, moreover, signals the abandonment of the gods, an abandonment that forms into distress [*Bedrängnis*], and which at the same time constitutes an awaiting [*Erharren*], and so a readiness [*Bereitschaft*[37]]: "As distress, [. . .] the distress of holy mourning becomes *readiness*. In this way, the fundamental attunement prevailing in this poetizing is first completed into its full essence."[38] The fundamental attunement of holy mourning is grounded in silence, since silence is that in which Being originates. Accordingly, Heidegger's most decisive statement on silence in the lecture course comes within the context (already referred to) where he is discussing poetizing and community:

> If we were to reflect philosophically still further back here regarding the essence and origin of language as originary poetizing [*Urdichtung*], we would have to recognize that language itself has its origin in silence [*Schweigen*]. It is first in silence that something such as "beyng" must have gathered itself, so as then to be spoken out as "world." That silence preceding the world is more powerful than all human powers. No human being alone ever invented language—that is, was alone strong enough to rupture the sway of that silence, unless under the compulsion of the God.[39]

Originary poetizing begins in silence, Heidegger says, and it is from out of silence that Being speaks and becomes world. It is silence, moreover, which brings about the holy in the manifestation of mourning. And the mourning that Heidegger finds in Hölderlin is, as noted, a disinterested mourning. What is of most importance, however, is that silence implies that meaning is secondary. If we place meaning as our primary objective, then we always end up stating something, explaining, or defining something. Meaning is thus never silent, but conversely, the holy is always silent. It has no meaning since it is, as Benveniste suggests, forbidden to human beings. Or as Rudolf Otto asserts in his *The Idea of the Holy*: "Not even music, which else can give such manifold expression to all the feelings of the mind, has any positive way to express 'the holy.' Even the most consummate Mass-music can only give utterance to the holiest, most 'numinous' moment in the Mass—the moment of transubstantiation—by sinking into stillness: no mere momentary pause, but an absolute cessation of sound long enough for us to 'hear the Silence' itself."[40]

We cannot reach the holy by dissecting it, analyzing it, or breaking it apart, but only fathom it in the blink of an eye, in the event [*Ereignis*] of poetizing.[41] When the holy appears, it is there only for an instant, and eludes being systematized or categorized, measured or accounted for. This is the difference, which Heidegger identifies in Hölderlin's "Germania," between the meaning the poem receives from an analysis of it in terms of form and content, or as the representation of the poet's "lived experience," as Heidegger calls it, and the significance that the poem expresses by silently hinting at that which cannot be heard. This hinting, or beckoning, figures itself in Hölderlin's poetry as the exposure of the silence of the gods in words, that is, as poetizing [*Dichtung*]. Thus, Heidegger says, the poetic [*dichterisch*] is "an exposure [*Ausgesetztheit*] to beyng, and as such exposure is the fundamental occurrence of the historical Dasein of the human being."[42] The gods beckon in silence, and they hint [*winken*], Heidegger says, "insofar as they *are*,"[43] and it is in the saying or telling [*Sagen*] that we as human beings come to know the gods. However, the saying is not what a poem, such as "Germania," presents to us as words on the page, but what is left unspoken. And it is in the unspoken of poetry that the holy speaks; it speaks, to borrow a phrase from Heidegger's reading of Trakl in "Language in the Poem," in a "withholding withdrawal," or as Heidegger puts it: "The holy bestows its arrival by reserving itself in its withholding withdrawal."[44]

In other words, the holy arrives as silence, which is to say it is a gift that does not announce its coming. This is why Heidegger insists that, in mourning and distress, we should prepare for the arrival of the holy by listening to the silence which Hölderlin's poetry enacts by leaving unspoken. If we do this, if we attempt to read Hölderlin's poetry as something else than what can be extracted from it by analyzing its form and content, or as the life world of the poet represented as poetry, Heidegger seems to say, we are preparing ourselves for what is yet to come, and so open ourselves up for building, in dialogue and in community, that which may become the ground and foundation—*grund und boden*—of our human Dasein, united and bound together in spirit.[45] This too, it seems, is what Goethe confidently states in his distich 68: "What is the holy? 'Tis that which binds many spirits in union. Bond, though ever so slight, like the grass on a wreath." Or better, in German: "*Was ist heilig? Das ist's, was viele Seelen zusammen / Bindet; bänd es auch nur leicht, wie die Binse den Kranz.*"

CLOSING REMARKS: HEIDEGGER AND THE HOLY

The preceding reflections have mainly focused on the holy in Heidegger's *Hölderlin's Hymns "Germania" and "The Rhine."* They have been an attempt to explore some of the keywords which can be seen to serve as the framework for the notion of the holy in Heidegger's lecture course. As such, these reflections are not, in any way, exhaustive when it comes to unravel the holy as a theme in his thinking, or even Heidegger's conception of the holy in Hölderlin's hymns "Germania" and "The Rhine." They should rather be seen as probing thoughts that will hopefully elucidate, from my chosen perspective, how Heidegger relates to the holy. One should bear in mind, furthermore, that the keywords I have chosen to highlight in the lecture course are, for the most part, words that can be found in Hölderlin's poetry, such as holy, mourning, silence, etc. This fact goes to show the importance Heidegger places on the singularity of poetry, that is, how each, in Heidegger's estimate, great poet, and thinker, for that matter, has his own peculiar or idiosyncratic way of expression, or rather poetizing [*Dichtung*]. This is also one reason why I have mainly referred to Heidegger's reading of the holy in Hölderlin, although I do make an exception when I invoke his reading of Trakl and the holy. This, since I believe the conception of the holy that Heidegger develops in his reading of Trakl has affinities with the one he develops in his exegesis of Hölderlin.

I have, for a similar reason, juxtaposed Benveniste and Heidegger. Reading them in apposition serves to contrast their respective notions of language and in particular the holy. Thus, the holy as both positive and negative, a sign of the divine, and that which is forbidden to human beings, provides a point of departure for reflecting on the holy and its significance in Heidegger's reading of Hölderlin. My most important comparison, however, comes with Goethe, who in his distiches 68 and 69 of *The Four Seasons* offers an intimation of what the holy can be thought to be outside of Hölderlin's work.

I want to conclude with a final reflection by once more following the path of Heidegger's reading of the holy. Accordingly, I would like to trace the path of the German word for holy, *Heilig*, and highlight its kinship with *Heilung*, healing or cure, which might have a special significance in the year 2020, considering the pandemic that struck us unawares. In emphasizing the connection between *Heilig* and *Heilung*, we could say that poetry, as poetizing, heals the broken, the wound left by the severed tie between the holy and the human. And from *Heilung* we get *Heilungsdauer*, recovery time, recovering the holy through poetry, dialogue, community, and that kind of mourning which does not mean a fall into utter hopelessness or self-pitying despair, but mourning as waiting, waiting for what is yet to come. This waiting does not take time, but gives time; holy mourning gives us time to wait for what Goethe names the most holy: "*Was ist das Heiligste? Das, was heut und ewig die Geister, / Tiefer und tiefer gefühlt, immer nur einiger macht.*"

NOTES

1. Hegel quotes from Goethe's *The Four Seasons*, "Autumn": "LXXVI. What is holy? 'Tis that which binds many spirits in union. Bond, though ever so slight, like the grass on a wreath. LXXVII. What is the holiest? That which binds to-day and forever, Spirits in sympathy close, union of soul unto soul." Johann Wolfgang von Goethe, *Goethe's Works*, Vol. 1, ed. Hjalmar Hjorth Boyesen (Philadelphia, PA: G. Barrie, 1885), 269. This quite free translation of Goethe's text calls for it to be given in German: 68 "*Was ist heilig? Das ist's, was viele Seelen zusammen / Bindet; bänd es auch nur leicht, wie die Binse den Kranz.*" 69 "*Was ist das Heiligste? Das, was heut und ewig die Geister, / Tiefer und tiefer gefühlt, immer nur einiger macht.*" Johann Wolfgang von Goethe, *Poetische Werke*, Berliner Ausgabe, Band 1, *Gedichte und Singspiele* (Berlin and Weimar: Aufbau Verlag, 1960), 264–65. Notice, in particular in 68, the connection and alliteration between "*bindet*, "*band*," and "*Binse*," that is, how the holy binds souls (*Seelen*) together, like the grass or rush (*Binse*) of the wreath, while also binding the poem together through language. Community is envisaged as a wreath, binding together and intertwining the individual with the many, while also being a circle, without beginning and end. It is this interrelation between souls, spirits, people, and poetry that enacts the holy as holy, which is also something that Heidegger develops in his reading of the holy in Hölderlin. As we will see, the threefold conception of the holy as disinterestedness that Heidegger finds in Hölderlin is intimated here in Goethe's enactment of the holy in distich 68 of *The Four Seasons*. When it comes to distich 69, a clarifying literal translation of it could be: "What is the most holy? That which makes, today and forever, felt deeper and deeper, the spirits everlasting in unity." The holy, in other words, binds the spirits together in time without end. This is what is the most holy, the act of achieving infinite unity, a unity of spirit and of people beyond their individual determination. Heidegger calls this *Gemeinschaft*, which he explains in similar words as Goethe, that is, *Gemeinschaft* is formed by binding human beings together, and so creating a bond between them: "[C]ommunity [*Gemeinschaft*] is through each individual's being bound in advance to something that binds and determines every individual in exceeding them." Martin Heidegger, *Hölderlin's Hymns "Germania" and "The Rhine,"* trans. William McNeill & Julia Ireland. (Bloomington and Indianapolis, IN: Indiana University Press, 2014), 66. Now, my aim in this essay is not to relate the holy to Heidegger's thinking of Being, specifically. This has already been admirably done by Richard Capobianco in his *Heidegger's Way of Being*. Capobianco interestingly mentions the wreath that binds together that which appears. It is in Heidegger's reading of Pindar's *Isthmian Ode 5*, when discussing the words "golden" and "gleaming," where we find the word *Kränz*, of which Capobianco states: "Nature (Being) shows itself as the gleaming 'whole' that allows all beings to be and may be likened to a 'shining wreath' that 'wreathes everything that appears'. As this radiant

'orb of the wholeness of the whole', Nature (Being) is the 'divine', *the holy*." Richard Capobianco, *Heidegger's Way of Being* (Toronto: Toronto University Press, 2014), 35. Lastly, in the context of community, one should not neglect to mention Jean-Luc Nancy, whose perhaps most well know work is *The Inoperative Community*. It is impossible to reduce into a few words Nancy's notion of community. However, what might speak to the theme of the present essay is that in the French edition of his book, Nancy quotes a few lines from Hölderlin's poem "Bread and Wine": "One thing is certain: a standard always exists, at noon / Or at midnight, common to all of us. But also / To each of us something personal is granted" ["*Fest bleibt Eins*; *es sei um Mittag oder es gehe / Bis in die Mitternacht, immer bestehet ein Maß, / Allen gemein, doch jeglichem auch ist eignes beschieden*"]. Friedrich Hölderlin, *Poems of Friedrich Hölderlin*, trans. James Mitchel (San Fransisco: Ithuriel's Spear, 2004), 9; "Brod und Wein," *Hölderlins sämtliche Werke und Briefe*, Band 1, ed. Franz Zinkernagel (Leipzig: Insel-Verlag, 1922), 305. From these lines it is not too difficult to infer Nancy's thinking concerning the one and the plural, the singular and the communal. Thus, on Nancy's view: "Community is given to us—or we are given and abandoned to the community: a gift to be renewed and communicated, it is not a work to be done or produced. But it is a task, which is different—an infinite task at the heart of finitude." Jean-Luc Nancy, *The Inoperative Community*, trans. Peter Connor, *et al.* (Minneapolis and Oxford: Minnesota University Press, 1991), 35. Even though Nancy's notion of community is not altogether reconcilable with Goethe's, Hölderlin's, and Heidegger's, for that matter, we can still find nuances that can be instructive of how we can conceive of community and the holy in Heidegger's reading of Hölderlin in what follows.

2. G. W. F. Hegel, *Aesthetics: Lectures on Fine Art*, Vol. 2, trans. T. M. Knox (Oxford: Oxford University Press, 1975), 638.

3. Giorgio Agamben, "Foreword: The Vocabulary and the Voice," trans. Thomas Zummer, in Emile Benveniste, *Dictionary of Indo-European Concepts and Society*, trans. Elizabeth Palmer (Chicago: Hau Books, 2016), xv.

4. Emile Benveniste, "The Semiology of Language," in *Semiotics: An Introductory Anthology*, ed. Robert E. Innis (Bloomington and Indianapolis, IN: Indiana University Press, 1985), 241–42.

5. Benveniste, *Semiotics*, 242.

6. Emile Benveniste, *Dictionary of Indo-European Concepts and Society*, trans. Elizabeth Palmer (Chicago: Hau Books, 2016), xxiii.

7. Benveniste, *Dictionary*, 459.

8. This double meaning in Icelandic is also present in Swedish, where we find *hälsa*, which as a noun means health, and as a verb means to salute someone.

9. Benveniste, *Dictionary*, 460.

10. Benveniste, *Dictionary*, 476.

11. Benveniste, Dictionary, 476.

12. The essay is also, in English translation, referred to as "'When the poet is once in command of the spirit'." See Friedrich Hölderlin, *Essays and Letters*, trans. Jeremy Adler & Charlie Louth (London: Penguin, 2009), 333–48. For the essay in German, see Friedrich Hölderlin, "*Über die verfahrensweise des poëtichen Gesites*," in

Hölderlins sämtliche Werke, Band 3, ed. Norbert von Hellingrath (Berlin: Propyläen Verlag, 1922), 277–303.

13. Martin Heidegger, *Hölderlin's Hymns "Germania" and "The Rhine,"* trans. William McNeill & Julia Ireland. (Bloomington and Indianapolis, IN: Indiana University Press, 2014), 77. [HHGR]
14. HHGR
15. HHGR, 77.
16. HHGR, 75. Heidegger's emphasis.
17. HHGR
18. HHGR, 78.
19. HHGR. McNeil and Ireland's translation corresponds better to Heidegger's reading of Hölderlin with his focus on *uneigennützig*, that is to say, the disinterested character of the holy, which in Adler and Louth's translation is rendered as selfless. Here is the passage in Hölderlin's German: "*Denn diss ist allein in schöner, heiliger, göttlicher Empfindung möglich, in einer Empfindung, welche darum schön ist weil (sie) weder blos angenehm un glüklich, noch blos erhalben und stark, noch blos einig und ruhig, sondern alles zugleich ist, und allein sein kann, in einer Empfindung, welched arum heilig ist, weil sie weder uneigennützig ihrem Objecte hingegeben, noch blos uneigennützig auf ihrem inner Grunde ruhend, noch blos uneigennützig zwischen ihrem innern Grunde und ihrem Object schwebend, sondern alles zugleich ist.* Hölderlin, "*Über die verfahrungsweise des poëtichen Gesites,*" 300–301.
20. Benveniste, *Dictionary*, 11.
21. In Heidegger's words: "Yet if ever a poet demanded a *thoughtful* coming to terms with his poetry, it is Hölderlin [. . .], this is so because Hölderlin is one of our greatest—that is, one of our most futural—*thinkers*, because he is our greatest *poet*. A poetic turning toward his poetry is possible only as a *thoughtful* encounter [*Auseinandersetzung*] with the *revelation* of *Beyng* [*Offenbarung des Seyns*] that is achieved in this poetry." HHGR, 5.
22. HHGR, 58.
23. HHGR, 59.
24. HHGR, 198.
25. HHGR, 198–99.
26. HHGR, 7.
27. HHGR, 199.
28. HHGR
29. Julia Kristeva, "Preface," in Emile Benveniste, *Last Lectures, Collège de France 1968 and 1969*, trans. John E. Joseph, ed. Jean-Claude Coquet and Irène Fenoglio (Edingburgh: Edingburgh University Press, 2019), 19.
30. Kristeva, "Preface," 20.
31. HHGR, 64.
32. HHGR
33. HHGR, 123.
34. HHGR, 125.
35. Earth should here be understood as what Heidegger calls homeland, which means "not as mere birth place, nor as mere landscape familiar to us, but *as the*

power of the Earth upon which the human being 'dwells poetically', in each case in accordance with his historical Dasein." HHGR, 80.

36. HHGR, 123–24.

37. It should be noted that the word *Bereitschaft* in addition to readiness also contains the meaning of preparedness, of being well prepared for what is to come, on standby in the event of an emergency, or as a country being prepared for war.

38. HHGR, 94.

39. HHGR, 199.

40. Rudolf Otto, *The Idea of the Holy*, trans. John W. Harvey (Oxford: Oxford University Press, 1958), 70.

41. In his reading of Hölderlin's "As When On a Holiday ..." Heidegger gives his most succinct characterization of the holy: "The holy bestows [*verschenkt*] the word, and itself comes into this word. This word is the primal event [*Ereignis*] of the holy." Martin Heidegger, *Elucidations of Hölderlin's Poetry*, trans. Keith Hoeller (New York: Humanity Books, 2000), 98.

42. HHGR, 34.

43. HHGR, 31.

44. Martin Heidegger, "Language in the Poem," in *On the Way to Language*, trans. Peter D. Hertz (New York: HarperCollins, 1982), 165. In the quoted passage, Heidegger uses the word "*verschenkt*" (translated as "bestows"), which invokes the notion of gift and giving into the way the holy arrives. The holy is a gift, *Geschenk*, which does not present itself as such, or rather, it does not present itself at all, but gives in silence, that is, in withholding its giving.

45. To refer again to Heidegger's reading of Hölderlin's "As When On a Holiday..." we find there a similar view of the holy and the grounding of historical Dasein: "In its coming, the holy grounds another beginning of another history. The holy primordially decides in advance concerning men and gods, whether they are, and who they are, and when they are." Martin Heidegger, *Elucidations of Hölderlin's Poetry*, 97–98.

Chapter 6

Heidegger and the Question and the Need of the Holy

Holger Zaborowski

I. HEIDEGGER'S EARLY THOUGHT: THE HOLY AS A VALUE AND THE CRITIQUE OF NEO-KANTIANISM

The "holy" is a key concept of contemporary philosophy of religion. Important studie, many of which exhibit a phenomenological outlook, have been devoted to the interpretation of this crucial concept or phenomenon.[1] There are many reasons for the widespread interest in the holy. After the critique of religion, in general, and of Christianity, in particular, and after the announcement of the death of God in the nineteenth century, the holy seems to allow for an understanding of religious phenomena that is not dependent on a specific religion nor on the presupposition of the existence of God. It does not come as a surprise that Martin Heidegger's thought, too, has significantly inspired the philosophical and theological examination of the holy.[2] Scholarship on Heidegger's own understanding of the holy normally focuses on his later, that is, his Being-historical thought.[3] But as an emerging scholar, too, during the time of his first lecture courses at the University of Freiburg, Heidegger dealt with this concept in a manner that not only reflects his own religious origins and his early theological interests[4] but also explains his silence about the holy in the 1920s and early 1930s and sheds light on his somewhat surprising rediscovery of the "holy" in the 1930s and later.

The young Heidegger knew well contemporary discussions of the holy. Rudolf Otto's famous study *The Idea of the Holy. An Inquiry into the Nonrational Factor in the Idea of the Divine and its Relation to the Rational*[5] (*Das Heilige. Über das Irrationale in der Idee des Göttlichen und sein Verhältnis zum Rationalen*), however, was met with grave disapproval by Heidegger.[6] A letter to his wife Elfride, written on October

27, 1918, shows how important he considered it to distance himself from Otto's understanding of the holy. The reason is that Heidegger, already on his way to his early hermeneutics of facticity, or of factical life, aimed at developing a radically different approach to what philosophy is and how it is to be pursued (suffice it to say here that the young Heidegger himself knew well what he rejected without being fully aware yet of what he was striving for). In this letter, he therefore declares that he intends to position the "problem of the holy" into "these new fundamental contexts—not only because they are entirely missing in Otto, but in a purely objective interest."[7] Otto was for him, as he writes a little later to his wife, on a "false trail."[8]

Presumably around this time, when he prepared in 1918 and 1919 a lecture course on "The Philosophical Foundations of Medieval Mysticism"[9]—a course that he contrived in parts, but never delivered because he did not feel he had coped with the subject—Heidegger also worked on a review of Otto's book that he eventually neither published nor even finished. In the dense and partly cryptic notes for the book review, it become clear what led to Heidegger's skepticism about *The Idea of the Holy*. He refers to the "principal problems" of Otto's approach which, as he points out, "demand initially, if not solution, at least to be named and outlined."[10] Heidegger explicitly names two problems of Otto's phenomenology of the holy that are closely intertwined: first of all, the "problem of historical consciousness" and, second, the "problem of the irrational."

According to Heidegger, "the holy may not be made into a problem as theoretical—also not an irrational theoretical—noema."[11] It should, as Heidegger points out under the significant influence of Schleiermacher, rather be interpreted "as correlate of the act-character of 'faith,' which itself is to be interpreted only from out of the fundamentally essential experiential context of historical consciousness."[12] Otto's phenomenology of the holy thus shows Heidegger the limits of any kind of phenomenology that examines the holy as an a priori idea and limits itself to the rational categories of the merely theoretical, even if it is the category of the "irrational." This kind of philosophy, Heidegger holds, is not open for the temporal and living "act-character" of human existence and for the phenomenon of historical consciousness that he increasingly discovered and explored in the late 1910s and early 1920s.

Heidegger did not go on to develop a distinct phenomenology of the holy on the basis of his criticism of Otto even though the comments that he made to his wife suggest that at some point he was, presumably because of his interest to understand his own religious faith philosophically and at the same time because of the influence of his teacher Edmund Husserl,[13] contemplating such an endeavor—a kind of new phenomenology of the holy as a genuine phenomenology of religion. He was too aware of the neo-Kantian undertones in Otto's book and in Wilhelm Windelband's *Das Heilige*,[14] which he briefly also mentions,[15] and considered the whole concept of the holy an invention that did not originate in an original experience. In the winter semester 1925–1926, he concluded that the "value" of the holy was devised in order to complement Kant's three *Critiques* by integrating religion into the philosophical system.[16]

In the context of his close readings of some of St. Paul's letters and of St. Augustine's *Confessions*, presented in lecture courses in 1920 and 1921, Heidegger, therefore, avoids the concept of the holy (and thus possible misunderstandings) and focuses on a phenomenology of religious life, that presupposes the "method" of formal indication, that is, an approach that does not objectify religious phenomena but helps understanding the lived religious experience. In so doing, Heidegger goes way beyond a theoretical interest in the holy as a key category of intellectually grasping the religious.[17] In the following years, the concept of the "holy" disappears altogether from his thinking—as, by and large, many other questions concerning religion or, more broadly speaking, the religious which he leaves, on the basis of his own distancing from the faith of his youth and from his concern with theological issues and against the background of his methodological understanding of philosophy as "a-theistic"[18] in relation to traditional theology.

This is, however, not to say that the phenomena that Otto describes as "holy" are entirely absent from Heidegger's thinking. On the contrary, Heidegger comes even close to some of Otto's observations regarding the holy as *mysterium tremendum et fascinosum* in his phenomenology of anxiety in *Being and Time*, in his approach to the experience of nothingness in "What is Metaphysics?" and even in his later thought.[19] As is often the case, if Heidegger disapproves of another thinker very strongly, there is a deep and often even on-going influence of this particular thinker on his thought, too. He would in many cases at least partly adopt an idea or view that he criticized and significantly transform it in an innovative manner—in his attempt at disclosing a radically original dimension of human life or, later, of Dasein or of the truth of Being.

All the more striking is the central position of the concept of the holy in his later thought after the turn toward Being-historical thinking or the thinking of the event of Being. When Heidegger, after his so-called turn, draws his attention to the poetry of Friedrich Hölderlin, a fellow Swabian, inspired by a deeply Nietzschean understanding of modernity, he uncovers the historical absence, or lack, of the holy in the contemporary age and finds an entirely new approach to this word and its possible significance that should leave an imprint on his thinking until his death.

II. HEIDEGGER'S MIDDLE THOUGHT: THE DEATH OF GOD AND HÖLDERLIN'S POETRY OF THE HOLY

In his encounter with Friedrich Nietzsche, Heidegger becomes aware of the implications of the death of God and of the completion of Western metaphysics in modern nihilism. His Being-historical reading of the history of Western metaphysics shows him the conditions of the traditional Christian and metaphysical concept of the holy (not only as a theoretical concept for the irrational but also as an attribute of God). Heidegger thus finds a justification for his early skepticism with respect to the philosophical significance of the holy. It is his close reading of Hölderlin's poetry, however, that allows him an utterly different approach to the holy, so much that the holy—understood not as a metaphysical category nor as a theological or religious concept, but as a "hint" (*Wink*)—takes a crucial place in Heidegger's middle and late philosophy.

Particularly famous is Heidegger's much cited reference to the holy in his *Letter on Humanism*: "Only from the truth of Being can the essence of the holy be thought. Only from the essence of the holy is the essence of divinity to be thought. Only in the light of the essence of divinity can it be thought or said what the word 'God' is to signify."[20] The further context of this passage is Heidegger's search for a new understanding, or thinking, of God that goes beyond what he conceives of as the onto-theological conceptualizations of God as "highest being" in which the holy, as it is often understood, participates or on which it depends. This metaphysical God, he maintains with Nietzsche and Hölderlin on his side, has died. If one wants to speak of God again, one should reorient oneself, think more primordially than metaphysics ever could think, and become attentive to the truth of Being of, or from, which Heidegger speaks. This, as Heidegger maintains, will also allow a new understanding of the holy "which indeed remains closed as a dimension if the open region of Being is not cleared and in its clearing is near to humans."[21]

In another important text, Heidegger clarifies the difference between "Being" and "holy" as well as their similarity: "Being" and the "holy," he writes, "call the same and yet not the same." While the holy is "experienced"—by Hölderlin, the poet—Being is "pre-thought" by Heidegger, the philosopher.[22] Both are not to be understood as "ground," "cause," or as an "absolute," but as that "what prevails (heals) and essences before the gods and human beings."[23]

Only on the basis of this new thinking of Being and of the holy, Heidegger maintains, is a new approach to God possible. This is why Heidegger does not only invert the common relation between the holy and God, in that he prioritizes, as it were, the holy over the divine and over God, while this relation is commonly understood conversely. He also makes the thinking of "divinity" and of "God" dependent on the thinking from the "truth of Being." Thus, Heidegger himself—as the thinker of, or from, the "truth of Being"—takes a central role for the possible new thinking of the holy and of God. The holy, then, is not merely something irrational nor can it empirically be observed. It is related to, or from a certain perspective even identical with, the disclosure of Being, understood Being-historically.

It is, therefore, not thinking alone that can find a new approach to the holy or the healing (Heidegger seems to use both words in the *Letter on Humanism* almost synonymously). It all depends ultimately on Being itself: "To healing Being first grants ascent into grace; to raging its compulsion to malignancy."[24] Thinking cannot effect the holy or its ascent. It has an altogether different, but no less important duty or possibility. Its task is to guide "historical eksistence, that is, the humanitas of homo humanus, into the realm of the upsurgence of healing [*des Heilen*]."[25]

It is at this point that Heidegger highlights that thinking is dependent upon a dialogue with poetizing. Their tasks, as has already been mentioned, are different: "The thinker says Being. The poet names the holy."[26] Here, Heidegger follows a trajectory that he first entered in his close reading of Hölderlin's poetry in the 1930s. As is well known, when he speaks of "the poet," he particularly and almost exclusively thinks of Hölderlin[27] who shows a path beyond the constraints of metaphysics and onto-theology for which "God can . . . descend to a cause, a *causa efficiens*."[28] In his "elucidations" of Hölderlin's poem "Remembrance" ("*Andenken*"),[29] first published in 1943, Heidegger characterizes what the poet Hölderlin pursues as follows: "For as the one who points, the poet stands between men and gods. Out of this 'between,' he thinks that which passes beyond both gods and men and makes them holy and is different from them both, and addresses itself to him as the poem which is to be uttered. Thinking like a mortal, he puts the highest into a poem."[30]

Heidegger thus reads the word of Hölderlin's poetry in light of a very special hermeneutics: "The word of this song is no longer a 'Hymn to' something, neither a 'Hymn to the Poets,' nor a hymn 'to' nature; rather, it is the hymn 'of the holy.' The holy bestows the word, and itself comes into this word. This word is the primal event of the holy. Hölderlin's poetry is now a primordial calling which, called by what is coming, says this and only this as the holy. The hymnal word is now 'compelled by the holy,' and because compelled by the 'holy,' also 'sobered by the holy.'"[31]

It is the holy itself that calls the poet and grants him his words that are themselves holy by virtue of both being disclosed by the holy and disclosing the holy. The holy is thus not something that can be experienced and analyzed theoretically. It is also not something that is founded in the performance of one's life or in Dasein's moods. It is the horizon within which experience—in the sense of receiving something on one's way of thinking and poetizing—is possible. Heidegger, the thinker of the history of Being, now interprets—similarly to the later "Letter on Humanism"—the holy as allowing a new disclosure of gods and of human beings: "Hölderlin's word conveys the holy thereby naming the space of time that is only once, time of the primordial decision for the essential order of the future history of gods and humanities."[32]

For Heidegger, Hölderlin serves as a new "prophet" of the holy—"prophet" literally understood as the "fore-speaker" or "fore-caster" of what is yet to come. Heidegger's own role in his thinking about the holy, however, oscillates. On the one hand, he limits himself as a thinker to merely elucidating the poetry of Hölderlin who, by virtue of being a poet, is closer to the holy. It is, on the other hand, the thinker Heidegger who understands what poetry really is and who, on the basis of this understanding, awards an eminent role to Hölderlin. It is as if Hölderlin's poetry is a new revelation that for Heidegger replaces both the Biblical revelation of the Judeo-Christian tradition, as well as the political revelation of National Socialism. While theology interprets biblical revelation and political action realizes the message of National Socialism, Heidegger's Being-historical thinking elucidates Hölderlin's poetry. Heidegger's approach to Hölderlin's poetry of the holy has, therefore, two important dimensions, one with respect to Heidegger's religious and theological origins and the other with respect to his political involvement with National Socialism particularly during the rectorate.

This claim becomes clear if we briefly remind ourselves of two important personal challenges that Heidegger faced in the mid-1930s. He mentions them in a letter that he wrote more than a year after he resigned from the rectorate, to Karl Jaspers. In this letter, he refers to two "thorns" in the flesh (thus alluding to St. Paul in 2 Cor 12:7), the "confrontation with the faith of my origins and the failure of the rectorate."[33] Heidegger, to be sure, had lost the religious belief of his youth and his interest in Christian theology that let him develop a particular interest in the concept of the holy in his very early career; he also increasingly lost his faith, as it were, in Hitler, in National Socialism, and in his own possibilities of shaping the German university, in particular, and German society, in general, under the new regime.[34] Vis-à-vis the "thorn" of this loss and this failure, Heidegger seems to interpret Hölderlin as an answer or solution to what he considered the philosophical key problem of his time. This is the problem of nihilism that, as he now holds, can neither be overcome by traditional religion—because of the death of God and also because of the close link between Christianity and metaphysics—nor by National Socialist politics.

It is Hölderlin's poetry—as poetry of the holy—that shows Heidegger a way of leaving nihilism behind. For "in its coming, the holy, 'older than the ages' and 'above the gods,' grounds another beginning of another history."[35] This "historical beginning," Heidegger writes in *On the Beginning*, is not to be understood within the framework of the opposition of religion and Christianity, on the one hand, and paganism (as, maybe, expressed in National Socialism), on the other.[36] It is to be understood as radically transcending and overcoming this traditional opposition—as does the holy that Hölderlin's word "conveys."

It goes without saying that this reading of Hölderlin's poetry of the holy remains deeply problematic as it is dependent on presuppositions that are far from being persuasive. Heidegger provides not many conclusive arguments for his approach to Hölderlin—however inspiring it may be. Among many other things, he aimed at overcoming the modern subjectivist perspective on the holy that, in his reading, has characterized the neo-Kantian approach to the holy. If he succeeded in doing so or not is a different question. It may be plausible to argue that a kind of subjectivism remains in the eminent roles that Heidegger attributes to himself and to poet Hölderlin. This reading of Hölderlin, one can argue, is indicative of the in-depth crisis of Heidegger's thought in the 1930s and early 1940s, symptomatic of his continuing search for understanding and orientation in a time of fundamental crises—on a personal, religious, political, and philosophical level.

III. HEIDEGGER'S LATE THOUGHT: THE LACKING OF HOLY NAMES AND A NEW WAY OF QUESTIONING

One of the last texts written by Heidegger stands under the title "The Want of Holy Names" (*"Der Fehl heiliger Namen"*).[37] In this text—a gift to the romanticist Hugo Friedrich on the occasion of his 70th birthday—Heidegger resumes his elucidations of Hölderlin's poetry and his interpretation of the contemporary epoch. The title of this short essay refers to Hölderlin's word in the last stanza of the elegy "Homecoming" (*"Heimkunft"*) "holy names are lacking." Heidegger calls this word "simple, all-explaining, and yet mysterious"[38] and reads it as a key to understanding the specific situation and "need" of "the technological age." This need, he points out, is hidden in the absence of the "presence of the divine."[39] According to Heidegger, we have not yet recognized this absence, and thus we have not yet captured the need of our time. If we were able to have insight into the character of this absence and its origin, "which presumably hides in the withdrawal of the holy,"[40] we would be able to understand this need. The technological age, Heidegger maintains, cannot understand itself—"the power of enframing that determines it"[41]—and thus fails to find the "region of the saving."[42] A new kind of "experience" is necessary.

It may appear, Heidegger writes, that modern thinking can lead to such an experience.[43] Heidegger, however, declines this possibility and distinguishes sharply between the modern post-Cartesian focus on methodology and the required path of thinking as being on a way.[44] For Heidegger, the poet can "let himself be said the pure call of the presence as such, be it even only and precisely a presence of the lacking and of the withdrawal."[45] Thinking, he goes on, can prepare the experience of the lacking and thus help the poet to understand—in the sense of "enduring"—"the need" of the lacking of holy names "which is forgetfulness of Being."[46] There is, therefore, in times of need the "possibility of an insight into that, what *is* today by lacking."[47] So Heidegger does not remain hopeless as there are still poets, such as Hölderlin, and thinkers, such as himself, who help one another in understanding the lacking of holy names.

At first sight, Heidegger may simply appear to continue his earlier thinking of poetry and of the holy. But the differences between his earlier and this reading of Hölderlin are remarkable. At this late stage, Heidegger calls Hölderlin's word "far-looking ahead" (*weitvorausblickendes*) and thus still takes his poetry in very high regard,[48] but he no longer interprets Hölderlin as the "prophet" of a new revelation of the holy nor his poetry as "word" or "event" of the holy. It is now the "need" of the holy itself that "urges" the poet "into saying."[49] Neither Hölderlin, the poet, nor Heidegger, the Being-historical thinker, are in positions of "certainty" and proper "understanding" as they seem to have been earlier when Hölderlin's word could "convey the holy" and Heidegger could self-confidently elucidate it. On his way of thinking, Heidegger's tone and temper have become significantly more careful, more tentative, more questioning, and, indeed, more humble than in his middle period. The short statement "questions over questions"[50] after a series of fundamental questions, frequent conjunctives, and the reference to a mere "possibility"[51] shows this important difference in both style and content.

It is almost as if the withdrawal of the holy has become even more pressing for the late Heidegger. The wider context for this transformation is that Heidegger, already beginning in the mid-1930s, increasingly moved away from a philosophy of will and decision that still had somewhat of an impact on his early Being-historical thinking and, thus, on his early reading of Hölderlin to his later thinking of radical releasement. He also dealt intensively in the year after the war with the question concerning technology and thus with the question concerning the completion of metaphysics as something that could not easily be "overcome" —not even by a philosopher as insightful as Heidegger himself or a poet as prophetic as Hölderlin. It seems that Heidegger, after a period of masterfully providing answers—most prominently shortly before, during, and immediately after the rectorate—has incrementally regained the radical questioning attitude of his very early way of thinking that had led him to question so blatantly Rudolf Otto's approach to the holy.

Heidegger's late approach to the holy, that is, to its absence, not to its "calling" the poet or the thinker, can not only be read as an interpretation of the radical godless and "holy-less" dimensions of late modernity—what Max Weber called from a different perspective the "demystification" (*Entzauberung*) of the world. It is also protective against the danger of finding too easily replacements for what is really holy, yet seems to remain absent, be it in the irrational as the opposite of the rational, in ideological religious or political movements, or in idolizing poets as "prophets" of the holy and a very specific way of thinking as bearing witness to these prophets. Thinking is no longer motivated by a hidden religious or political agenda—and be it the agenda to replace religion and politics by thinking and poetizing. All that is left to do, the very late Heidegger, suggests, is to address the absence of the holy, to continue to raise questions, and thus to remain on the way.

IV. AFTER HEIDEGGER: FROM THE ANONYMITY OF THE HOLY TO THE HOLY OF REVELATION AND TO THE HOLINESS OF THE HUMAN BEING

One simple, yet mysterious word such as the "holy" allows an understanding of Heidegger's complex way of thought—from his early beginnings over the attempts to establish a new kind of thinking of the 1930s and early 1940s to the serenity of his very late thinking which takes questioning to be its piety. What is needed is to stay on one's way of questioning. This approach to the holy in late modernity—as an approach to the absence of the holy—may be Heidegger's lasting contribution to the phenomenology of the holy.

There is, however, something irritatingly lacking, as it were, in Heidegger thinking of the holy. This lack may even explain the radical focus on the absence of the holy in the late Heidegger. The holy, understood along the lines of Heidegger's interpretation, as an almost anonymous holy—as "a life experience" or, later, as an event—may truly be absent and, indeed, even questionable. Closer to us—to use another key word of the late Heidegger—may be the possibility of an altogether different holy, of the holy, or the healing, as revealed and promised salvation (*Heil*) or of the holy in concrete human form. Heidegger's particular perspective—the absence of the possibility of divine revelation and salvation and of the saint, of the holy human being—shows the extent to which Heidegger left the Jewish and Christian perspective on the holy behind.

Two thinkers who were both deeply influenced by Heidegger have focused on divine revelation and salvation and the conditions for the possibilities of understanding it, on the one hand, and on the possibility of the holiness of the human being, on the other. On the basis of Heidegger's understanding of Being (*Seinsverständnis*), the theologian and philosopher Bernhard Welte has examined the understanding of the holy or of salvation (*Heilsverständnis*) as the transcendental horizon within which the event of Biblical revelation and the promise of something that is fundamentally "healing" can be understood. While Welte adopted Heidegger with respect to Christian theology, the Jewish philosopher Emmanuel Levinas did so with regard to a deeply and radically ethical thinking. In a phenomenology that goes beyond the borders of phenomenological thinking, he distinguished sharply between the sacred and the saint and explored the dimension of holiness as ethical saintliness in the face of the Other.[52] However different their approaches are, they both show the inspired dimension of Heidegger's thought on the holy—in its achievement as well as in its failures. They show, in other words, what it means to be and to remain on the way of thinking toward the holy.

NOTES

1. See particularly *Wiener Jahrbuch für Philosophie XLIX* (2017) (Rudolf Langthaler and Michael Hofer (eds.), *Das Heilige. Eine grundlegende Kategorie der Religionsphilosophie* (Wien and Hamburg: New Academic Press, 2017); Jörg Splett and *Die Rede vom Heiligen. Über ein religionsphilosophisches Grundwort* (Freiburg/München: Verlag Karl Alber, 1985), 2nd edition).

2. See, for example, Hal St John, *The Call of the Holy. Heidegger – Chauvet – Benedict XVI* (London and New York: Bloomsbury T & T Clark, 2012); not only Jörg Splett (cf. fn. 1), but also Bernhard Welte and his students Bernhard Casper, Klaus Hemmerle, and Peter Hünermann were influenced by Heidegger in their discussions of the holy (see Bernhard Welte, *Hermeneutik des Christlichen, eingeführt und bearbeitet von Bernhard Casper* (Freiburg, Basel, and Wien: Herder, 2006); Bernhard Casper, Klaus Hemmerle, and Peter Hünermann, *Besinnung auf das Heilige* (Freiburg im Breisgau: Verlag Herder, 1966)).

3. For discussions of the holy in Heidegger's thought see particularly Stephanie Bohlen and *Die Übermacht des Seins, Heideggers Auslegung des Bezuges von Mensch und Natur und Hölderlins Dichtung des Heiligen* (Berlin: Duncker und Humblot, 1993); Holger Helting, *Heideggers Auslegung von Hölderlins Dichtung des Heiligen. Ein Beitrag zur Grundlagenforschung der Daseinsanalyse* (Berlin: Duncker und Humblot, 1999); Emilio Brito, *Heidegger et l'hymne du sacré* (Leuven: University Press, 1999); Marius Johan Geertsema, *Heidegger's Poetic Projection of Being* (Springer International Publishing, 2018).

4. For Heidegger's religious and theological background see my A "Genuinely Religiously Orientated Personality. Martin Heidegger and the Religious and Theological Origins of His Philosophy," in *The Companion to Heidegger's Philosophy of Religion*, ed. Andrew Wiercinsky and Sean McGrath (Amsterdam: Rodopi, 2010), 3–19.

5. Rudolf Otto, *Das Heilige. Über das Irrationale in der Idee des Göttlichen und sein Verhältnis zum Rationalen* (Breslau: Trewendt & Granier, 1917) (mit einer Einführung zu Leben und Werk Rudolf Ottos von Jörg Lauster und Peter Schüz und einem Nachwort von Hans Joas, München: Beck, 2014); for the English translation see: *The Idea of the Holy. An Inquiry into the Nonrational Factor in the Idea of the Divine and its Relation to the Rational*, trans. by John W. Harvey (Harmondsworth: Penguin Books, 1959).

6. For Heidegger's interpretation of Otto's book see Annalisa Caputo, *La filosofia e il sacro. Martin Heidegger lettore di Rudolf Otto* (Bari: Stilo, 2002); Ben Vedder, *Heidegger's Philosophy of Religion* (Pittsburgh, PA: Duquesne University Press, 2007), 27, 48 f.; Pierfrancesco Stagi, *Der faktische Gott, Würzburg: Königshausen & Neumann*, 2007, 62–64; Hal St John, *The Call of the Holy. Heidegger – Chauvet – Benedict XVI* (cf. fn. 2), 104–108.

7. *Mein liebes Seelchen! Briefe Martin Heideggers an seine Frau Elfride, 1915-1970*, hrsg., ausgew. und kommentiert *von* Gertrud Heidegger, München: Deutsche Verlags-Anstalt, 2005, 88 (for an English translation see Martin Heidegger, *Letters to His Wife, 1915-1970*, selected, edited and annotated by Gertrud Heidegger, translated by R. D. V. Glasgow (Cambridge, UK: Polity, 2008)).

8. *Mein liebes Seelchen! Briefe Martin Heideggers an seine Frau Elfride, 1915-1970*, 100.

9. GA 60: 301–37.

10. GA 60: 332.

11. GA 60, 333.

12. GA 60: 333.

13. Cf. here Edmund Husserl's letter to Heidegger of September 10, 1918, in: Edmund Husserl, *Briefwechsel, in Verbindung mit Elisabeth Schumann hrsg. von Karl Schumann, Bd. 4: Die Freiburger Schüler* (Husserliana — Edmund Husserl Dokumente 3.4) (Dordrech/Boston/London: Kluwer, 1994), 132.

14. Wilhelm Windelband, *Das Heilige. Skizze zur Religionsphilosophie* (1902), Tübingen: Mohr, 1916 (also in: Wilhelm Windelband, *Präludien II. Aufsätze und Reden zur Philosophie und ihrer Geschichte*, 5th edition (Tübingen: Mohr, 1915, 295–332)).

15. GA 60: 334.

16. GA 21: 83.

17. GA 60: 1–299.

18. For Heidegger's understanding of philosophy as atheistic see Martin Heidegger, *Phänomenologische Interpretationen zu Aristoteles. Ausarbeitung für die Marburger und die Göttinger Philosophische Fakultät (1922)*, ed. Günther Neumann (Stuttgart: Philipp Reclam jun., 2002), 28.

19. For this see Hal St John, *The Call of the Holy. Heidegger – Chauvet – Benedict XVI*, 104–108; for Otto's influence on Heidegger see also Pierfrancesco Stagi, *Der faktische Gott*, 62.

20. GA 9: 351.
21. GA 9: 351.
22. GA 71.
23. GA 71.
24. GA 9: 360.
25. GA 9: 359.
26. GA 9: 312.
27. See GA 12: 40 for a reference to Georg Trakl as a poet of the holy.
28. GA 7: 27.
29. GA 4: 79–151.
30. GA 4: 123; 145.
31. GA 4: 76.
32. GA 4: 76.
33. Martin Heidegger and Karl Jaspers, *Briefwechsel 1920–1963*, ed. Walter Biemel and Hans Saner (Frankfurt and Munich, 1990), 157.
34. For this see my *"Eine Frage von Irre und Schuld?" Martin Heidegger und der Nationalsozialismus* (Frankfurt am Main: Fischer, 2010).
35. GA 4: 76; 97.
36. GA 69: 31.
37. GA 13: 231–35.
38. GA 13: 232.
39. GA 13: 232.
40. GA 13: 232.
41. GA 13: 232.
42. GA 13: 232.
43. GA 13: 233.
44. GA 13: 233f.
45. GA 13: 234.
46. GA 13: 234.
47. GA 13: 235.
48. GA 13: 232.
49. GA 13: 232.
50. GA 13: 232.
51. GA 4: 76, 97.
52. Emmanuel Levinas, *Totality and Infinity*. See here my "*Die Heiligkeit der Person und der heilige Gott. Anmerkungen zu einer Hermeneutik des Heiligen*," *Wiener Jahrbuch für Philosophie* XLIX (2017): 58–72.

Chapter 7

Through Being to the Holy
Learning to Ask the Question of Being
Joeri Schrijvers

Commentators agree that around 1935 an important new phase in Heidegger's work starts. Right around this time Heidegger starts to speak of the holy, of things gathering the divinities around us mortals living between the earth and the sky. Needless to say, however, that many are struck by Heidegger's poetic, and at times even enigmatic, writings in this period (and after). This essay proposes therefore to take Heidegger at his word, both when it concerns his statement that thinking in effect can be learned and that, through such thinking, a passage through Being to the holy can be attempted.

On the one hand, from at least *Being and Time* onward, Heidegger instructed us about the question of Being. It is no exaggeration to say that Heidegger's grand endeavor was precisely to teach us how to move away from beings in order to ask, once again, the question of Being. Such a move, however, was to be accompanied with a specific experience. "We of today," Heidegger once stated, "are scarcely able any longer properly to raise even the *question* of the Being of beings—to raise it in a way which will put into question our own being so that it becomes questionable in its relation to Being, and thereby open to Being."[1] There is also Heidegger's explicit recognition that, when properly asked and thus when properly questioned by Being, the experience of the question of Being can open the way to an experience of the holy. This essay will therefore try to trace these steps through Being to the holy.

I. TURNING (AWAY FROM *BEING AND TIME*)

What happened, then, around 1935? Andrew Mitchell argues that "ecstatic existence is no longer a privilege of Dasein. [Whatever] appears within a world [. . .] must appear ecstatically."[2] If in *Being and Time* such ecstasy was reserved to Dasein, in that it reaches into the past, the present, and out to the future, it is now up to the thing to call the mortal forth toward its unique temporality. If it was up to Dasein to create the meaning of Being, the mortals now discover meaning in the interplay between world and earth. Slowly but surely, the quite formal structures of existence *Being and Time* outlined find their material counterpart in the later work: the mortals deal with bridges, jugs, and temples whereas Dasein could do nothing but hammer. For some, such as Benjamin Crowe, Heidegger's talk of God and gods presents an "affective coloring" of the basic structure of being-in-the-world: with the earth in a sense, the transcendental structure of "being-in-the-world" materializes and takes on specific spatial and temporal contours.[3] This makes it possible for Crowe to see in the Greek polis, with its temples and its offerings, the "Greek being-in-the-world" or, as Jussi Backman attempts, to see in a simple desk already the contours of the somewhat lofty "thing" Heidegger imagines.[4]

This thing, then, is meant to be a counterpart both not only to the stale *Gegenstand* (or object) of modernity but also to the reductive stance towards beings of the metaphysical tradition reducing them to displaying merely a visible form of an invisible essence. Such things will show us how to appreciate, for instance that "the *full* meaning of my desk [. . .] is never 'equal' in two instants but always different. It is now first and foremost a storeroom for my books, now a support for my computer, now a surface on which to place my cup of coffee, now an example to be used in my text, and so on."[5] Yet for Backman, it is clear that Heidegger here is also pointing beyond mere whatness and mere matter:

> Whereas matter only can only individualize a thing spatiotemporally as a particular specimen [. . .] of a common [. . .] type, the fourfold context individuates each instant of presence. Even instances of a thing that is the "same" in the sense of numerical identity—for example, one and the same jug—are not equivalent to one another in meaning: a jug is now a holder for for a libation of the gods, now a vehicle for pouring a drink to friends, and so on.[6]

These things like desks and jugs point us toward an understanding of beings beyond the metaphysical and modern tradition and even beyond *Being and Time*. Whereas the tradition taught us to see in this particular desk the instantiation of the deskness of the desk—every desk will always and everywhere display the idea of deskness—*Being and Time* taught us to see that the deskness of the desk *also* lies in our use of the desk in and through a context of the desk's ready-to-handness—the desk is a being used *to* put my coffee on—Heidegger's idea of the "thinging of the thing" calls forth entirely new *horizons of meaning* just to understand the presencing of these simple beings as jugs and desks.

Yet these jugs and desks can be part of the *Gestell* just as well. This *Gestell*, which Heidegger uses for our own modern era, brings about what Mitchell has beautifully called "the birth of the commodity."[7] Objects present themselves exclusively as object and their presencing as things is forgotten or at least attenuated. What so comes to the fore is a throw-away culture in which everything and all becomes manageable and replaceable. There are a few instances in which Heidegger pointed to what would become our consumption culture.[8]

For our purposes, we need to keep in mind that for Heidegger, however, any object can become a thing just as all things can (and will) be reduced to objects. What we have called earlier the need to learn to experience Being is just this— Heidegger's endeavor teaches us to move from objects to things. For objects have nothing *unheimlich* about them[9]: the human being will forget that not everything is manageable, consumable, and replaceable. Heidegger saw intimations of this in transcendental and idealist philosophy: if for Kant (and Husserl) the object was exhausted in the subject's transcendental categories or in phenomenology's constitutions which conditions the object's appearance, then Hegel's idealist philosophy took this one step further by arguing that these objects are created even by the subjects. With all this, Heidegger argues, "the most radical withdrawal [*äußerste Entzug*] of Being begins [and] the essential provenance of Being can never come into view as a question and as worth questioning."[10]

It is for these inexhaustible horizons of meaning that the thing brings about that Heidegger found it necessary to turn to religious language: this language speaks of what beings (or things) ought to be, of their purpose, and of the inexhaustible reserve of meaning these things present. There always is a discrepancy or *Unfug* between what these things show us and what we can say of beings. The question, then, remains: how are we to experience this inexhaustibleness of meaning and what, if anything, does this have to do with God and the Gods? Are these more than figures that show the purposivesness of meaning, that is, its adjustment and its insertion into Being as an ideal and as a goal for human presence and culture (as Backman holds), more than cultural givennesses, and a heir to the heroes that already in *Being and Time* functioned as exemplars for a given culture (as Young holds), even more than mistaking these cultural givennesses with a theological realism (as Crowe seems to hold)?[11]

II. THE THING, THE HOLY, AND THE QUESTION OF BEING

Let us for this, first, listen to Heidegger's understanding of such a fourfold. In 1950, Heidegger writes:

> The things that were named [the snowfall and an evening bell], thus called, gather to themselves sky and earth, mortals and divinities. The four are united

> primally in Being toward one another, a fourfold [. . .] This gathering [. . .] this letting-stay is the thinging of the things. The unitary fourfold [. . .] which is stayed in the thinging of things, we call: the world.[12]

It is clear that we need to see the thing first as an expansion of the world. The world is no longer made up of mute beings which are only present-at-hand or ready-to hand; the world now contains things which open up the world to its other, to the heavens and the divinities (mostly—this much should be noted by Catholic thinkers—by pointing to the very materiality of the earth). The thing *gathers*: it is ecstatic, which means it cannot contain itself and reaches out to us mortals and to the earth on which we dwell; it comes (and goes) from beyond the beings-within-the-world. From this, it is clear to that Heidegger is gesturing already toward a presencing and meanings that are not to be reduced to its presence *to* and meaningfulness *for* human beings alone, through ready-to-handness or present-at-handness. Heidegger's abandonment of transcendental thinking, simply put, mean this: objects within-the-world present themselves not to me, my transcendental ego, alone, but *presence around* us and *for* us all.

Through readings of several poets, Hölderlin principally, but George and Trakl too, Heidegger will point out that the thing offers a *gleaming* and a *radiance* to the world. It is quite correct to state that here Heidegger proceeds to a re-enchantment of the modern scientific world.[13] Heidegger does not hesitate to name this radiance holy. Such a *holy radiance* is not a spectacle, nothing exceptional or sensational in which nothing of these beings would remain concealed and would lose, as we will see, its uncanny character. In its stead, things bring before us "the permanently essential, the simple and ownness of beings."[14] Insofar things are allowed to emerge as the things they are, one might say, they simultaneously allow human beings as the mortals that they are. Human beings *find* themselves before these things, not as a final answer to a riddle, but as the questions that they are and have to be amidst the coming and going of beings. It is from this stress on what is simple and uncomplicated that, understandably but not entirely correctly, the pastoral and parochial interpretations of Heidegger take their cue.

Yet one must not forget that the holy is not something present: it is not before us as an object nor already facing us a simple being would. At best, the holy *presences*—it is a process rather than a product, a movement rather than a completed action. Quite some exercise, however, is needed for the human being to be "in tune" with these movements.

In his *What are Poets for?* (1946), Heidegger says:

> The turning of an age does not occur at just any time by the eruption of a new god or by the new eruption of an old god from an ambush. Where is he supposed

to turn, upon his return, if human beings have not already prepared for him his sojourn? How could there ever be for God a sojourn for God unless the radiance has already begun to appear in all that is.[15]

Most often in effect, there is nothing holy in this world. The holy is exempt from all conditions and creations on the part of human beings—one used to call this *transcendent*. It should not become (although it will) part of the *Gestell* that rages through our era. Heidegger's lines thus set the human being a task: the mortals are to prepare a sojourn for the gods (and Heidegger is thus preparing us for the experience of such a sojourn). They must learn to perceive the radiance in all that appears. For this, one might say, human beings must first learn to dwell on earth themselves: they must see that "dwelling is the essence of being-in-the-world."[16] Heidegger, in a way, is teaching us how to have such an experience.[17]

However, there is no guarantee that even when one learns to dwell the gods will appear: "Man does not decide whether and how beings appear, whether and how God and the gods [. . .] come forward into the clearing of Being."[18] One should note that Heidegger is here far removed from the metaphysics of Neoplatonism, in which what diffuses from the One will sooner or later return to the One, as well as from Christianity in which what is created will one day be redeemed from sin and so safely return to its creator. There is, for Heidegger, to be no certainty that, were the human being to prepare a divine abode, the divinities are prepared to "show up" and present themselves within Being. Some have imagined Heidegger's thinking of the unity of Being as one of pure loss, an endless outpouring of beings evident only in their finite coming and going.[19]

Yet there is much to learn here: if the Gods are to dwell with us, we must first learn to dwell. Heidegger poetically describes our dire situation amidst commodities as follows: if we are lacking in names that are holy (Hölderlin), and if no things are if the words are failing (George) then surely this means the holy in fact *is* not (yet). And it is not even certain that it will come.

One must first learn to dwell in Being (if the Gods are to appear) and one must learn to speak of beings anew (if beings are to appear properly). It is here that Heidegger's attention to language, to the intimate relation between the word and the world, comes into play. It is through the word that the thing attains (its) being just as much as beings and things call for proper wordings. Long before Austin's *How to do Things with Words*, Heidegger could in effect write that "essential words are deeds": words bring about things just as much as things invite us to speak.[20]

We are therefore not to take lightly Heidegger's steps, as it were, through Being and beings to god and the gods. This step is however occasioned through the mediation of the thing. Let us read with care:

> Only from the truth of Being can the essence of the holy be thought. Only from the essence of the holy is the essence of divinity to be thought. Only in the light of the essence of divinity can it be thought or said what the word "God" is to signify. Or should we not first be able to hear [. . .] these words [. . .] if we are [. . .] to experience a relation of God to man?[21]

Whereas most commentators jump right into the question of the holy, as if the holy is always present and up for grabs, it pays to take Heidegger here at his word and begin at the beginning, namely, with the question of Being and beings he taught us to ask: why are there beings rather than nothing? For if we are to prepare a sojourn for the Gods, we need first to ask about beings (in their Being).

III. BEING AND THE HOLY: LEARNING TO THINK—LEARNING TO QUESTION

We need to realize that the event of Being or the event of world (in which things come to presence) is not of our own making. We do not decide whether and how beings appear, we are rather thrown in the world in which beings present themselves. Or, as Heidegger later has it, "we are thrown into the open."[22] Recall how *Being and Time*, and the works around this period, mentioned anxiety, death, and boredom as those particular moments in which an awareness for Dasein was raised that it is and has to be nothing but this span of eighty odd years or so between its birth and death. Now we should wonder whether Heidegger's thing provides a similar momentum for us mortals. Whereas Dasein is chased outside to recover its authenticity from out of its dealings in the world, the mortals are already in the open. They enact an *Innestehen*—in the Open, in the *Lichtung* or clearing—from out of which they need to learn to properly tend to beings which are also in the open. For this, a double movement seems required. The mortals are the ones that follow, trace, and seek after the throw that throws them in their thrownness in the open. "What throws" the mortals in the open clearing "is not man, but Being itself."[23]

But how can we perform this double movement, from out of beings (surrounding us) in which we find ourselves thrown, to that which has thrown us in the first place, Being itself? In this regard, it is important to note the thematics of the *Sprung* in Heidegger. In one way or another, from *Being and Time* onward, we need to *jump away* from beings, be this through a sort of fading away of the omnipresence of beings (in anxiety and boredom) or through beings that can show us the way away from beings. The thing turns out to be just such a pointer or messenger.

Such a movement might be considered along a certain passage-way: first we cling to beings, then we jump into the open region, only then to rediscover beings again. We will now trace consecutively these jumps and jolts (through which the mortal ones end up being slightly out of joint).

In his *Introduction of Metaphysics*, Heidegger proceeds this way:

> "Why are there beings at all?" If we ask in this way, we start out from beings. They are. They are given to us, they are in front of us and can thus be found before us at any time [. . .] Now the beings given to us in this way are immediately interrogated as to their ground [. . .] Such a method just broadens and enlarges as it were, a procedure that is practiced everyday.[24]

The question (too?) quickly receives an answer: the ground of beings is what all will call God. Heidegger will here insinuate already that this ground, itself, will be conceived as itself *a* being, made in any case of the substance of beings. To avoid such an answer, Heidegger proposes to add to the question asked "and why not nothing." This addition allows us to "hold out [these beings] into the possibility of not-Being." A lot has happened: we have moved away from an everyday manner of questioning: what is caused by what or by whom? We have moved away from a tendency to cancel, almost unnoticeably, the contingency of the beings surrounding us (and that we ourselves are). Heidegger is however not satisfied and wants us to query further:

> [This] question is a foundational metaphysical question, which is metaphysically answered through the fact that an explanation [*Erklärung*] of beings is reached from out of a *cause* and a ground. [The] Being-historical thinking asks all metaphysical questions silently slightly different insofar it does not rank beings within explanations but rather asks about the primacy [*Vorrang*] of beings itself. The answer comes from the knowing about the abandonment by Being of beings [. . .] Being leaves to beings such preponderance.[25]

Why indeed would this or that being tell us everything we need to know about Being? Would it, for instance, not be better to ask about Being qua Being—an avenue Heidegger indeed will pursue? Beings have a tendency, then, a preponderance, to stand in the way of the question of Being just as the human being "at first clings always and only to beings."[26] Similarly, Being just leaves beings out in the open, to themselves.

We then need to unlearn our addictiveness to beings and the tendency to "explain [*erklären*] Being by way of some sort of being"[27] even if it would be the highest. This movement was, in *What is Metaphysics* of 1928, described as a "repelling gesture" in which "beings as a whole" are involved "in a parting gesture."[28] Here the experience of nothing (in particular) lets beings fade away in order to let appear "an original openness of beings as such": nothing particular is revealed, except that beings reveal themselves in their appearance in the openness of world and that, now, this appearing of appearing can be noted. Somewhat metaphorically, one might say: what appears is (almost) nothing, but it (still) is (Being). What one is aware of is now no longer the finitude of one's own appearance in Being but rather that such finite coming and going needs to be extended to all that appears in the openness of Being *and* that this open clearing of Being makes clear that, as the appearing of appearing, its revelation is so simple that it seems to be nothing at all. At the same time, this appearing of appearing or this event of world is essential: without its event, one would not even have appearances of beings at all.

Heidegger's *Introduction* to *Metaphysics* has a slightly different take on this Being of beings (or the appearing of this appearance). More and more Heidegger wants to attain Being through *thinking* which, certainly for Heidegger, was an experience in itself. In this regard, Being seems to be everywhere although it is nowhere and resembles nothing (in particular) more than anything else: "Being, that which pertains to every being whatsoever and thus disperses itself into what is most commonplace, is the most unique of all."[29] Although Being is omnipresent, and dealt to every being alike, it allows itself no comparison to anything else. Moreover: "compared to beings which are immediately accessible, Being manifests the character of holding itself back, of concealing itself in a certain manner."[30]

Yet how to attain Being? It is here that Heidegger's insistence on the *Sprung* becomes relevant, because the task of unlearning, of kicking the habit of dwelling amidst beings is never once and for all attained. Heidegger is clear about this unlearning: "we moderns can learn only if we unlearn at the same time. Applied to the matter before us: we can learn thinking only if we radically unlearn what thinking has been traditionally. To do that, we must at the same time come to know it."[31] At this point, Heidegger's thinking will evolve and he will no longer hold that a single jump outside of metaphysics is possible. The thinking of Being first, however, needed a place "where only the leap will help us further. [This] leap takes us abruptly to where everything is different, so different that it strikes us as strange [*uns befremdet*]."[32] In the same years, mid-1950, Heidegger also writes that this "leap is the vault out of the [. . .] principle of reason as a principle of beings into the saying of Being qua Being," away, that is, from the practice of explaining beings through beings, of finding a foundation and ground for what "is," which is a practice, in Heidegger's words, of "*Ergründen und Begründen*" that determines our "*Tun and Lassen*."[33]

Yet here still Heidegger seeks for beings that can aid us on our way to Being. The *Introduction to Metaphysics* will therefore point to artworks as signaling the very Being of beings: written around 1935, it is no surprise that it overlaps with the short essay *On the Origin of the Work of Art* in which he first speaks of understanding the thing *as* thing.[34] It is through the workings of the work of art as a thing—the work of art is a thing but not all things need be works of art—that "the work holds open the open region of world."[35] Throughout one finds the same principle as it were: "The open is itself the immediate. Nothing mediated, be it a God or a human, is therefore ever able to reach the immediate immediately."[36] Just as one cannot look at the sun directly, one first notices that these beings are in the light of the sun, only then to see the sunlight, indirectly, *through* its light on particular beings.

IV. UNUSUAL BEINGS

We have noted that this thinging of the thing is but a step on the way to see the shimmer of Being. This shimmer of Being is a preface to the question of the holy and the Gods. Yet most often we do not pose the question of Being, let alone do we encounter the holy. According to *What is Called Thinking?*, one needs to recall it is not just scientists who do not think, the most remarkable fact remains that *we* do not yet think.

How can thinking let Being light up and shine? What is it that we are to experience and perceive? How is one to comport oneself if one is to name the holy and experience God's relation, if any, to us? This is, if you will, a third step in the question of Being. It raises an awareness, one might say, a sensibility perhaps, a contemplative interruption amidst everyday preoccupations. If Schopenhauer finds that the mark of a philosopher is the ability to imagine that everything that is going on might be just a dream then Heidegger would insist that a sure sign of a philosopher is a dissatisfaction with what commonly assumed to be common and usual.

Let us look at this last moment in our encounter and experience of Being which started with moving away from beings only to move into an appreciation of the strangeness of Being. In *What is Metaphysics?* Heidegger walks a fine line between the anxiousness that marked his existential analytic and the more positive experiences of homecoming and marvel that are present after *Being and Time*. Here one reads:

> Only because the nothing is manifest in the ground of Dasein can the total strangeness of beings overwhelm us. Only when the strangeness of beings oppresses us does it arouse and evoke wonder. Only on the ground of wonder—the revelation of the nothing—does the "why?" loom before us. Only because the "why" is possible as such can we in a definite way inquire into grounds, and ground them.[37]

We have seen that, later, Heidegger will loosen his focus on this why-question (because of its tendency to bring only beings before us). It is to be noted that here already Heidegger points to the strangeness and *Befremdlichkeit des Seienden* if we are to marvel at Being. Something must strike us a strange or uncommon if we are to pose the question of Being. In the *Origin of the Work of Art*, these artworks, as things, similarly bring us to a region in which "everything is other than usual"—*anders wie sonst*.[38]

Yet the work of art and the thing do not reveal something new or something that we did somehow overlook. There is no spectacle in Heidegger. Neither are we in the region of transcendental-phenomenology whose ego could align its intuition of the artwork to its intentionality if only the ego could make a sufficient amount of adumbrations of this particular artwork. Instead, the thing reveals what is already there in a different way. Through the work of art one learns, Heidegger says, that what is common, namely that everything around us just *is*, is actually uncommon.[39] Two years later, in the *Grundfragen der Philosophie* (1937–1938), Heidegger will elaborate on such wonder, adding that in wonder "the common itself becomes [. . .] uncommon."[40] This process is however best described in Heidegger's *Parmenides* (1942–1943). Here it becomes clear that anything can become a distinctive thing and that this was perhaps misleadingly expressed by the high cultural examples of Greek temples and Van Gogh's shoes Heidegger had used earlier. Heidegger now states:

> the uncanny, or the extraordinary, shines throughout the familiar ambit of beings we deal with and know, beings we call ordinary [. . .] What shines into beings, though can never be explained [*Erklärbare*] nor constructed out of beings, is Being itself.[41]

The *question* of Being, then, teaches us the "*Aushalten des Unerklärbaren*," to realize, at least, how strange and uncommon it is to be."[42] This is what simple and essential: the "passing over into the more wakeful intimation of wonder [that] a world worlds around us at all, [that] things are [and] that we ourselves in their midst are."[43] In this sense, the question of Being teaches us not to take for granted what is granted to us.

We now need to understand the role of the *thing* in its relation to this question. In the terminology of Heidegger's *Parmenides*, the thing is what *winks* and hints at the uncanny *from within* the canny and the common.[44] One should again note the interplay between beings and Being. Where in *Being and Time* Dasein projected itself onto Being through the leap away from beings (in anxiety), here, because of the ecstasy of the thing, Being *reaches out to us* precisely through the mediation of the thing. The thing, and its interplay between heaven and earth, spills over into the world and hints at a meaning that *is* not yet, that perhaps is still is to come and that at least does not stifle into the full presence of an essence as metaphysics was wont to think. Heidegger would still affirm that "higher than actuality stands possibility" but would now say that the meanings that are still to come (among which, perhaps, are the holy and the Gods) are not things to be created, projected, or constructed by the human being. Mitchell even argues that Heidegger's last God arrives in the mode of "only ever arriving":[45] it will always remain possible that God will come even if, if one is to follow Mitchell, who is influenced here more by Jean-Luc Nancy than strictly following Heidegger, this God never "presents" Godself in the present.[46]

It is tempting to phrase these turns in Heidegger as a transcendental first phase and a later realist phase.[47] This would, however, perhaps not completely represent or show how Heidegger frames our encounter with Being:

> *No* way of thought, not even the way of metaphysical thought, begins with man's essential nature and from there goes on to Being, nor in reverse from Being and then back to man. Rather, every way of thinking takes its way already *within* the total relation of Being and man's nature or else it is not thinking at all.[48]

It is not that the human being is a meaning-making machine that, from time to time, asks about Being. It is not, in turn, that Being addresses the human being without a role to be played by (human) beings. If Being *braucht* beings then the reverse is true as well; human beings are dependent on their very relation to Being. If anything, a transcendental framework (from man to Being) would, for Heidegger, need to be properly placed within the realist framework in which Being is given for and to the human being. It is not that these projections of meaning never attain anything more or other than world. Rather, these meanings coming, and sent, to the human being are made of the stuff of possibility to such an extent that a demarcation of these meanings within a transcendental framework would deny Heidegger's emphasis on Being as evading every man-made construction and explanation. It is the event of Being and world that conditions and constitutes any and all constitutions that the transcendental ego could or would want to make.[49]

One needs to focus on this "total relation" between the human being and Being if we are to understand what the holy can mean for Heidegger. For what do we attain when we attain Being? Nothing present-at-hand, nothing that can become a *Gegenstand*. At best, one attends to a movement or a happening: through the light that shines on beings in a clearing (of about eighty odd years) we attain the *Lichtung* of Being. Heidegger's critique of humanism sheds some light on what this can mean for the questions of religion and theology. For this address of Being, toward the beings that we are, through the beings that we encounter (and even though this address is somewhat uncanny and strange) at least speaks of "a concern about man" on the part of Being.[50]

It is up to the mortals to meet the demands of Being—Heidegger would say *Entsprechen*—and display, at least, a "care for the light" a care, that is, for Being's concern for us.[51] Heidegger will never allow the possibility that beings other than human can meet this demand. Here the central role of language is clear—only through words are beings revealed (and the demand of Being "to be brought to speech" is met). In Heidegger's Schelling essay an elucidation of the role of human beings is given.

> [In] the human being the word fully expresses. The human being itself speaks and essences in language. With this, the human being is uplifted above the light of reason; he moves not only in something lit up [*Gelichteten*] like the animal but speaks about this light.[52]

Yet this speaking about the *Lichtung*, this movement from the *Gelichteten* to the *Lichtung*, from what appears to the appearing of appearing is not something at our disposal. Rather, a thing abides only *for a while*. "First and foremost," there seem to be no things at all. Let alone do we notice the presencing of Being or name the holy within the dimension of Being.

V. THE TIME OF THE THING: FOR A WHILE

The concept of the "while" became important in Heidegger's work in the forties and names the temporal interplay between Being's approaching beings and beings' care for the concern or *Bemühung* that Being shows in their regard. For this interplay seems to be governed by time: time might be safe from Being/beings; it is clear that Being and beings are not safe from time. It is clear too that the showing up of Being in and through beings, if only rarely appreciated, shows something like a finitude of Being and time—a realization Heidegger used to conclude *Being and Time*. Despite the realization, Heidegger still thought that Being "always and everywhere" would be the same, whereas the "Being-historical" Heidegger will clearly state that Being is in each epoch differently.

"The while" names the presencing of the thing, for instance, the happening of the artwork as a being "that never was before and never comes to be again": the work turns the usual into the unusual for a while only.[53] The presencing of the thing therefore names an event and a beginning: something shows up that we had not seen in this way and will likely never see again in this particular way. The artwork *arrests* our attention. It, as every other thing, gathers the fourfold around its happening. Yet "appropriating the fourfold, it gathers the fourfold's whiling into something that is there for the while [*in ein je Weiliges*]: into this thing."[54] It begins with a simple recognition: where *Being and Time* pointed out that we *are* this span of eighty odd years between our birth and death, we now need to realize that an expiry date comes along in all that appears. All of us are here together for a while only.

For such an event to happen, everything must align in the right manner. Commentators mention an ultimate relationality in Heidegger here, for in the thing one notices precisely such a "mutual belonging," a being confined to one another, *einander zugetraut sein*.[55] Mitchell explains that here "each one is a movement out to the other"; Heidegger's essay on Schelling beautifully mentions our "*wesensmäbige Weisung an der Andere*," our essential directedness (if not being confined) to the other.[56] Yet this alignment, this presencing of all with all, is fragile and, as we will see, a bit suspect.

For now, one needs to realize that this happening, of truth, of Being, of the truth of Being (in which, through beings, we let our addiction to beings go for a while) is generally a joyful gathering, so much so that commentators wonder what happened to the anxiety so central to the work of a youthful Heidegger, although these joys an jubilations never seem to occupy center stage as much as anxiety did.[57] Yet, for Heidegger's interpretation of the holy, it is important to know that Heidegger's thinking of the *Weile* is related to his readings of feasts and festivals in Hölderlin's poetry. One *sings and dances* at festivals: not something one usually does for the God of onto-theology, a cold *causa sui* that supposedly is the ground of all Being.[58]

Two more things need to be mentioned about this "while." First, it is the occasion for Heidegger to conceive of another, perhaps more phenomenological, account of causation. Second, it speaks of a *Fug* (fittingness) in and of Being which seems to know no longer of any *Unfug* (disjointedness) and for this reason is, for someone like Derrida, somewhat suspect. In this regard, one recalls Derrida's deconstructions of the infamous *Schlag* (blow or strike), which set in motion an entire critique by Derrida— the entire *Geschlecht* series centers around the *Schlag* that the one, united humanity suffers before it falls apart in multitudes and plurality, and finds its division between, among others, friends, and foes. In the same manner in the Heidegger's concept of the thing, all is gathered in such a way that a unity with no division whatsoever seems intimated. Such a unity would, in more than one way, resemble for instance the metaphysics of the Neoplatonist One, where all loss is ultimately recovered when such a loss of Being will be united again with the One. It was examples such as these that urged Derrida to wonder whether or not Heidegger was not simply repeating metaphysics' grand gestures rather than overcoming or overturning metaphysics.[59]

One should note, though, that in *The Principle of Reason* Heidegger once relates the concept of the "while" to our everyday practice of looking for reasons and grounds. Throughout Heidegger is commenting on Silesius' saying that "the rose is without why: it blooms because it blooms." Heidegger hears a different form of causation here: not what exactly has caused this rose to bloom but rather to see what is happening with this blooming *while* it is blooming. In German, the *"weil"* points to a different sense of causation. It is not an answer to the "why-question": the rose simply blooms while she blooms. This might help us to see our own "without why". We are "the there" in the clearing while we are "there"—for some odd years, we are in Being and witness its event.

For Heidegger, this event of blooming is an aid in coming to understand what exactly pertains to Being when it comes to the question of time, to understand this temporality of Being (from within these few year we witness this event of Being). In a sense, it comes naturally to us to frame this event of time from out of what is present and lies before us. If we have seen one rose, we *basically* have seen them all. We frame time, when asking about the essence of time, as follows: "'In Being' means: being present. Beings are more in Being the more present they are. Beings come to be more present, the more abidingly they abide, the more lastingly [*bleibend*] they abide. What is 'in time' is present and therefore of the present. Only the 'now' is of the present at each given moment."[60] What is most present will be therefore (and henceforth) be configured as "eternal." When we see this rose blooming, we see a process that in any individual case and at any given moment is the same: given the right circumstances, any rose and all roses will bloom. "The idea of Being sees them as in their being [the rose in this case] as independent of time."[61]

Metaphysics, when canceling contingency, cancels time altogether: it fails to ask about the relation between time and eternity, between, one might just as well say, the presencing of beings and the presencing of the eternal (or not) God. Metaphysics, Heidegger's late *Zur Sache des Denkens* will argue, takes for granted the "the passing away constantly" of time and, from here, it will forget the "remaining" of time in its very fading away: to every being, there pertains a certain time, but such time will remain after the fading away of this particular being.[62] It is tempting, for metaphysics (and for us all) to "[determine] time by a kind of being," to see time as a being that is granted to us, likely, by a highest being or as a being that we can "manage" as today's mantra goes.[63]

This procedure stalls the movement of Being (in and as time) toward us: "To talk of presencing, however, requires, that we perceive [. . .] abiding in lasting as lasting in present being. What is present concerns us, the present, that is: what, lasting, comes toward us, us human beings."[64]

This is what the blossoming of the rose teaches: its blossoming *lasts as long as its lasts*. The blossom obeys a certain *timing*, in Spring for instance, for which there is no reason to assume that this blossoming here and now will be the same come next Spring (if, that is, Spring will come again for me, for us). It is this "timing" of time that makes for the fact that for Heidegger it is time that grants beingness rather than the other way around (which what, roughly, metaphysics taught). Yet this granting of time to us and to everything, in no way whatsoever, makes the question of the holy and the eternal (or not) God any less pertinent—if anything, it calls for a reconfiguration of these questions.

This is exactly what Heidegger intends when he likens the blossoming of the rose to the "while": it blossoms *while* it blossoms and, *especially* when we are to think about the coming of God and the Gods, we should not look passed its presencing in Being (as a being) and in time. One learns what its blossoming is from its very blossoming (here and now before us) *since* and *as long as* it is blossoming. It would not be wrong to interpret this as bringing phenomenology back to its very grounding. The rose is without why means that it both blossoms because it is blossoming and needs no further reason for this (what metaphysics will nonetheless provide, showing—for Heidegger—it is somewhat off track) and that "there is" (*es gibt*) a certain timing for these things to happen. For all these reasons, Heidegger asks, citing Goethe:

> "you stick to the *because* but ask not *why*": What does the while [*das Weil*] mean? It guards against investigating the "why," therefore, against investigating foundations. It balks at founding and getting to the bottom of something [*das Begründen und Ergründen*]. For the "while" is without "why," it has no ground, it is ground itself.[65]

One can conclude that Heidegger finds here the phenomenological origins of our obsession with causation. In *The Principle of Reason*, Heidegger traces this process from Hegel's idealism (which ultimately *creates* the objectness of the object before the subject) through Kant's transcendentalism (which still receives the "appearing of the appearing" but is ready to trace it back to the condition of the subject) back to the Greek experience of being/s, which speaks of a "lying before us" of beings that have, as Richard Capobianco calls it, "[emerged] from out of pure emerging itself."[66] This Greek experience knew about causation too; it simply did not turn its effects into the building-blocks of scholastic and modern systems (in which the principle of causation *rules* even over God as the first cause).[67] The Greek *aition* for Heidegger is rather simple. If, for instance, the wind blew the pen off the table, one says that the wind is what changed the appearance of the table, what made for the fact that this table now appears and presences differently.[68]

One can therefore argue that Heidegger returned phenomenology to its beginnings in what emerges "of itself" echoing the definition of the phenomenon in *Being and Time*.[69] Heidegger thus traces the "self-showing" of the phenomenon. The danger of a metaphysics, of asking for an ultimate why, is to stick to the being that so shows itself (and ultimately, in our era, to see this as manageable and controllable) and to forget that in this appearance and self-showing there lingers the event of the appearing of appearing: "the It gives [*Es gibt*] withdraws in favor of the gift which It gives."[70] Throughout his career, Heidegger will prefer natural appearance over and against fabricated appearance: the blossoming of the rose too is supposed to "manifest itself on its own."[71] It is tempting to read in Heidegger a manifesto for ecology and a nature mysticism as some are minded to do. The question here, to Heidegger and to such interpreters, is whether this is phenomenologically correct at all: the rose may well blossom on its own, but if the rose bush were not trimmed and cut by the gardener, this blossoming might not appear.[72]

Be this as it may, it is clear that the later Heidegger found language other than phenomenology to name this process of emergence. It might turn out this is another, no less appropriate, language *for* phenomenology.

CONCLUSION

We have seen Heidegger moving *from* presence and the present *to* the presencing of such presence, *then* to the realization that this presencing in a given epoch is not free of time itself, and *lastly*, to realize that this presencing in different epochs itself comes from out of an interplay reaching through them all. It is for this last interplay that Heidegger has reserved, from time to time, the name of the holy. As an awe-inspiring event, that presences each time differently, this event—for which Heidegger found the name "Being" not always appropriate—that is *set apart* and *distinct* from that which, through this event, presences in each case, namely the diverse beings, this event would have deserved a holy name. Heidegger would thus have retrieved (and repeated Derrida would add) the most traditional meaning of what is holy (separated, distinct, out of the ordinary). Yet *the experience* of this event, one might say, is one of ultimate mediation. One might say: one never reaches purely into that which is reaching out to us. One can approach Being's approach only through mediations—we think what other have thought about this event, while these others, in turn, thought what their predecessors, and so on. This is why the past and the tradition will become increasingly important for Heidegger. Thinking after the end of metaphysics cannot occur without incorporating what metaphysics has already thought. Long gone now is the *leap* outside of metaphysics.

If, however, Being approaches beings, and if God is to gesture toward beings, then such a God will "take the hint" as it were and, from out of a "pleasing nearness," accommodate to the conditions of the receiver, knowing well that the receiver will distort and, well, deconstruct this very approach. If God then chooses to appear (and this freedom, contrary to what theologians as Jean-Luc Marion think, is not contradicted here) then God will appear in Being and as a being.[73] The *Offenbarung* will therefore accommodate to the *Offenbarkeit* and unconcealment of beings. In this way, Heidegger is quite close to how the theological tradition configured God's revelation. Aquinas, for instance, developed a similar stance in the dictum that God's revelation to humankind always and already occurs according to the mode of the receiver (e.g., *Summa Theologica* 1a. q.75 a.5)—a dictum to which Heidegger's discourse on Being has, to my mind, always remained faithful.

Heidegger remained most of the time silent about his personal beliefs. It is, however, not to be excluded that the question of the holy, and the appearance of the holy, in Being, remained a real possibility. As a philosopher, however and even though the "methodical atheism" of *Being and Time* was, if not abandoned then at least softened, Heidegger did not have to grapple with questions that a genuine theology of Being would need to ask; he just needed to show that it was a genuine possibility.

All of this means that, if theology is to learn from Heidegger, it will need to take the question of Being seriously and start from the beginning as it were. All Heidegger had to show, as a philosopher is "that the address [*Anspruch*] of the divine, which is grounded in Being itself, is taken up by man into dictum and sayings" and thus that the "relation to the divine being rests in Being [*im Sein beruht*]."[74]

NOTES

1. Martin Heidegger, *What is Called Thinking?* (San Francisco, CA: Harper and Row, 1968), 78.

2. Andrew Mitchell, *The Fourfold. Reading the Late Heidegger* (Evanston: Northwestern UP, 2015), 14, also 181–83.

3. Benjamin Crowe, *Heidegger's Phenomenology of Religion. Realism and Cultural Criticism* (Indiana, IN: Indiana UP, 2008), 119.

4. Crowe, 119. Crowe does not elaborate how the "Greek" being-in-the-world would relate to a "medieval" being-in-the world. These would be ever so many givennesses of world. Yet Crowe intriguingly traces Heidegger's idea of the fourfold back to his reading of Ernst Cassirer's "mythical Dasein" in 1928, see 107ff. For Backman, see *Complicated Presence. Heidegger and the Postmetaphysical Unity of Being* (Albany, NY: SUNY Press, 2015), 165ff.

5. Backman, *Complicated Presence*, 165.
6. Backman, 202.
7. Mitchell, *The Fourfold*, 36.
8. See GA 7, 8n.a and GA 15, 367–69.
9. See for this Heidegger, *The Principle of Reason* (Indiana, IN: Indiana UP, 1991), 82.
10. *The Principle of Reason*, 88.
11. See respectively Backman, *Complicated Presence*, 142–43, Julian Young, *Heidegger's Later Philosophy* (Cambridge: Cambridge UP, 2002), 96–97 and Crowe, 141–42.
12. Heidegger, *On the Way to Language* (San Francisco, Harper and Row, 1982), 197.
13. Cf. Jean-Yves Lacoste, *Experience and the Absolute. Disputed Question on the Humanity of Man* (New York: Fordham UP, 2004). For the matter of "gleaming" in Heidegger's thinking, see especially Richard Capobianco, *Heidegger's Way of Being* (Toronto: University of Toronto Press, 2014), Chapter 2.
14. Heidegger, *Hölderlin's Hymn "Remembrance"* (Indiana, IN: Indiana UP, 2018), 59.
15. Heidegger, *Off the Beaten Track* (Cambridge: Cambridge UP, 2002), 201.
16. Heidegger, "Letter on Humanism," in *Basic Writings*, ed. D. F. Krell (New York: HarperCollins Publishers, 1993), 260.
17. Cf. Heidegger, *What is Called Thinking?*, 15.
18. Heidegger, "Letter on Humanism," 234.
19. See Mitchell, *The Fourfold*, 209.
20. Heidegger, *Schelling's Treatise on the Essence of Human Freedom* (Ohio: Ohio UP, 1985), 25.
21. Heidegger, "Letter on Humanism," 253.
22. Cf. "Letter on Humanism," 252.
23. "Letter on Humanism,", 241.
24. Heidegger, *Introduction to Metaphysics*, 29–30.
25. GA 67, 19. For a short, brilliant summary of Heidegger's take on this question, see GA 66, 267–77.
26. Heidegger, "Letter on Humanism," 234.
27. Heidegger, *The Principle of Reason* (Indiana, IN: Indiana UP, 1991), 68.
28. All citations: "What is Metaphysics?" in *Basic Writings*, 103.
29. Heidegger, *Introduction to Metaphysics*, 83.
30. Heidegger, *The Principle of Reason*, 63.
31. Heidegger, *What is Called Thinking?*, 8.
32. *What is Called Thinking?*, 12.
33. Heidegger, *The Principle of Reason*, 61 and 11, respectively. The German makes clear that Heidegger here uses the same terms he uses to delineate "onto-theology" in *Identity and Difference* (Chicago: Chicago UP, 2002), 57ff. See *Der Satz vom Grund* (Pfüllingen: Neske, 1997), 26.
34. Heidegger, *Introduction to Metaphysics*, 65 and 140 and "On the Origin of the Work of Art," in *Basic Writings*, 157ff.

35. Heidegger, "Work of Art," 170.
36. Heidegger, *Elucidations of Hölderlin's Poetry* (Amherst, NY: Humanity Books, 2000), 83.
37. Heidegger, "What is Metaphysics?" 109.
38. Heidegger, "Work of Art," 197.
39. "Work of Art," 190 and *Introduction to Metaphysics*, 178.
40. GA 45, 166.
41. Heidegger, *Parmenides* (Bloomington, IN: Indiana UP, 1992), 105–106.
42. GA 45, 172
43. Heidegger, *Hölderlin's Hymn "Remembrance,"* 58.
44. Heidegger, *Parmenides*, 99 as a translation of *"in das Geheure herein Winkenden und Zeigenden,"* in GA 54, 147. One should note that Heidegger still uses the concept of the leap here, cf. 150.
45. Mitchell, *The Fourfold*, 171.
46. Mitchell seems to display here what we have elsewhere called the Protestant trait of postmodern thinking, according to which the divine can never really "show up," "make an appearance" in Being, see *Between Faith and Belief. Toward A Contemporary Phenomenology of Religious Life* (Albany, NY: SUNY Press, 2016).
47. The different perspectives are represented by Thomas Sheehan, *Making Sense of Heidegger. A Paradigm Shift* (Lanham: Rowman & Littlefield, 2015), and Richard Capobianco, *Engaging Heidegger* (2010) and *Heidegger's Way of Being* (2014) (Toronto: Toronto University Press), and his forthcoming *Heidegger's Being: The Shimmering Unfolding* (Toronto: University of Toronto Press, 2022).
48. Heidegger, *What is Called Thinking?*, 80.
49. See for this the intriguing discussions between Heidegger and Husserl on the famous Britannica piece defining phenomenology, see Edmund Husserl, *Psychological and Transcendental Phenomenology and the Confrontation with Heidegger* (Dordrecht: Kluwer, 1997), 138.
50. Heidegger, "Letter on Humanism," 223.
51. Heidegger, "Letter on Humanism," 262.
52. Heidegger, *Schelling"s Treatise on the Essence of Human Freedom* (Ohio: Ohio UP, 1985), 141–42.
53. Heidegger, "Work of Art," 187.
54. Heidegger, "The Thing" in *Poetry, Language, Thought,* trans. A. Hofstadter (New York: Harper and Row, 2001), 194 modified.
55. "The Thing," 194.
56. Mitchell, *The Fourfold*, p. 281 and Heidegger, *Schellings Abhandlung über das Wesen der Freiheit* (1809) (Tübingen: Niemeyer, 1995), 153, 127 in the translation.
57. Capobianco, *Heidegger's Way of Being*, 32.
58. Reference is to Heidegger's famous saying in *Identity and Difference*, 72.
59. The best entry into the debate is the imagined dialogue between Heidegger and "the theologians" in Derrida, *Of Spirit. Heidegger and the Question* (Chicago: Chicago UP, 1989), 109.
60. Heidegger, *What is Called Thinking?*, 101.
61. *What is Called Thinking?*, 102.

62. Heidegger, *On Time and Being* (New York: Harper and Row, 1972), 3.
63. *On Time and Being*, 3.
64. *On Time and Being*, 12.
65. Heidegger, *The Principle of Reason*, 127.
66. Richard Capobianco, *Heidegger's Way of Being*, 70.
67. Heidegger, *The Principle of Reason*, 26.
68. *The Principle of Reason*, 109–10.
69. Heidegger, *Being and Time* (San Francisco, CA: Harper and Row, 1967), 51.
70. Heidegger, *On Time and Being*, 8
71. Heidegger, *The Principle of Reason,* 64.
72. For Heidegger on this very question, consult: "On the Being and Essence of *physis* in Aristotle's *Physics*, B, 1," in *Pathmarks* (Cambridge: Cambridge University Press, 1998).
73. On the contrary, already in 1957, Heidegger mentioned a concern with regard to the principle of reason *ruling* even over God, see *The Principle of Reason*, 26.
74. Heidegger, *Parmenides*, 114 and 105.

Chapter 8

The Holy in Heidegger's Reading of Greek Tragedy

Necessity, Measure, and Law

James M. Magrini

When speaking of Heidegger's philosophy after "the turn" (*die Kehre*), the writings of the 1930s and beyond, Richard Capobianco rightfully observes that Heidegger's thinking was "rigorously philosophical"—but that it also "attained the poetic."[1] In one sense, Western philosophy (metaphysics/ontology) is already an expression of theology as onto-theology, and second, since the onto-theological tradition has forgotten or obscured the concern with Being qua Being ("fallen into the oblivion of Being"), it privileges what Heidegger calls "objectifying thinking and saying."[2] In the "Appendix" (1964) to the lecture, "Phenomenology and Theology" (1927/28), Heidegger warns that if objectifying thought is left unchecked, this "scientific-technical manner of thinking will spread to all realms of life."[3]

Thus, when exploring the Holy in relation to the loss or fleeing of the gods, Heidegger seeks a form of thought and speech that is non-objective in nature. Heidegger finds in Rilke, and to a far greater extent, Hölderlin, a form of non-objectifying thinking and saying that is *"poietic,"* related to *Dichtung*, which Heidegger views as a revelatory form of "singing," which is not a way of speaking and thinking "about" things, but rather an attuned manner of dwelling in their *presence*. "The singing saying of the poet," insists Heidegger, does not covet or solicit that which "is ultimately accomplished by humans as an effect," it does not "posit and represent anything as standing over and against us or as an object," for non-objectifying thinking and saying instantiates the "simple willingness that wills nothing, counts on no successful outcome,"[4] and as we learn, it holds the unique potential to facilitate the emergence of the Holy, which is essential if we are to once again dwell and prosper in the presence of the divine gods.

Heidegger's sustained engagement with Hölderlin's poetry, which includes the confrontation with ancient Greek tragedy, is grounded in the pressing issue of the loss of the Holy in our lives, for when attuned by *das Gestell* of technology (*Enframing*), we experience the "world's night," the default or flight of the gods from our lives. In relation to the sense of Holy, it is crucial to note that not only have "the gods or the god fled, but the divine radiance has been extinguished in the world's history."[5] Our experience of this destitution, as William McNeill contends, stands in stark "contrast with the golden age of the Greeks, who were exposed to the 'fire from the heavens' [the Holy]."[6] Heidegger claims that the gods will return at the "right time," and Hölderlin establishes this time, for in the midst of the world's night the poet sings to the "fugitive gods" and poetizes the Holy. This is because Hölderlin remembers (*Andenken*) what has been—a time when the Holy radiated in a powerfully luminescent manner—and foretells what might be the futural reawakening of humanity to the lost sense of the Holy, heralding in his poetry the return of the gods as the "site of the wedding festival of men and gods."[7]

This historical occurrence (*Ereignis*), according to McNeill, "comprises the 'incipient greeting' in which humans and gods are greeted by 'the holy,'" and the Holy inspires a form of attunement (*Stimmung*) "more primordial (*anfanglicher*) and more originary" (*ursprünglicher*) than every other human attunement,"[8] and that is the attunement Heidegger names *das Festliche*. As stated, Hölderlin poetizes the flight of the gods because he recognizes the absence of the Holy. His poetry anticipates their return and arrival because it first prophesizes the return of the Holy and humanity's re-awakening to its presence. Turning to Greek tragedy provides a vista into what it means to already dwell in the presence of the Holy, an experience that has been lost to us. Although there are numerous references to Greek tragedy in Heidegger's vast corpus, herein we focus on three of Heidegger's readings of Greek tragedy, offering an interpretation of the Holy, elucidating the manner in which this concept is foundational to his reading of Greek tragedy, which opened the ancients to the Holy and invited their participation in and potential appropriation of its "truth" for the sake of their historical destiny.

Heidegger's notion of the Holy stands in contrast to the holy or holiness of God found in the primary doctrines of both Judaism and Christianity, where, as William Barklay asserts, it is God that makes the world a place of *holy* dwelling and *not the reverse*, that is, the holy is not a phenomenon conceived as somehow antecedent to God.[9] It is possible to grasp this Christian view by turning to Plato's dilemma presented in the *Euthyphro*, where we encounter Socrates posing the following question to the priest Euthyphro when discussing piety, or the issue of the holy: "Is that which is holy [*hosion*] loved by the gods because it is holy [thus commanding the Gods' reverence], or is it holy because it is loved by the gods [thus the phenomenon of the holy is dependent on the gods]."[10] We note that the Attic Greek "*hosiotes*" indicates that the holy is the property of the gods, "not *appropriated* or *permitted to man's use.*"[11]

Christianity relates to the second horn of Plato's dilemma, whereas Heidegger's understanding of the Holy relates to the first. For in Heidegger's view, the gods are only *as* gods in the first instance because they dwell within the presence of the Holy, and with the loss of the Holy as described, the gods become fugitives from the scene because they are dependent on the Holy for their divine and sacred stature, and with this view, Heidegger's philosophy is irreducible to either theology or Christian philosophy,[12] for Heidegger is emphatic that the Christian tradition has impeded and even obscured "our coming to know the Greek world."[13] For Heidegger, the Holy is more primordial than and antecedent to the sacred, the divine, and the gods; the Holy is "the essential sphere of divinity, which in turn alone affords a dimension for the god and for God."[14] It is the Holy, when radiating as the "prevailing" power itself, that is necessary for the gods to be *as* gods and for Holy names to gather their power to communicate what is sacred and divine. As related to the *Euthyphro* dilemma, based on Heidegger's interpretation of Hölderlin's poetry, "The holy is not holy because it is divine; rather the divine is divine because it is 'holy,'"[15] and the Holy itself *is* nature (*physis*), and *physis* holds "everything, even the gods, in 'life'."[16]

I. INTIMATING THE HOLY IN GREEK TRAGEDY: AESCHYLUS, PROMETHEUS, AND NECESSITY

In Heidegger's analysis of world and historical founding art, "The Origin of the Work of Art" (1935/36), we encounter the ancient Greek temple that gathers worshippers in community, and through their participation in the "truth-happening" of the temple's "work-being," their world or open relational context is revealed and given legitimacy as it is firmly set upon the Earth, which rises and "juts through the world."[17] The Earth is a primordial power that emerges and lights up the Greeks' historical dwelling, consecrating the ground upon which they founded their existence, and as Heidegger contends, the "Greeks early called this emerging and rising in itself and in all things *physis*."[18] When the Greeks came to worship, in the rising presence of the Earth, which alone granted the gods their divine power, the statue erected as the center-piece of the temple was never present before them as a cold, sterile marble likeness of one or another deity. Rather, in the "work-being" of the temple, the statue came alive; they were in the presence of the "god himself."[19] The unique experience of the Greeks in the midst of the Holy revealed a world alive with historical potential, permeated by a sense of wonder, and according to Heidegger, the ever-present sense of the Holy common to the Greek experience was also gathered and communicated through linguistic works, for example, poetry and most specifically Greek tragedy, both of which poetize the Holy.

To poetize the Holy in Greek tragedy, in a "proto-philosophical" manner, as McNeill observes, is not merely to depict narrative, dramatic events, but instead to give life to an essential "poietic dwelling, accomplished in its being by the *poiesis* of a world that occurs in each case as *mythos*."[20] Poets and tragedians do not simply employ words in an ordinary manner; rather they allow language to speak through them. This is the basis of what Heidegger calls "projective saying."[21] As stated, Greek tragedy was anything but a staged spectacle depicting and re-presenting dramatic events for the purpose of entertainment or *cathartic* release. Instead, as Heidegger emphasizes, Greek tragedy poetizes the struggle between the old and new gods as waged and fought in the "work-being" of the tragedy—"the place of all nearness and remoteness of the gods"[22]—within which the Greeks in attendance participated as preservers of the work. In such attuned moments, "the holy and the god is invoked into the openness of his presence,"[23] and in the midst of the opening of the Holy, the ground is consecrated and the sacrifices and dedications to the god acquire legitimacy. So powerful was the Greeks' encounter with the Holy, occurring through the rising of Earth, that it attuned and transformed their world, and in every instance they fought a battle and put up for decision and choice, "what [was] holy and what unholy, what [was] great and what is small, what [was] brave and what cowardly, what lofty and what flighty, what master and what slave."[24]

We introduced the notion of *physis,* which Susan Schoenbohm defines as an originary process that "enables and allows the presence of things to come into appearance,"[25] and thus *physis* is inseparable from unconcealment and *aletheia.* Beyond this, Heidegger claims that *physis* had a broad and expansive meaning for the Greeks; it referred to "heaven and earth" and "human history as the work of humans and the god," and, in addition, the Greeks understood *physis* as the "event of standing forth arising from the concealed and thus enabling the concealed to take its stand for the first time."[26] Capobianco highlights the "arising" and subsequent "enabling" power of *physis* within his perceptive reading of the *Ur*-phenomenon, making the distinction between that which *prevails* and *prevailing* as such. First, *physis* as unaided bringing-forth is set off from *techne,* the knowledge associated with aided bringing-forth; *physis* indicates, "whatever prevails" and persists (unaided) in its manifestation. Second, *physis* "points beyond 'what prevails' to 'the prevailing of whatever prevails,' 'prevailing as such (*Walten als Solches*).'"[27] This is expressive of the omni-presence of *physis,* which Heidegger links with the primordial Earth component as paired with the world in relation to historical founding works of art, for the Earth is the "sheltering (*Bergen*) that is intrinsic to *physis*."[28] For Heidegger, drawing on Hölderlin's poetry, the Earth is living and dynamic, everything arises from the Earth and returns to it, the Earth, as a "sheltering agent"[29] is revelatory, but it is also, in a more primordial and essential way, "concealing and continually self-secluding."[30] Heidegger observes that "Hölderlin names nature [*physis*-Earth] 'the holy'"[31] and claims that the Earth is "older than the ages and above the gods,"[32] that is, the Earth, "is the holy [*Heilige*]," and always remains "unbroken and whole [*heil*]."[33]

Capobianco observes that *physis*-Nature "structurally precedes and exceeds any kind and level of meaning"; it can never be mastered, as Greek tragedy shows us, and "is never exhausted by sense or meaning,"[34] and here we refer to the understanding and mastering of *physis*-Nature through "calculative knowledge" (objectifying thinking) commonly associated with the applied sciences. McNeill echoes these thoughts when observing that what is given in tragedy, "is never secured by knowledge alone, not even the highest philosophical knowing, that of *theorein*," which is a finite mode of knowing, but instead is "implicated in a [non-objectifying] poiesis that is not merely human or within the control of the finite human perspective on the world."[35] Related to the Holy and Greek tragedy, it is crucial to note that Heidegger claims, "it was not in natural processes that the Greeks first experienced . . . *physis*, but the other way around: on the basis of a fundamental experience of Being in poetry and thought."[36]

Heidegger first seriously turns to Greek tragedy to illuminate his developing philosophy of history, necessity, and destiny in the Rector's address, "The Self-Assertion of the German University" (1933), with the focus on re-conceptualizing the power of human knowledge, or as Veronique Foti asserts, the relationship between "German *Dasein* [and] the original Greek essence of science (*Wissenschaft*)."[37] Heidegger introduces Aeschylus' tragedy, *Prometheus Bound*, highlighting a view of heavenly or Holy "Necessity," which as Foti contends, offers an interpretation focused on a "static figure of the [Holy] enigma" that is later replaced in Heidegger's further analyses of tragedy with "Being's historicality and temporality."[38] We return to this issue of stasis, and to a lesser degree, temporality, in relation to Necessity after examining Heidegger's brief interpretation of the exchange between Prometheus and the chorus, which initially appears to dramatize the resignation of Prometheus to his fate. However, Heidegger understands things differently, he reads the tragedy as poetizing something revelatory and heroic in philosophical terms relating to what can be understood as a pervasive, enigmatic, and primordial divine force that transcends both humans and divinities.

Zeus chains Prometheus to a rock of adamantine and tortures him for stealing fire from the gods, with the aim of delivering technological power (*techne*) to humanity. The chorus expresses sympathy for Prometheus, pleading: "Do not, after helping men to your own hurt/Neglect to save yourself from torment." To which Prometheus responds, "Fate fulfills all in time," indicating that his freedom will come only after enduring "countless pains," and Prometheus' rejoinder continues, serving as the focus of Heidegger's reading: "Cunning [*techne*] is feebleness beside Necessity [*Ananke*]."[39] Heidegger translates the Greek, *"Techne d' anankes asthenestera makro,"* as "knowledge is far less powerful than necessity," and he observes that into the speech of Prometheus, "Aeschylus puts an adage that expresses the [concealed] essence of knowledge,"[40] and the prophetic message is that all human knowledge of things remains in advance "at the mercy of overpowering fate and fails before it."[41] According to Heidegger, it is Prometheus's recognition that human knowledge is radically limited in the face of what is destined beyond the human being that qualifies him as the first philosopher. Prometheus, through philosophical insight, is attuned to the preordained, ontological inevitability that historical necessity is a power beyond human wisdom, manifesting in the radical indeterminacy of human destiny that this tragedy seeks to understand, and this for the ancient Greeks, as we have indicated, is found in their authentic relationship to that which lies beyond their sure and certain grasp, inspiring their openness to and receptivity of the enigmatic force of the Holy.

The single line quoted from Aeschylus, as Dennis Schmidt observes, is presented by Heidegger without context, there is no analysis of the overarching mythological story inspiring Prometheus's recognition and assertion,[42] and if we look closer at the dialogue following the line Heidegger cites, an undeniable sense of the Holy emerges, a view within which even the so-called "power of fate" is under the charge of because it is less powerful than Necessity. We note that the chorus, rather than focusing on "fate," asks Prometheus whether or not Zeus holds power over Necessity: "And whose hand on the helm controls Necessity?"[43] In relation to the Holy in terms of the *prevailing* that *prevails as such*, the tragedy poetizes the Holy as an immemorial force, which is personified in the female cosmic goddess (*protogenos*) Necessity (*Anangke/Adrastia*),[44] who instantiates all that is inescapable and inevitable—a Holy power that is unassailable. Necessity in Greek myth rules the heavens and commands the *Moirai* (Three Fates) and the *Erinyes* (The Furies), and even the gods can't escape her supreme power and rule, for example, Prometheus is clear that Zeus is below Necessity, and for the chorus, the Daughters of Oceanus, this astonishing revelation represents the supreme "Holy truth" that had hitherto remained concealed, cloaked "in mystery."[45]

The goddess Necessity is often portrayed as bearing a heavenly torch as she shelters, radiates, and wields the gleaming, luminescent light of the Holy, the originary fire from above, and for the Greeks, as Heidegger contends, tragedy inspired the Greeks awakening to the "blazing brightness" of the "Heavenly fire."[46] This image and theme of fire and light continues through our analysis, because for Heidegger, it is fire that ultimately signifies the essence of the Holy, not only as it streaks across the ancient skies but also as it rises up and through the flames of the homely "hearth," which is the center of Being for the Greeks as Heidegger understands this issue.

Capobianco provides insight into the phenomenon of glowing and gleaming in Hölderlin's poetry as this is related to Nature as the luminous *Ur*-phenomenon as captured in the German word *das Glänzen*, noting that "Nature does not just 'shine,' it 'gleams'," and this "gleaming is a '*höheres Erscheinen*,' a 'higher appearance' or 'higher revealing,'" which also suggests "something more elevated, sublime, and 'holy.'"[47] This notion of gleaming, as consistent with our analysis, is inseparable from the unconcealment (*aletheia*) of Holy Nature, indicating that it stands higher than, and shines brighter than, and first makes possible, the conception and experience of nature as "landscape" (*Landschaft*), or collection of natural entities.

In relation to our reading of the Holy, we return to explore Foti's claim that Heidegger, in "The Self-Assertion of the German University" provides us with the static, reified figure of the enigmatic Necessity (*Anangke*), and only later, in *Introduction to Metaphysics,* moves to offer a more dynamic, fluid, and indeterminate model grounded in the relationship between historical *Dasein* to Being's historicality and temporality. Is there a way to embrace a sense of "stability" in relation to Necessity and the Holy in Heidegger's reading of 1933 without invoking the onto-theological idea of a reified or hypostatized notion of the Holy, which would run contrary to Heidegger's thought? It is possible, if we turn to Capobianco's enlightening reading of what we have termed *physis*-Earth or *physis*-Nature (the Holy), for there we encounter a view that retains and necessitates both the sense of stability and the indelibility of the primordial Temporality (*Temporalität*) of the Holy. It is also possible to explore this issue without granting a radical turn or change to Heidegger's view of the Holy as encountered in other readings, for example, as we find in Heidegger's reading of Sophoclean tragedy in Hölderlin's *der Ister* lecture course (1942), which is analyzed in the next section.

Exploring Heidegger's reading of Hölderlin's late poem, "The View," Capobianco contributes to the understanding of the essential "perdurance" of Nature: "That nature completes the images of the seasons/That nature stays, as the seasons glide along in haste/Is from fulfillment; then high heaven gleams/Upon the people."[48] Nature is the Holy and it "stays" because it is "whole," for "all that is *given* comes and goes, arrives and departs," the seasons, the suffering of Prometheus, the indeterminate historical dwelling of Dasein, "but the *giving itself*," as Nature and the Holy, stays and perdures, "remains one, whole, simple, complete";[49] and this understanding, as Capobianco carefully notes, "does not speak to any kind of traditional onto-theology,"[50] but reflects instead a radically anti-anthropocentric view that expresses profound reverence for Nature as the Holy. This concept, as related to what was introduced as Nature (*physis*-Earth) in terms of "the *prevailing as such*," perdures as a primordial temporal phenomenon, indeed, the finite temporality (*Zeitlichkeit*) of *Dasein* is "structured as it is only because it is correlated to the temporality (*Temporalität*)" of *physis*-Earth as that which *prevails as such,* as that which remains and perdures while the world's events *glide along in haste*. It is Necessity that, as the Holy, in its unwavering omnipresence that "keeps everything together in the undamaged immediateness of its 'film law.'"[51] In Heidegger's reading of Aeschylus, the Holy as Necessity (*Anangke*) is at once "the *prevailing* of whatever prevails" and "*prevailing as such*."[52]

Anticipating our analysis of Sophoclean tragedy, Robert Bernasconi emphasizes that the "holy is both on the one hand, the immediate, chaos, and on the other hand, it is mediacy, law."[53] Moving forward, we further develop Heidegger's claim that *physis*-Earth "does not derive from the gods," but rather "the gods themselves have their being by virtue of nature's powers."[54] Hölderlin inspires the view that the "Holy, 'older than the age' and 'above the gods,'" is what essentially decides "in advance concerning men and gods, whether they are, and how they are, and when they are."[55] For in the presence of the Holy, the Greeks displayed their "perseverance in the face of [the Holy], a stance that was initially one of wonder and astonishment."[56] Heidegger argues, in relation to the Greeks' relationship to the Holy, that tragedy nurtures and facilitates their attunement and transformation, and in such moments, all that is questioned becomes truly question-worthy, for in the presence of the Holy questioning is no longer "simply a preliminary stage to the answer as knowledge, a stage that we can put behind us, but questioning will itself become the highest form of knowledge."[57] We learn from both the Greeks and Heidegger that authentic or "essential" questioning compels us to "simplify our gaze to the extreme in order to focus on what is inescapable."[58]

II. SOPHOCLEAN TRAGEDY AND THE HOLY: OEDIPUS, ANTIGONE, MEASURE, AND LAW

When Heidegger turns to Sophoclean tragedy in *Introduction to Metaphysics* he focuses on both *Oedipus Rex* and briefly on *Oedipus in Colonus* and, in far greater detail, the *Antigone,* and this tragedy is reinterpreted in the lecture course *Hölderlin's Hymn "Der Ister."* Schmidt makes the observation that in

Heidegger's reading, it is not deeds such as the murder of Laius or marriage to his mother Jocasta that are responsible for his suffering, rather it is "the excessive sight of Oedipus, the excess of [his] speculative power."[59] This notion of excessive sight is expressed by Hölderlin within the lines of the poem, "In lovely blueness": "Perhaps King Oedipus has/One eye too many,"[60] and we explore this idea as we move from *Introduction to Metaphysics* to Heidegger's later essay, "Poetically Man Dwells" (1951).

Interpreting Hölderlin's poem, taking a lesson from Oedipus, Heidegger shows what is required by Dasein to poetically dwell on the earth under the heavenly sky in the presence of the mystery and enigma we call the Holy, that is, an attuned relationship to that which exceeds us in holding our potential for the appropriation of our destiny, our historical dwelling. *Oedipus Rex* is a tragic study in human subject-hood, decision, and choice, highlighting the unfolding of the "essential relationship between *physis* and *aletheia*,"[61] the primordial antagonism between concealment and unconcealment, with the foreboding sense that often times self-knowledge is inseparable from the annihilation of the self. For Heidegger stresses that Oedipus's self-knowledge occurs in relation to and in terms of the openness to *physis* and its self-concealing essence, "for Dasein, withholding such openness," facing potential dangers that have been brought to light—for example, language first opens Dasein to the threat of losing its Being—"means nothing other than giving up its own essence."[62] It is possible to state that Oedipus hubristically overstepped bounds, and when his own essence was revealed to him in the clarifying light of unconcealment, "he can endure only by gouging out his eyes—that is, by placing himself outside of all light," and in his blindness he is most clearly "revealed to the people as the man he *is*,"[63] the vile plague of Thebes that he zealously sought to eradicate.

Heidegger observes, "There always remains the question whether [Oedipus's] blindness derives from some deficit and loss," a naturally occurring physical affliction, or in the boundary-shattering (hubristic) abomination of "abundance and excess."[64] Although Heidegger does not invoke this notion, Oedipus's tragic fate is relatable to the cosmic relationship between *hubris* and *Nemesis,* a goddess linked to Necessity (*Ananke/Andrastia*) who is assigned the task of meeting out divine punishment when the cosmic order has been assaulted through hubristic acts that defy established limits and flagrantly violate the divine or holy order (*cosmos*). The Greek "*nemein*," means to mete out one's just share or administer justice and retribution for hubristic, limit-destroying or boundary-shattering actions. In Oedipus's case, it is a form of hubris that leads to his destruction and tragic fall, and when the chorus listens in horror to the messenger's recounting of Oedipus's self-blinding with the brooches of Jocasta, they appear to have already peered into the heart of the matter that Hölderlin poetizes, namely, that Oedipus has transgressed what we might call "Holy" boundaries: "Oh, unhappy man, what madness has come on you? Who is the unearthly foe that, with a bound of more than mortal range, has made your ill-starred life his pray?"[65]

This *bound* or *boundary* of which the chorus speaks is indicative of the range, scope, and power that is beyond us, but required, as Heidegger contends, if we are to come to our proper dwelling place on the earth beneath the sky and divinities, for it is against the Holy (the heavenly) that we must measure ourselves in order to receive the true measure and breadth of our mortal Being-in-the-world. Hölderlin's observation that King Oedipus has *one eye too many* serves as a warning regarding the fundamental condition grounding Western culture, that we are lost to the fate of clinging to scientific or technical knowledge grounded in metaphysics, which is erroneously embraced as a salvific force, and this constitutes the tragic belief in the invincible power of human progress. Oedipus shows us that we require an "entirely different metaphysical depth," we need what the Greeks experienced, namely, "a fundamental relationship to the Being of beings [*physis*] as a whole, a relationship that is well founded and built truly,"[66] which indicates that we must learn to dwell near and where the authentic saving power resides, opening the potential for embracing a view of knowledge and self that outstrips all "modern subjectivisms and psychologisms."[67]

In "..Poetically Man Dwells," this understanding of a poetic earthly dwelling and self-knowledge that is well founded and truly built, is expressed in Heidegger's view of what we have referenced as "Holy measure," which is engendered by Hölderlin's poetry. As stated, we arrive at the proper gauge for our dwelling only when "measuring [ourselves] against the heavenly,"[68] the "unknown god." However, we note that it is *not* the divine god that truly serves as the human's *metron,* instead, as our analysis makes clear, it is the Holy itself. For it is the case that when measuring our finite existence (that which prevails) against the *prevailing as such,* to find the proper *metron* for human dwelling, we do *not* submit to the god, but to the appearance in the sky and heavens of the "alien element to which the unknown god has yielded,"[69] that is, the self-concealing Holy enigma (*physis*-Earth).

The "measure-taking" required is not a common measure, a quantitative (Cartesian) calculating of some distance in space, consisting of points and coordinates. Indeed, what Heidegger terms our "unpoetic dwelling," our inability to take Holy measure, is rooted in the "curious excess of frantic measuring and calculating."[70] Instead, the measure of which Heidegger speaks is an essential *ontological* form of measuring in which Dasein first comes into its authentic temporal-historical dwelling by gauging itself against the awesome and incalculable powers of the Holy—in the presence of the unknown God—while spanning and holding itself in the "dimension" *between* heaven and earth, *between* the sky and the ground that bears up

Dasein's dwelling. In order for Dasein to come into its authentic historical dwelling, it must locate, establish, and continually reestablish its ties to the Holy, for "man does not undertake this spanning [measure-taking] just now and then; rather, man is man at all in this spanning."[71] As related to our analysis of the Holy and upward-looking measurement, Bernasconi describes the Holy as "immediate in the sense that it does not arise from mediation," and when considering the relationship between gods and human beings, "which both belong to the holy, the holy is strict mediacy."[72]

Thus, from Greek tragedy it is possible to receive the proper gauge for assessing our potential historical "vocation," our potential way of building, thinking, and dwelling poetically that is wholly unique to our historical epoch. What Hölderlin poetizes about our relationship to the sublime and enigmatic sway of the Holy, in the precarious and dangerous search for self-knowledge, as related to *Oedipus Rex*, is captured accurately in the *Delphos grammati*: "Know Thyself." Importantly, as opposed to indicating that self-knowledge is possible through meditative and sustained self-reflection, the internalization of consciousness, this epigram serves as a warning to learn and abide by human limits, which are revealed, as we have learned through Heidegger and Hölderlin, when we measure ourselves against that which is beyond us, that which *prevails as such* and is itself ontologically beyond all measure.

As classicist Jean-Pierre Vernant notes, "Know Thyself" (*gnothi seauton*) meant for the Greeks, "learn your limits; know that you are a mortal man; do not attempt to be the gods' equal," and this epigram is in no way urging the Greeks to "turn their gaze inward to discover themselves inside their 'I'," or the interiority of the ego, for as Vernant contends, learning for the Greeks always took the form of turning outward, or looking upward, searching for inspiration through *measure*.[73] This is why Heidegger stresses that we must return to the Greeks in order to learn from Oedipus that the human application of knowledge, as it is understood, shaped, and guided by Western metaphysics (onto-theology), "does not demand what is authentic," for the "concealed will to transform beings for the openness of Dasein calls for more,"[74] and is indeed grounded in that which is beyond us, that which prevails over our ephemeral, earthly dwelling.

Heidegger's 1942 reading of the *Antigone,* in the lecture course *Hölderlin's Hymn "The Ister,"* is crucial to our interpretation of the Holy. In Heidegger's reading of Oedipus, we encountered the "evasiveness" or blindness to the opening (unconcealment) and approach of his destiny from out of the depths and concealed essence of the Holy; Oedipus failed to take measure of the Holy and hubristically overestimated the power of human knowledge while ignoring the Lawful limits set in advance of human concerns. Conversely, Antigone's actions and her story demonstrate an intimate understanding (*phronein*) of human limits, and the essence of the tragedy lies in Antigone taking upon herself the "unhomely" to arrive at her Being-at-home in relation to the Holy. As earlier stated, in *Introduction to Metaphysics,* Heidegger provides an extensive analysis of the chorus in the *Antigone,* in which, as Capobianco points out, the human's essence is primordially "unsettled" and "*unheimlich,*" and thus is not at home (*unheimisch*) "in relation to Being and the Overpowering."[75]

Yet Heidegger's return to *Antigone* in 1942 is in no way a "repetition as some have suggested,"[76] and in fact represents a *reversal*. Capobianco brings our attention to what Heidegger states in his reading that is often overlooked by commentators—and this is the "care" (*Sorge*) to "become at home," which reveals that the human being, as the "unhomely one, is nonetheless primordially *at-home* in Being,"[77] but is initially unaware of "Home *as* Home."[78] Antigone must find her way through the unhomely in a resolute manner, as if through a "foreign land," in order to "come to recognize Being *as* Home and to dwell at the Source."[79] The Hearth, the originary site of Being and *becoming-homely,* in this reading is no longer "the site of inauthentic Dasein," as we encounter in the 1935 reading, and is rather the "site of Being at home in a primordial way," for as related to our analysis, the chorus is actually "pointing 'beyond' the human being's 'unsettledness' unto the *hearth,*" the site of the Holy, "the 'place' where human beings primordially belong."[80] Exploring this issue, we return to the understanding of *evasiveness* as introduced in our reading of Oedipus, for as Antigone comes to terms with what is indeed most "homely" within the "unhomely," the evasiveness we describe relates to the inauthentic turn from the site of the home, the Hearth, and the Holy.

Heidegger's initial concern is with two Greek terms in the choral ode: "*Polla ta deina kouden anthropou deinoteron pelei,*" and the key terms are "*deinon*" and "*pelei,*" and these terms are intimately related to and consistent with what we have thus described in relation to the Holy in Greek tragedy. *Deinon* can be understood as that which is wondrous or awe-inspiring, but also refers to "the fearful, the powerful, the inhabitable," in that what is *deinon* "essentially exceeds everything habitual,"[81] an understanding derived from Hölderlin's poetizing of Sophoclean tragedy. Capobianco observes that *deinon* indicates that the human being is "'*das Unheimlichste*' the most unsettled, and therefore, '*unheimisch,*' 'not at home,' or 'unhomely.'"[82] In Heidegger's earlier reading of *Antigone*, Capobianco notes that the "unsettled nature" of human beings is "intrinsically 'unhomely' because it constitutively forgets Being," for in and through its immersion in beings, it "can find no 'home'—no ultimate ground or meaning—among beings."[83] Yet, as Capobianco further observes, in Heidegger's second reading in 1942, Being as "home" is the proper destination of the human being, and this is the leitmotif of the reading.

Antigone comes to be-at-home when recognizing, and further, appropriating, the ontological truism that her Being, her being-toward-death, and her ultimate possibilities for existing, are granted by *physis*-Earth (the Holy), that which stands beyond and prevails above even the gods. With this idea, Heidegger removes the tragic Greeks, who were proto-philosophical, from the latent philosophical subjectivism that haunts Western metaphysics (onto-theology). When discussing the term *"pelein,"* Heidegger states that in "Homer and Hesiod, *pelein* is the usual word for *einai*, which we translate as Being."[84] We include in this initial definition the idea that *pelein* also refers to what is "more uncanny" and "looms or stirs beyond the human being"; *pelein* is the "stirring and looming, abiding in itself amid change, emerging from out of itself," and this, as we are already familiar with, "is what the Greeks otherwise call *physis*"[85]—that is, *physis*-Earth. In terms that are now familiar, Heidegger indicates that *pelein* and its persistence and movement, is the *prevailing* of that which *prevails as such,* for *pelein* "stirs itself of its own accord," and does not "flow away but remains and abides within itself, in its surging"; and in the depths of its abysmal essence, in "its concealed presencing," lies a "stillness and tranquility amid constant unconcealed absencing and presencing."[86]

Heidegger's claim in this 1942 reading of the tragedy is that there is a tendency for us to turn from our "homely" essence and flee-in-the-face of it to expend our energies in all directions, and through a multiplicity of actions (*pantoporos-aporos*)—as a form of *ontological escapism* or the *evasiveness* that resists *the homeward turn*—we arrive "everywhere and yet everywhere come to nothing," for none of these activities, once we have fled from and ignored our essence for Heidegger, ever prove "sufficient to fulfill and sustain [our] essence."[87] We flee-in-the-face of what is essential because we are, the *katastrophe*—we instantiate the ontological potential of the tragic "reversal that turns [us] way from [our] own essence."[88] This notion we might say is the *authenticity* of Antigone in relation to her finding and choosing her proper place of dwelling, appropriating her destiny within the world as it is given in advance by a force that remains silent and unnamed in the tragedy. This is described as taking up or bearing up—a suffering under as *pathein*—the full weight of the *deinon,* and when choosing her essence, she is informed in advance by what Heidegger labels *"phronein,"* or what we might term intuitive "tragic" wisdom, which originates "from the innermost middle of human essence."[89]

McNeill also asserts that *phronein* is the "all-determinate origin of her actions,"[90] the understanding of what she must do in accordance with a Law that by necessity stands beyond both the gods of the higher realm, such as *Zeus,* and the gods and goddesses of the lower realm, *Dike,* and is, as Heidegger claims, "something that pervasively attunes human beings," and yet is neither born of nor traceable to any human ordinance, for human ordinances have no rule or power over this Law, because human laws "fall emphatically below what prevails even beyond the gods."[91] Indeed, Capobianco's reading highlights the sense of Antigone's attunement to the Law of the Holy, her "being in awe and in admiration before that which commands respect and awe."[92] Antigone's actions, her anointing the body of Polyneices and in a ceremonial manner, covering his corpse with dirt in order for his soul to find rest, is the moment of choosing her essence, and this choice is inexplicable in terms of familial duty born of blood or responsibility to human morality, laws of the polis, or edicts passed by Creon, but rather her choice instantiates what is promised in advance to a higher power and Law, to what is "fitting and what is destined to her from the realm [the Holy] of whatever prevails beyond."[93] And, as McNeill stresses, although what prevails from beyond is "nothing determinate," it nevertheless "prevails and even 'lives' (*Waltet*),"[94] with an undeniable immediacy and pressing force, and yet the Holy as we have described it, as stated, remains unsaid and unnamed by Sophocles in the drama.

Heidegger observes that when Antigone is brought before Creon, he demands to know why Antigone has transgressed the law he has established forbidding the burial of Polyneices, the precise type of law (*nomos*), as stated, that gives structure and organization to the human *polis*. Antigone defiantly informs Creon that his laws have no authority over her, and she steadfastly declares that no mortal law of the state "could override the unwritten and unfailing statutes of heaven; for their life is not of today or yesterday, but [prevailing] for all time; no man knows when they were first put forth."[95] Prior to being led off by Creon's guards, Antigone cries out, "See what I suffer, and from whom, because I feared to cast away the fear of Heaven."[96] Although Creon sentences Antigone to death, it is she who actually chooses death, and despite Creon later overturning Antigone's sentence on the advice of the chorus, his new decree holds no power, for Antigone has already taken her life, and in doing so has traversed, endured, and overcome her "unsettledness," the "fearful and inhabitual experience"[97] of the not-at-home. For Heidegger, Antigone's death is ultimately her becoming homely, constituting her "belonging to Being."[98] So, in her choosing to ceremoniously bury her brother and end her life, in service to what stands above the gods and human law, Antigone accepts and then appropriates her un-homeliness— *pathein to deinon touto*—and, as McNeill recognizes, "knowingly takes upon herself her being-towards-death," the dying that is Antigone's belonging to Being, which is her homecoming from out of the experience of being unsettled. This is the "dying that belongs,"[99] not to Antigone, but rather to Being or the Holy itself. Here, we must return to Heidegger's words when speaking about Antigone and the attuned choices she makes, the essence of her Being-at-home is the return to the site of the Holy, which for the "Greeks is *physis*,"[100] and hence traceable to the Earth.

Homecoming for Antigone is a return to her primordial belonging to the Holy Earth, her enlightened recognition and appropriation of the source, which is possible in the first instance because she is immersed in the pervasive unfolding of *physis* (*pelein*), in its movement from out of concealment and back. Importantly, Capobianco emphasizes that at the heart of the "unsettled" experience of Dasein, there is already an *intimation* of this sublime, primordial "home," which we have identified as the Holy. However, it is obscured because of Dasein's immersion in and attention to beings, manifesting as the *fear* "before that which commands respect and awe," the power, in the sense of "standing out into the powerful itself," and the *unusual*, indicating the sense of potentially "going beyond the habitual and accustomed to stand out into what is extraordinary."[101] Antigone is attuned to the homely source, the Holy, and so chooses the necessary path to traverse the path of the "unhomely," taking up and suffering (*pathein*) under the *deinon*, and Heidegger names this her "ultimate action," which *is* the choosing of a "destiny as that which alone is fitting," and in her actions and undertaking, Heidegger locates "the supreme action and proper history of humankind,"[102] for to move through the foreign, the unhomely, in order to experience the return home is to accomplish Dasein's homecoming.

By means of *phronein*, Antigone knows precisely what is "fitting and destined to her from the realm of whatever prevails beyond."[103] We have referred to what is destined as the Holy, the Law of Necessity, that which engenders authentic measure for humanity, beyond *Zeus, Dike,* and all human *nomoi*. In Hölderlin's poetizing of Sophoclean tragedy, as related to our reading of Antigone's actions and her death, the Holy is "the law which ordains its measure in a different way than does human law," the Holy "reigns above all dispositions," and is properly "above men and gods."[104] Based on the ground covered, we know that "what essentially prevails as that which is to be poetized [as the Holy] cannot be a being,"[105] or supreme deity as in traditional mono-theistic religions, and since it is not a being or entity, it cannot be identified as "something actual," and as a result, "therefore always appears to be nothing,"[106] and so it can only be said, intimated, or sung through a language that poetizes, or given through, as we have shown, the poetizing *mimesis* of the *mythos* of Sophoclean tragedy.

CONCLUDING THOUGHTS

We Who Are Banished From the Hearth, the Site of the Holy

The chorus in the *Antigone* emphatically declares that those who have forgotten their indebtedness to the Holy and refuse to take up the full weight of *to deinon* will continue to live in the destitute time of the flight of the gods, never to return and reside in their company. As Capobianco recognizes, in inauthenticity we remain "unsettled" because we have forgotten that we are "primordially at home in nearness to Being, the source of all beings," and unlike Antigone, we fail to "take up [our] unsettledness and unhomeliness resolutely."[107] It might be said that we are the "unsettled" ones that the chorus claims cannot be entrusted to their sacred hearth, which is the Being-present to the homely "Hearth." It is the Hearth where the illuminating and generative flames of the Holy rise up to the heavens, for example, within the gods' temples and in the warmth of the home's hearth and, as with "all sites of human habitation." As Heidegger points out, this is where the fire from Heaven "has its secure local and, as this local," lit and engendered by the spirit of the Holy, it "gathers around it all that properly occurs (*sich ereignet*) and is bestowed."[108] Cathy Leblanc raises the issue of the "usefulness" of Heidegger's thought, concluding that to learn from Heidegger, we must first *listen* to his language, allowing ourselves to be *attuned* by its sway and oscillation to the end of inspiring and installing a mood, which holds the positive and transformative power to lead us to the consideration of ideas overlooked by Western metaphysics, leading us down new and potentially rewarding paths of thought. For Leblanc, Heidegger's philosophy offers the potential "to counter the scattering effect of today's timing, today's often distressful way of life," which is highlighted by agitation and unmanageable "stress."[109] Let us briefly consider a philosophical, or thoughtful, lesson from our reading of the Holy in Greek Tragedy.

In this *Anthropocene* era, which John Gray links to the devastating effects of secular humanism, we are now experiencing and indeed participating in the domination and seemingly inevitable destruction of the planet.[110] The rise and domination of secular humanism is a phenomenon spawned by a certain metaphysics of presence as described so often, in so many different contexts, by Heidegger, who radically challenges this anthropocentric view, the subjectivism that is detrimental to the human community. As we have argued, it is the Earth or *physis* that should serve as the true measure for the human being, and as Capobianco observes, Heidegger wants us to understand, through an event of re-attunement, that we have "lost the ability to 'hear' the names of Being as the Greeks heard them."[111] If we are able to truly hear these names again, then we will, in Capobianco's words, come to recognize that "there is more, always more, to manifestation—a richness of showing, a reserve of appearing, that can never be fully tapped. *Physis* endlessly arising and we endlessly astonished."[112]

When addressing the issue of subjectivism, Heidegger is clear that what is required for the originary community is the relationship to the Holy as we have discussed. In the lecture course, *Hölderlin's Hymns "Germania"* and "The Rhine" (1934–1935), the notion of the originary community is intimately linked to Dasein's historicality (*Ereignis*), occurring only when "each individual is bound in advance to something that binds and determines every individual in exceeding them," that is, based on our interpretation, the Holy must be allowed to manifest for appropriation in a way where its advent is neither reducible to "the individual taken alone" nor to the human "community as such."[113]

According to Heidegger, the potential exists to experience the return of the Holy only when the loss and absence of the Holy strikes with existential immediacy, when our historical Dasein, in a mode of fundamental attunement, "endures the need of its godlessness and its fragmentation."[114] Heidegger philosophizes a double loss: The "default of the god forebodes something even grimmer," for it is not only the case that the gods have fled, "but the divine radiance has [also] become extinguished in the world's history."[115] This is because the flight of the gods has been obscured in our unsettled times, and Heidegger claims that we become aware of the flight of the gods and our destitute state only when we are transformed within the revelatory power of the attunement of "Holy Mourning" (*heilige Trauer*), which occurs in relation to the power of the Holy Earth. Holy Mourning must not be conceived as expressing "an isolated whining over some loss or other," neither should it be thought of as a "burdensome sadness about everything and nothing."[116]

Instead, it is a knowing that takes seriously the matter; we take the loss of the gods to heart, and this attuned knowing, is the purest form of "remaining with the gods" and the divinity that is no "longer fulfilled."[117] Holy Mourning gives rise to "distress" and engenders our authentic search for the traces of the fugitive gods, which includes the anticipatory listening for the reticent hints of their potential return while abiding in the darkness of the "world's night," suspended in the deafening silence of the gods' abandonment. The knowing associated with attunement is *An-denken* or "remembrance," which is "thinking of" what has been, in "distinction to what is simply past," and it is at once thinking in anticipation of what is on the approach, but not yet fulfilled. What is on the approach is the festival, which is sent by the Holy and finds its "determinate ground in the holy."[118] As stated, this festive attunement is more primordial that all other forms of human attunement, and as McNeill brings to our attention, this indicates it is more primordial than either "mourning (*Trauer*) and joy,"[119] and the attunement of the festival occurred for the ancients through their participation in Greek tragedy, an event inspiring the communion of humans and gods, united in the presence of the Holy.

In returning to the Greeks and tragedy, Heidegger shows us what once was, and beyond, what might be or become, revealing to us through Greek tragedy "the time of primordial decision for the essential order of the future of gods and humanity."[120] To move into the "truth" of tragedy, that which tragedy poetizes, requires that we encounter the gods and once again speak their essence, and Heidegger suggests that we already, although in an obscured and concealed manner, intuit what lies beyond the gods, and that is the true "living potential of spirit," that is, the "power of nature"—the Holy—that essentially works in its prevailing to give life to and maintain "the sacred,"[121] harboring the potential to inspire our earthly dwelling under the sky and the heavens to new and unforeseen heights. Heidegger, turning to Heraclitus, provides an analogy to our discussion of the Holy in the Greek experience of tragedy when translating Fragment 119: "*Ethos [ēthos] anthropo daimon*," which is usually rendered, "A man's character is his *daimon* [destiny]." However, Heidegger is unsatisfied with this translation, claiming that it "thinks in a modern way and not a Greek one."[122]

Heidegger offers a unique reading that suggests "*ēthos*" actually refers to the open region of Being. For Heidegger does not read *ēthos* in terms of what is commonly understood as "ethics" (*ethike*) in Aristotle, instead Heidegger claims *ēthos* refers to the more original sense of an adobe or intimate place of dwelling, and beyond this, Heidegger identifies *ēthos* as the primordial site of the Holy, that which "pertains to the essence of the human being," as that which "resides in nearness to him."[123] When attuned to the Holy, all human dwelling instantiates the vocation and task of respectfully preserving, holding near and dear, "the advent of what belongs to the human being in his essence,"[124] that is, the arrival (advent) and manifestation of the Holy. Concluding, along with Heidegger, with a slight modification, it is possible to understand Heraclitus as poetizing the following: The human being authentically dwells [*ēthos*] in his essence as a human being only in the enigmatic pervasiveness and perdurance of the omnipresent Holy. Through Hölderlin we learn that tragedy is a hymn in praise of and in celebration of the Holy, and it is Greek tragedy that poetizes what is above and beyond humans, bringing "it together into the sharpness and force of the unique ray through which [the Holy] is allotted to man, in order to bestow it."[125] This is where Hölderlin's brilliance lies, according to Heidegger, in recognizing that the "essential condition of the poet," much as for the ancient Greeks, "is grounded not in the reception of the god, but in the embrace of the holy."[126]

NOTES

1. Richard Capobianco, *Heidegger's Way of Being* (Toronto: University of Toronto Press, 2014), 49.

2. Capobianco, *Heidegger's Way of Being*, 54.

3. Martin Heidegger, "Phenomenology and Theology" in *Pathmarks*, ed. William McNeill (Cambridge: Cambridge University Press, 1998), 60.

4. Heidegger, "Phenomenology and Theology," 61.

5. Martin Heidegger, "What are Poets For?" in *Poetry, Language, Thought*, trans. Albert Hofstadter (New York: Harper & Row, 1971), 91.

6. William McNeill, *The Time of Life: Heidegger and Ethos* (Albany, NY: SUNY Press, 2013), 151.

7. Heidegger, "What are Poets For?" 93.

8. McNeill, *Time of Life,* 151.

9. William Barclay, *The Mind of Jesus* (San Francisco, CA: Harper-Collins, 1976), 99.

10. Plato, "Euthyphro" in *Plato: Complete Works,* ed. J. M. Cooper (Bloomington, IN: Indiana University Press, 1997), 10-b (25).

11. H. Liddell and R. Scott, R. *A Lexicon: Abridged From Liddell & Scott's Greek-English Lexicon* (Mansfield Centre: Martino Publishing, 2015), 50.

12. Thomas J. J. Altizer. *The Call to Radical Theology* (Albany, NY: SUNY Press, 2012), 73–74.

13. Martin Heidegger, *Holderlin's Hymn "The Ister"* trans. William McNeill and Julia Davis (Bloomington, IN: Indiana University Press, 1996), 77.

14. Martin Heidegger, "Letter on Humanism" in *Pathmarks,* ed. William McNeill (Cambridge: Cambridge University Press, 1998), 258.

15. Martin Heidegger, "As When on a Holiday..." in *Elucidations of Holderlin's Poetry,* trans. Keith Hoeller (New York: Humanity Books, 2000), 82.

16. Heidegger, "As When on a Holiday..." 87.

17. Martin Heidegger, "Origin of the Work of Art" in *Basic Writings,* ed. David F. Krell (San Francisco, CA: Harper & Row, 1993), 174.

18. Heidegger, "Origin of the Work of Art," 169.

19. Heidegger, "Origin of the Work of Art," 168.

20. McNeill, *Time of Life,* 193.

21. Heidegger, "Origin of the Work of Art," 203.

22. Heidegger, "Origin of the Work of Art," 198.

23. Heidegger, "Origin of the Work of Art," 169.

24. Heidegger, "Origin of the Work of Art," 169.

25. Susan Schoenbaum, "Heidegger's Interpretation of *Physis* in *Introduction to Metaphysics*" in *Companion to Heidegger's Introduction to Metaphysics,* ed. Richard Polt and Gregory Fried (New Haven, CT: Yale University Press, 2001), 146.

26. Martin Heidegger, *Introduction to Metaphysics,* trans. Richard Polt and Gregory Fried (New Haven, CT: Yale University Press, 2000), 16.

27. Capobianco, *Heidegger's Way of Being,* 53–54.

28. Capobianco, *Heidegger's Way of Being,* 64.

29. Heidegger, "Origin of the Work of Art," 168.

30. Heidegger, "Origin of the Work of Art," 174.

31. Heidegger, "Origin of the Work of Art," 80.

32. Heidegger, "As When on a Holiday..." 82.

33. Heidegger, "As When on a Holiday..." 85.

34. Capobianco, *Heidegger's Way of Being*, 63.
35. McNeill, *The Time of Life*, 193.
36. Heidegger, *Introduction to Metaphysics*, 15.
37. Veronique Foti, "Heidegger, Hölderlin, and Sophoclean Tragedy" in *Heidegger Toward the Turn: Essays on the work of the 1930s*, ed. James Risser (Albany, NY: SUNY Press), 169.
38. Foti, 169.
39. Aeschylus, *Prometheus Bound*, trans. Philip Vellacott (UK: Penguin Books, 1961), 35.
40. Martin Heidegger, "The Self-Assertion of the German University" in *The Heidegger Controversy: A Critical Reader*, ed. Richard Wolin (Cambridge: MIT Press, 1998), 31.
41. Heidegger, "The Self-Assertion of the German University," 33.
42. Dennis Schmidt, *On Germans and Other Greeks: Tragedy and Ethical Life* (Bloomington, IN: Indiana University Press, 2000), 234.
43. Aeschylus, *Prometheus Bound*, 35.
44. C. Kerenyi, *The Gods of the Greeks* (New York: Thames and Hudson, 1998), 94.
45. Aeschylus, *Prometheus Bound*, 35.
46. Heidegger, "As When on a Holiday..." 92.
47. Capobianco, *Heidegger's Way of Being*, 29–30.
48. Capobianco, *Heidegger's Way of Being*, 36.
49. Capobianco, *Heidegger's Way of Being*, 37.
50. Capobianco, *Heidegger's Way of Being*, 35.
51. Capobianco, *Heidegger's Way of Being*, 89.
52. Capobianco, *Heidegger's Way of Being*, 53–54.
53. Robert Bernasconi, *The Question of Language in Heidegger's History of Being* (New York: Humanity Books, 1985), 31.
54. Heidegger, "As When on a Holiday..." 87.
55. Heidegger, "As When on a Holiday..." 97–98.
56. Heidegger, "The Self-Assertion of the German University," 33.
57. Heidegger, "The Self-Assertion of the German University," 33.
58. Heidegger, "The Self-Assertion of the German University," 33.
59. Schmidt, *Tragedy and Ethical Life*, 243.
60. Martin Heidegger, "Hölderlin and the Essence of Poetry" in *Elucidations of Hölderlin's Poetry*, trans. Keith Hoeller (New York: Humanity Books, 2000), 64.
61. Heidegger, *Introduction to Metaphysics*, 107.
62. Heidegger, *Introduction to Metaphysics*, 183.
63. Heidegger, *Introduction to Metaphysics*, 112.
64. Martin Heidegger, "Poetically Man Dwells" in *Poetry, Language, Thought*, trans. Albert Hofstadter (New York: Harper & Row, 1971), 228.
65. Sophocles, *The Complete Plays of Sophocles*, trans. Sir Richard Claverhouse Jebb (New York: Bantam Books, 1982), 109.
66. Heidegger, *Introduction to Metaphysics*, 113.
67. Heidegger, "Poetically Man Dwells," 222.

68. Heidegger, "Poetically Man Dwells," 220–21.
69. Heidegger, "Poetically Man Dwells," 225.
70. Heidegger, "Poetically Man Dwells," 228.
71. Heidegger, "Poetically Man Dwells," 221.
72. Bernasconi, *The Question of Language,* 39.
73. Jean-Pierre Vernant, *The Greeks,* trans. Charles Lambert and Teresa L. Fagan (Chicago: University of Chicago Press, 1995), 16.
74. Heidegger, *Introduction to Metaphysics,* 113.
75. Richard Capobianco, *Engaging Heidegger* (Toronto: University of Toronto Press, 2011), 56.
76. Capobianco, *Engaging Heidegger,* 58.
77. Capobianco, *Engaging Heidegger,* 60.
78. Capobianco, *Engaging Heidegger,* 63.
79. Capobianco, *Engaging Heidegger,* 63.
80. Capobianco, *Engaging Heidegger,* 62.
81. Heidegger, *The Ister,* 67.
82. Capobianco, *Engaging Heidegger,* 59.
83. Capobianco, *Engaging Heidegger,* 60.
84. Heidegger, *The Ister,* 71.
85. Heidegger, *The Ister,* 108.
86. Heidegger, *The Ister,* 72.
87. Heidegger, *The Ister,* 84.
88. Heidegger, *The Ister,* 84.
89. Heidegger, *The Ister,* 107.
90. William McNeill, "A 'Scarcely Pondered Word' and The Place of Tragedy: Heidegger, Aristotle, Sophocles" in *Philosophy and Tragedy,* ed. M. de Beistegui and S. Sparks (New York: Routledge, 2000), 172.
91. Heidegger, *The Ister,* 117.
92. Capobianco, *Engaging Heidegger,* 59.
93. Capobianco, *Engaging Heidegger,* 59.
94. McNeill, "A 'Scarcely Pondered Word,'" 184.
95. Sophocles, *Oedipus Rex,* 128.
96. Sophocles, *Oedipus Rex,* 138.
97. Heidegger, *The Ister,* 104.
98. Heidegger, *The Ister,* 104.
99. McNeill, "A 'Scarcely Pondered Word,'" 194.
100. Heidegger, *The Ister,* 112.
101. Capobianco, *Engaging Heidegger,* 59.
102. Heidegger, *The Ister,* 109.
103. Heidegger, *The Ister,* 117.
104. Martin Heidegger, "Remembrance" in *Elucidations of Hölderlin's Poetry,* trans. Keith Hoeller (New York: Humanity Books, 2000), 128
105. Heidegger, "Remembrance," 120.
106. Heidegger, "Remembrance," 120.
107. Capobianco, *Engaging Heidegger,* 63.

108. Heidegger, *The Ister,* 105.
109. Cathy Leblanc, "The Usefulness of Heidegger's Thought," *Gatherings* (2013): 159.
110. John Gray, *Straw Dogs: Thoughts on Humans and Other Animals* (New York: Farrar, Straus and Giroux, 2007), 4.
111. Capobianco, *Heidegger's Way of Being,* 39.
112. Capobianco, *Heidegger's Way of Being,* 63–64.
113. Martin Heidegger, *Hölderlin's Hymns "Germania" and "The Rhine,"* trans. William McNeill and Julia Ireland (Bloomington, IN: Indiana State University, 2014), 74.
114. Heidegger, *Hölderlin's Hymns,* 82.
115. Heidegger, "What Are Poets for?," 91.
116. Heidegger, "What Are Poets for?," 89.
117. Heidegger, "What Are Poets for?," 97.
118. Heidegger, "What are Poets For?," 128.
119. McNeill, *Time of Life,* 157.
120. Heidegger, "As When on a Holiday..." 98.
121. Heidegger, *The Ister,* 29.
122. Heidegger, "Letter on Humanism," 269.
123. Heidegger, "Letter on Humanism," 269.
124. Heidegger, "Letter on Humanism," 269.
125. Heidegger, "As When on a Holiday..." 90.
126. Heidegger, "As When on a Holiday..." 91.

Chapter 9

Retrieving and Constructing a Spatial-Phenomenology of the Holy in the Early Heidegger

Paul Downes

In the short trajectory of time from *Being and Time*[1] to *Basic Problems of Phenomenology*,[2] Martin Heidegger fled from space. Viewed historically against the prolific output of Heidegger's whole corpus, the distance between these two works is barely an interval. Yet many shifts are in this interval. Whereas space is interwoven with temporality as transcendence in *Being and Time*, the Heidegger of *Basic Problems* goes to almost excruciating lengths to excise space from time. He treats space as mere interval. The reasons for and artificiality of this project of excision, of diametric oppositional splitting of space from time, need to be explored as part of an argument for a spatial condition of the holy.

The focus here is not primarily on the totality of the holy but on a key spatial condition for the experience of the holy, for the holy to unfold, unveiled in experience. This may be a manifold unveiling, including through disparate sense modalities and states of content of experience, yet it arguably shares a common supporting condition in spatial structural terms, framing experience. The holy is Being postulated as a spatial framing projection underlying key features of Heidegger's thought, a movement of relative expansion and openness in experience, in both experiential structure and content.

I. THE MATTER IN *BASIC PROBLEMS* AND INTRODUCING THE DYNAMIC BETWEEN DIAMETRIC AND CONCENTRIC SPACES

The process of unveiling bears a heavy burden of explanation in *Basic Problems*, while the unconcealment of truth as *aletheia* is a pervasive dimension of Heidegger's later thought, invoked also in *Being and Time;* and *aletheia* is explicitly associated with unveiling in *Basic Problems*.[3] In *Basic Problems*, unveiling is invoked for a wide array of phenomenological dimensions, namely, time, world, nature, transcendence, truth, perception, intentionality, cognition, and poetry, while also being a feature of inauthenticity, as an inauthentic unveiling, and not simply an authentic one. It is as though this unveiling operates as a fractal structure, repeating itself at different levels and modes of experience—a repetition that occurs in dynamic structural terms.

Whereas Hans-Georg Gadamer notes that both Heidegger and Hegel share a concern with unveiling, as indeed does Heidegger himself when acknowledging that Hegel "wrested concealed things from their hiding-places,"[4] Gadamer recognizes that Heidegger's unveiling is not the reflected light of Hegel's self-consciousness but a prior concern with unveiling.[5] In Heidegger's words, this is *"before* all reflection."[6]

This dynamic unveiling structure is intimately related also with projection. From this, it is a further step to envisage this key unveiling process as a concrete spatial projection, a dynamic spatial structural movement. In *Basic Problems*, Heidegger expressly links projection and unveiling, "with the projection, with the forthcast world, that is unveiled from which alone an intraworldy extant entity is uncoverable,"[7] "unveiling must itself somehow see, as unveiled, that upon which it projects."[8] This intertwining of unveiling and projection. is also linked to temporality. Heidegger asks, "how is projection grounded in temporality? In what way is temporality the condition of possibility for the understanding of Being?"[9]

Projection, phenomenological construction, and reduction as retrieval are key methodological concerns of the current argument. For Heidegger, Being "must always be brought to view in a free projection. This projecting of the antecedently given being upon its being and the structures of its being we call *phenomenological construction.*"[10] A phenomenological construction of the holy is Being postulated as *concentric spatially structured* experiential conditions. The holy as a space, a spatial structure of experience, is Being understood as an expanded spatial capacity for experience. Expansion is necessarily a relative term, so such a spatial mode of experience is to be distinguished from space as an absolute position (of Kant); it is neither the terrain of a monistic fusion as obliteration of self in Nietzschean Dionysian rapture[11] nor the "empty" "mere nonentity" space of Cartesian abstraction.[12] While it may be embedded at times in an immersion as dwelling in place, it is to be distinguished from mere space as place or change of place.

Heidegger states, *"For us* phenomenological reduction means leading phenomenological vision back from the apprehension of a being . . . to the understanding of the Being of this being (projecting upon the way it is unconcealed)."[13] This essay will also explore this space of the holy through a retrieval from *loss* of this space of the holy. *This loss is not simply a mere nothing but it itself spatially patterned, postulated as diametric space.*

Projection and unveiling coexist as the dominant governing processes of *Basic Problems*. Both of these spatial structural dimensions require amplification in terms of concentric and diametric spaces *of* relation *in* relation, as part of a phenomenological construction and retrieval of the holy. Projection is a fundamental process of movement, prior to causal relations.

Very basic aspects of experience (separation-connection, symmetry, relative closure-openness) are proposed as meaningful in spatial terms as concrete projected structures of diametric and concentric space. This proposed spatial-phenomenological approach also adopts a self-referential approach to interrogate the unthought spatial projections underpinning Heidegger's own thought, as projected structures of Being. This ambit of inquiry on specific spatial projections in the assumption structure of Heidegger's thought is resonant with early Heidegger's propensity for self-referential thinking. For example, Heidegger of *Being and Time* is concerned with "The historizing of history"[14] and "the temporalizing of temporality" when asking, "Is there a way which leads from primordial time to the meaning of Being."[15] A similar self-referential questioning occurs when Heidegger asks about the background domain itself over which the ideal and real, *intellectus* and *res* correspond, noting that "it is not enough to simply presuppose this relational totality."[16] Thus, Heidegger asks if this background domain is itself "real or ideal in its kind of Being or neither of these?"[17] The current spatial-phenomenological approach to uncovering the holy in Heidegger's phenomenological period can be construed as a *spatializing of spatiality*. This self-referential background questioning invites a focus on *background* space itself to challenge metaphysical dimensions of an abstract non-sensory "beyond."

A diametric spatial structure is one where a circle is split in half by a line which is its diameter or where a square or rectangle is similarly divided into two equal halves (see figure 9.1, top). In a concentric spatial structure, one circle is inscribed in another larger circle (or square); in pure form, the circles share a common central point (see figure 9.1, bottom), a co-center.

Jacques Derrida interrogates projections of embodied experience into language and thought to go beyond the Platonic priority given to the visual, for example, to uncover the ear of the other and the haptic.[18] Interrogating fundamental experiential projections into texts is taken in another direction here for primordial experiences of spatial relations that are prior to the five senses, for example, experience of breathing. This is resonant with diverse traditions of associating breath with spirit and with the later Heidegger's references to breath, explored in the final part of this essay. It is these concentric and diametric primordial breath spaces for experience that are

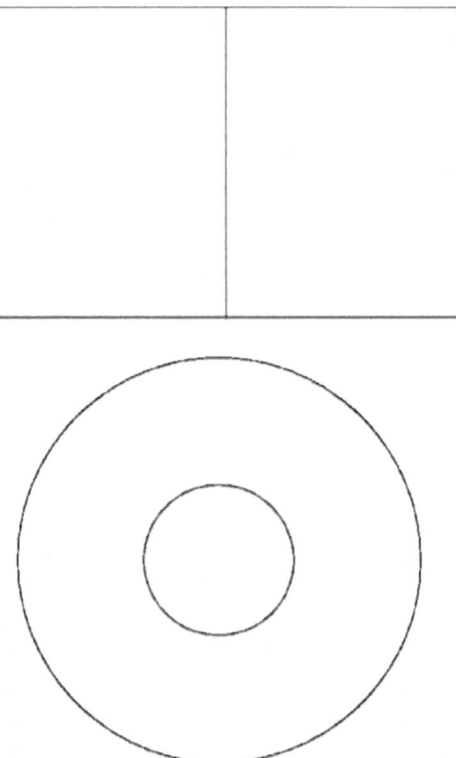

Figure 9.1 Diametric Dualism (top), Concentric Dualism (bottom)

unwittingly projected into texts, including Heidegger's seminal concepts. While these breath experiences may be experienced self-consciously, they need not be self-consciously experienced to operate as projected spaces.

Without needing to take on board the epistemological commitments of Claude Lévi-Strauss's structuralist reliance on linguistics for interpreting myths, his empiricism or all of his accounts of such contrasts, it is Lévi-Strauss' key explications of diametric and concentric structures of relation in myth, as well as in physical structures, across diverse cultures[19] that open a pivotal horizon of questioning pertaining to a spatial-phenomenology of Being. Lévi-Strauss apprehended this spatial horizon in rudimentary fashion, without addressing its ramifications for wider domains such as phenomenology. Diametric and concentric spaces can be understood as mutually interacting spatial projections. This must not, however, be reducible to the anthropocentrism of "an existentially a priori anthropology";[20] these spaces are wider than merely subjectivist anthropocentric projections.

Space is to be examined as an interactive tension between diametric and concentric structures. A purportedly key distinguishing feature of concentric and diametric structures, observed by Lévi-Strauss, is that they tend to coexist in "functional relation."[21] Lévi-Strauss recognizes that they are fundamentally interlinked, so that an increase in one is compensated by decrease in the other. Meaning is in their relative differences, rather than in either space considered in isolated, absolute, or atomistic terms. Three geometric contrasts will be identified between concentric and diametric spaces regarding connection/separation, symmetry, and relative openness/closure.

Concentric and diametric space cannot be treated simply as absolute positions, as merely positional states, if they are to be fundamental for a Heideggerian questioning. A relative and directional component to both spaces is required. Extracting Being from one tethered to categorial assumptions, including mere assertion, in *Basic Problems*, Heidegger continues his task of disentangling a conception of existence from Kant, to challenge a Kantian view of existence as absolute position: "the Kantian explication of the concept of being or the concept of existence: being equals position, existence equals absolute position."[22] This is an interpretation of Being and existence in spatial terms, if only to challenge space as positionality for Being.

Concentric and diametric spaces are not mere categories but rather a *relation*, in relational directional tension. Despite subsequent emphasis on the open, on *aletheia* as disclosure in what is tantamount to a spatial excavation of Being, in *Basic Problems*. Heidegger not only relies on temporality rather than spatiality as central to the question of Being he also directly retreats from a spatial questioning. This essay not only questions this spatial retreat but treats it as a point of departure for a prior questioning.

Concentric space is not Being proposed as an abstract, non-sensory mode of experience, but as an accelerated expansion of the sensory through experience of the breath. This spatial-phenomenological questioning is a phenomenology *through* space and not simply *of* space. This phenomenological concern with the holy is not to reduce the holy to mere subjectivism or simply to Dasein. Moreover, concentric space is not Being simply equated with the holy, it is an experiential condition and spatial projection to open to the holy, in a structural affinity with the holy.

The current predominant focus is on a *projected spatial structure* of the holy, rather than primarily on accounts of lived experience of the holy as experiential *content*. Early Heidegger's emphasis on restructuring of time in his reinterpretation of St. Paul's understanding of the *parousia* as arrival beyond a simple event in linear historical time[23] offers some affinity with restructuring of experience in space. The current emphasis on space for phenomenology and the holy is not to impose a diametric splitting from temporal considerations.

Referring additionally to other texts of Heidegger, this essay takes *Basic Problems* and to a lesser degree *Being and Time* as its main points of departure, while recognizing that the holy is more obviously central to much earlier and later writings of Heidegger. The focus on a spatial-phenomenology of the holy implicit in early Heidegger examines the unthought in his work, and despite some strong affinities with some key aspects of the later Heidegger on the holy, it also requires differentiation from the later Heidegger's accounts of the holy specifically with regard to both the festive and the fatherland in Hölderlin's hymn "Remembrance."[24]

While this essay will mainly focus on structural dimensions as projections of concentric and diametric space, a preliminary account of concentric space as lived experiential content can be outlined. The holy as concentric space can be understood as an experiential attunement. In the words of Heidegger in *The Fundamental Concepts of Metaphysics*, "Attunements are not side-effects but are something which in advance determine our being with one another . . . It seems as though an attunement is . . . like an atmosphere in which we first immerse ourselves . . . which then attunes us through and through."[25] This spatial atmosphere for attunement with the holy, as a more open expansive de-compressed space for attunement to the breath in concentric structured spatial-relational experience, can contrast with the compressed closure of the sealed space of diametric opposition. It is notable that Henning Nörenberg's interpretation of Rudolf Otto's numinous qualities in terms of "atmospheric quality,"[26] including an atmosphere that "condenses,"[27] implies a spatially relevant dimension to the holy in experiential content terms.

The open expansive movement of concentric space as a dimension of experience and breath offers affinity with Jean-Louis Chrétien's concerns with spacious joy in mystical and poetic traditions, specifically with his foregrounding of a spatial expansion in experience as dilation. Chrétien describes a "radiant"[28] circular movement "spreading out in waves and circles,"[29] as "heavenly liqueur,"[30] citing Paul Claudel's "liquid breathing."[31] Carl Jung's constellation of concentric mandala structures spontaneously emerging in the crisis of individuation offers another resonance with concentric space.

II. RETRIEVING THE HOLY FROM A COVERING UP THROUGH DIAMETRIC SPACE AS *GEGENSTAND*, AS STANDING AGAINST, STANDING OPPOSITE, SIDE-BY-SIDE

Heidegger's categories as a dimension of Dasein are envisaged by him as prior to Kant's categories of nature as quantity, quality, relation, and modality, which he notes were treated by Kant in *Critique of Pure Reason* as the sole categories and as distinct from the ego. Heidegger highlights that these categories informed the metaphysical tradition's account of four basic determinations of the soul, in terms of substance, simplicity, selfsameness, and existence. These treated the soul as immaterial, imperishable, persisting, and existing in reciprocity with a body. These "determinations of spirituality, in the concept of spirituality"[32] in metaphysical psychology are to be distinguished from Heidegger's concerns with the holy.

Heidegger seeks a prior realm not simply to the Kantian categories but also to the Kantian ego. Whereas Heidegger locates this realm in temporality, as distinct from the natural time of sensibility of Kant, a conception of structured categories prior to these Kantian categories can be understood in terms of space, though in a more dynamic sense than categories *per se*. Heidegger's quest for a more fundamental truth and experience can be construed here as opening a pathway to the holy that is not sidetracked down metaphysical alleyways of spirit and soul as metaphysical categories absorbed by Kant.

A key consequence of the relative differences between concentric and diametric space needs to be established to interrogate spatiality in *Basic Problems*. A claim is not being made that entailments of the relational differences between concentric and diametric spaces are qualities that are in some way essential or intrinsic to either structure, considered as mere categories, or as individual isolated structures, abstracted from the context of their mutual relation. A key relative difference, overlooked by Lévi-Strauss' empiricism, is nevertheless ascertainable in principle. It is evident that inner and outer poles of concentric space are fundamentally attached to one another, unlike in diametric space. It is a self-evident entailment of concentric relation that both concentric poles coexist in the same space—a co-center—and thus, the outer circle overlaps the space of the inner one; the outer circle surrounds and contains the inner circle. The opposite that is within the outer circle cannot detach itself from Being within this outer shape. That the outer circle can move in the direction of greater detachment from the inner circle notwithstanding, it cannot, in principle, fully detach itself from the inner circle in concentric relation (even if the inner circle becomes an increasingly smaller proportion of the outer). Full detachment could conceivably occur only through destroying the very concentric structure of the whole opposition itself.

The inner concentric circle is *prima facie* interpretable as a mode of "being in" the outer and, for Heidegger of *Being and Time*, "Being-in is not a 'property' which Dasein sometimes has and sometimes does not have";[33] it is a fundamental feature of Dasein's existence. Concentric space offers a relation that allows for distinction between an inner and outer pole, while retaining an underlying connection.

In contradistinction, in diametric space, no pole is *in* the other; both oppositional realms are basically detached and can be further smoothly detached from the other. These conclusions operate for both spaces, whether two or three dimensional. A concentric space assumes connection between its parts, and any separation is on the basis of assumed connection, whereas diametric space assumes separation, and any connection between the parts is on the basis of this assumed separation. In Bachelard's words, pertinent to diametric space, "simple geometrical opposition becomes tinged with aggressivity."[34] This is not a predilection for geometrical or mathematical models in general, rather, it is for this specific spatial tension based on geometric contrasts meaningful also for experience and as will be argued, built into the assumption structure of core dimensions of Heidegger's thought.

Concentric and diametric spaces are being examined as fundamental directions of movement rather than as simply static structures. Likewise, Heidegger seeks a dimension of directionality to space, while attributing this to view Aristotle, "We must not take the places as a pure juxtaposition of the there and here. Instead we must take this there as 'away from there' and this here as 'toward here.'"[35] Juxtaposition here is diametric spatial opposition of poles juxtaposed into static here/there opposites bereft of the dynamism of movement.

Heidegger not only links projection to the inauthentic but also to the realm of *things*:

"as though the Dasein's can-be were projected by the things, by the Dasein's commerce with them . . . This inauthentic self-understanding by way of things."[36] Thus, we "lose ourselves in and with" things;[37] this can be understood as part of a loss of the holy in an inauthentic projection. Yet further scrutiny of this loss as an inauthentic projection[38] uncovers a specific mode of relation as *diametric opposition*:

> by this characterisation of beings as objects, and in that sense as entities that stand over *against* [*Gegenstände*], I no longer have as a problem the being in its own self in regard to the peculiar mode of being belonging to it.[39]

The realm of objectness is a standing against, as in the German word for object, *Gegenstand*, "but instead the being *as standing-opposite, as standing-over-against*"; diametric space underpins this opposition as "an object . . . counterposed to the subject."[40] Heidegger does not take the further step of interpreting this spatially imbued oppositional standing against, this counterpositioning, as being a concrete spatial structure of diametric opposition. Heidegger reiterates his stance of *Being and Time*, when stating in *Basic Problems*, "Authenticity is only a modification but not a total obliteration of inauthenticity."[41] This opens the door to examination of diametric space as a space for modification and restructuring to concentric space, in the turning shift between these interacting spatial poles. It invites a phenomenological shift *to the spaces themselves*, from a Husserlian concern with *the things themselves.*

This diametric spatial *standing against* is built into the mode of perceiving an object, "But does an object require a subject ? Of course. For something standing-over-against always stands-over-against for a perceiver. Certainly."[42] This diametric structure of relation is also a spatial precondition for self-consciousness, as object of self-perception and for intentionality, which requires an object. Heidegger's assault in *Basic Problems* is on "an extreme version" of Descartes' and Kant's thought in German Idealism's (Fichte, Schelling, Hegel) concern with self-consciousness.[43] A spatial concomitant of this assault is the silent condition of diametric space, as the standing-against needed for self-consciousness.

If holiness is associated with a primary mode of self-disclosure of Being, it must be untethered from self-consciousness for Heidegger. As a spatial projection, the holy is not spirit as self-consciousness, "Since projection unveils without making what is unveiled as such into an object of contemplation."[44] The self is not its own object of contemplation in the unveiling projection. Yet a further step must be taken, namely, to *reconstruct* a way of being from one based on diametric spatial relation—a different space is needed for the holy. A concentric spatial-relational way of being challenges the assumed separation of a diametric spatial way of being founding self-consciousness. Diametric space is a distanciation and leveling down of experience flattening away the possibility for concentric space of experiential attunement for the holy.

Another feature of diametric space pertinent to Heidegger's understanding of space is *side-by-sideness.* Spatiality of being-in-the-world is expressly linked in Division One, III, 21c of *Being and Time* with the earlier discussions of being-in and the two modes of "categories" and "existentialia." Heidegger challenges the primacy of "side-by-sideness" or the separation built into two entities as categories in order for them to be "side-by-side." He overcomes a diametric relation between Dasein, Being, and "world" in his description of "being-alongside" the world, "There is no such thing as the 'side-by-sideness' of an entity called 'Dasein' with another entity called 'world'."[45] Both diametric spatial poles exist side-by-side each other in assumed separation, as parallel silos, rather than as a mutual overlapping of encountering.

Heidegger explicitly equates the "touch" of encountering with the mode of being-alongside.[46] For Heidegger, entities such as a table, chair cannot even potentially be encounterable. Relations between solid objects in space are diametric, as there is a basic assumed separation between each object as an object. Both objects exclude each other from occupying the same space. This assumed separation means they are not "encounterable"; encountering overcomes the remoteness of assumed separation. Concentric space expresses a "being-alongside" model of relatedness, where one pole dwells within and alongside the other, surrounded and in assumed connection.

In its entwinement with Being, the holy is not a mere category or positional state, but a prior mode that disinters the stasis in the categorial and positional. This proposed transition to concentric space and from diametric space is as a way of being in dynamic relative interaction rather than treating the holy or concentric space as frozen abstract categories in absolute spatial terms. Concentric space is not reinstantiation of a category for the holy, it is a spatial movement, a directional process of expanse beyond the merely categorial, so it is not tantamount to a static labeling of a person as holy.

III. STRETCH, CONTINUITY, TRANSITION, AND THE OPEN AS CONCENTRIC SPACE: THE EXCISION OF A CONNECTIVE SPACE FROM TEMPORALITY IN *BASIC PROBLEMS*

Heidegger tussles with space throughout *Basic Problems* through his pervasive reliance on spatially imbued concepts of unveiling and projection in this work. This tussle becomes an overt struggle with space in his attempted revival and development of Aristotle's "initial"[47] understandings of time that he builds from to accelerate a radical split from space. This overt argument to split space from time is, however, itself sustained through invoking spatially imbued concepts of stretch, transition, continuity, and open expanse to describe temporality. Heidegger thus invokes a "peculiar" domain for time that is purported to be firmly nonspatial.

In *Basic Problems*, temporality, light, being, projection, transcendence, purity, being-true, nature, poetry, world, motion, possibility, cognition, intentionality, and perception are all pivoted on a quasispatial axis of unveiling. Disclosedness and uncovering are also features of unveiling, while assertion is not. Yet in *Basic Problems,* this is treated as a peculiar nonspatial phenomenon. This excision of space from temporality in *Basic Problems* is in stark contrast with Heidegger's mutual entwinement of space and temporality in *Being and Time* where "the ontological meaning of 'care' is temporality"[48] and "Dasein can be spatial only as care,"[49] with care a key component of "the *temporalization-structure* of temporality" (italics in original).[50] Beyond a cursory mention,[51] care is nowhere to be seen in *Basic Problems*, in striking contrast to *Being and Time*. *Basic Problems* also lies in tension with the later Heidegger's recognition of "time-space"[52] as a mutually coalescing relation between space and time. In *Basic Problems*, Aristotle's time is a pathway, however initial, toward this "more original"[53] temporal questioning, as an expansion, building from rather than rejecting Aristotle.[54]

Assailing Bergson's interpretation of Aristotle's time in terms of space, Heidegger in *Basic Problems* views Aristotle's *Physics* as linking time with motion and not space. Bergson was "misled" as:

> he took continuity in the narrower sense of the extensional magnitude of space. Aristotle does not reduce time to space nor does he define it merely with the aid of space, as though some spatial determination entered into the definition of time. He only wants to show that and how time is something connected with motion.[55]

Commenting on Aristotle's dimensional character *megethos,* Heidegger states:

> This determination *megethos*, extension or magnitude, also *does not have a primarily spatial character*, but that of stretch. There is no break implied in the concept and essential nature of 'from something to something;' it is, instead, a stretching out that is closed within itself.[56]

Space is only conceived here *in diametric spatial terms of assumed separation as "break,"* as interval, rupture, whereas the stretching expansion of assumed connection is explicitly demarcated as a realm that is *not* spatial.

Stretch is a key concept for Heidegger's temporality, "A stretchedness which enters into expressed time is already originally present in the ecstatic character of temporality," being equated with it, "temporality qua ecstatic is stretched out within its own self. As the primary outside-itself, temporality is stretch itself."[57] The connective space lost to Aristotle's space as break regarding time is reconfigured into stretch to convey a connective concept of movement. This is argued for current purposes to be a concentric spatial movement, though the Heidegger of *Basic Problems* adopts a retreat from space into a supposedly connective *non*-spatial movement.

Stretch as a directional movement process is embedded with continuity, a continuous movement, "this continuity itself" as "stretching out (extension)."[58] The assumed connection of continuity of concentric spatial movement is allocated to a non-primarily spatial realm *on the assumption that space's key feature here is rupture as "break," in other words, that diametric space is the primary feature of space*. An underspecified conception of "dimension" is invoked for stretch and its related term, transition, "The now is not correlated as a point to a fixed point . . . It has dimension within itself; it stretches out toward a not-yet and a no-longer," and because of this *dimensional content* the *now* has within itself the *character of a transition*."[59] The term dimensional content has vitiated any role for space. Heidegger continues, "It is intrinsically transition. Because it has this peculiar stretching out within itself, we can conceive of the stretch as being greater or less."[60] Stretch is characterized as "peculiar" as it is purportedly nonspatial. Heidegger's rejection of space within time imports this quasi-spatial vocabulary of stretch, continuity, and transition against a backdrop of a "peculiar" "dimension."

In *Basic Problems*, Heidegger offers further conceptualization in implicitly concentric spatial terms, "Given that time embraces beings, it is required that it should be before beings, before things, moving and at rest, encompassing them. Kant calls time the 'wherein of an order.' It is an embracing horizon within which things given can be ordered with respect to their succession."[61] These are all also apt descriptions—*embracing, encompassing, an embracing horizon*—of concentric space of assumed connection between its poles.

Echoing Aristotle's view, for the Heidegger of *Basic Problems*, "geometrical relationships and their contents are extra-temporal, because they are not in motion and consequently are not at rest. A triangle is not at rest because it does not move. It is beyond rest and motion, and therefore in Aristotle's view, it is neither embraced nor embraceable by time."[62] Heidegger's objection to space as pertaining to temporality is through invocation of a geometrical truth, as a timeless ahistorical state, as mere mathematical rationalism. However, a geometric space is available that is not mere abstraction, not mere non-sensuous stasis and not one as absolute position; it is a geometric space embedded in experience, as a relational space, a space in dynamic interaction, as a directional movement. This concentric geometric space encompasses a dynamic connective quality characterizing Heidegger's descriptions of stretch, continuity, and transition, while a diametric geometric space as assumed separation offers a concrete structure of "break" and juxtaposition.

Heidegger seeks movement and continuity as well as a boundedness (closedness) to this movement for time, purportedly excised from space. Heidegger's solution of a "peculiar" spatiality that is purportedly a non-spatial "dimension" to avoid geometric connotations of a Western metaphysics as timeless abstraction risks going too far here in rejecting space *in toto* for temporality and not merely diametric spatial models. "Peculiar" non-spatial yet spatially imbued concepts risk importing a metaphysical abstraction and "beyond" for this connective quasi-spatial "dimension" in *Basic Problems*; it risks flight into metaphor with all of its metaphysical baggage of the *meta*.[63] It evades realization that his fundamental concepts are thoroughly saturated anyway with geometric spatial assumptions and language.

An obvious reference point for a conception of the holy specifically in *Basic Problems* is Heidegger's *instant*, as a primary original authentic dimension, "the instant belongs to the Dasein's original and authentic temporality and represents the primary and authentic mode of the present as enpresenting."[64] Any entwinement of the holy in the instant must interrogate projection, as the instant is embedded in this projective movement of enpresenting, "*enpresenting,* whether authentic in the sense of the instant or inauthentic, *projects that which it enpresents.*"⁶⁵ The instant is associated with authenticity, whereas projection pertains to both authenticity and inauthenticity. This interrogation of the instant invokes *spatial assumptions of closure*, additional to those of belonging:

> The present pertinent to the Dasein's temporality does not constantly have the character of the instant. The Dasein does not constantly exist as resolute but is usually irresolute, *closed off to itself* in its own most peculiar ability to be . . .⁶⁶ (my italics)

"Peculiar" here refers to a purportedly non-spatial dimension.

This issue of relative closure and openness pertains to a key entailment of the differences between concentric and diametric spaces, identified by Lévi-Strauss, regarding foreground–background interaction versus non-interaction. Lévi-Strauss argues that self-sufficiency and a split relation to the outside environment is a general quality of diametric systems:

> In a diametric system . . . virgin land constitutes an irrelevant element; the moieties are defined by their opposition to each other, and the apparent symmetry of their closed structure creates the illusion of a closed system.⁶⁷

Lévi-Strauss rejects closure for *concentric* structures, by implying that the relation of the *background* to both poles of the dualism is governed by the relation *within* the dualism itself, "cleared land is to waste land as waste land is to [background] virgin land."⁶⁸ Thus, as the concentric poles are in assumed connection to each other, they are also in assumed connection to the background; this assumed connection to background resists closure within the concentric structure. In contrast, diametric structures' relation within their own poles is one of assumed separation that maintains an assumed separation of minimal interaction with background.

The holy exists as the instant, closed off as diametric space and to be opened to concentric spatial movement. This concentric space is not merely unbounded openness but a dynamically structured one. Preoccupation with the open expanse, as an open region and movement, is a pervasive feature of the later Heidegger's thought. This is a theme also in *Basic Problems*, with Heidegger referring to "a peculiar openness . . . the horizon is the *open expanse* . . . The *carrying-off opens up this horizon and keeps it open.*"⁶⁹ Again this ineluctably spatial concept of openness is displaced from a spatial understanding as it is characterized as "peculiar." Nevertheless, this "peculiar" feature of the open as expanse is a *directional* feature of concentric spatial *movement*, with the open *region* as a more *positional* concentric spatial dimension.

With stretch, continuity, transition, and open expanse, Heidegger offers a space that is not a space, but rather a "peculiar" mode pertaining to time that is purportedly non-spatial. A more parsimonious explanation is that these are spatial phenomena but in a different nontraditional sense of space, akin to Heidegger's treatment of illumination and light that is to be distinct from a Platonic tradition. Each of these dimensions are not pieces arbitrarily stuck together, rather these dimensions of connective space (stretch, transition, continuity), the open, open expanse as movement, concealment and unconcealment, all cluster together not only in general spatial terms but in specific spatial terms, as an oscillation between concentric and diametric spaces. This clustering of a space-structure of concentric space and concentric spatial movement is a key phenomenological condition for experience of the holy.

A variant of the entailment of relative closure for diametric structures is that they bring decreased permeability (transparency) relative to the increased permeability (transparency) of concentric structures. The more fluid, open boundaries of concentric space are more permeable and transparent than the hard-walled boundaries of diametric space. Relative to concentric structures, diametric space provides an increased, tightened closed boundary between two domains, as diametric structures sever active interaction between its two parts.

The closed boundaries of diametric space offer an implication for consideration of the holy in terms of a radiance of light. Diametric boundaries close off a space to be permeable through light, whereas the more open concentric spaces offer a permeability for light. Diametric space's *thick partition* of boundaries renders experience opaque to light; concentric space opens up walls from the center of diametric space, to create an open axial point of symmetry, a clearing, a translucent center for permeability through a radiance of light.

These features of lack of permeability and opacity in the boundaries of diametric spatial closure and of relative transparency in the more fluid boundaries of concentric spatial openness are pertinent to a Heideggerian thematic of the holy in terms of light. Heidegger in *Basic Problems* refers to unveiling a hidden light as pertaining to Being, "The eye can unveil only in the light. All unveiling requires an antecedent illuminating," referring to "Being's *specific illumination*,"[70] with "the function of light, of illumination, for all unveiling of beings."[71] This offers some resonance along with Richard Capobianco's emphasis in the later Heidegger on the "distinctive ... *gleaming, glistening, glimmering, glittering, glowing*" connotations for Nature in Hölderlin's exploration of *"Das Glänzen der Natur"* as a *"higher revealing"* in the opening line of his late poem "Autumn."[72]

The Open as a direction is in direct contrast with the compression and closure of diametric space as a directional movement. A fundamental shift in the center of the opposition occurs in the movement open from diametric to concentric space; the diametric spatial center is a wall, a veil, a dividing boundary between the poles, whereas the common center (co-center) of concentric poles is fundamentally open and transparent as a clearing. The instant is opened away from diametric space through movement of the concentric space-structure.

Capobianco contrasts the theme of light (*lux*) in the early Heidegger with the later Heidegger's emphasis on the "spatial" in discussing *die Lichtung*, "the clearing." Capobianco suggests that this is due to a concern of the later Heidegger to distance his *Lichtung* concerns from a Platonic metaphysical tradition of light, as well as to express one that does not oppose light and darkness, with *aletheia* as "both light and darkness in the clearing."[73] In other words, Heidegger sought a prior relation of light to darkness than one of a diametric spatial opposition. Moreover, Heidegger's earlier concern with light was not simply a perceptual one but is prior to perception in the unfolding of Being as *aletheia*.

The entailment of relative openness of concentric space is primarily a spatial concern with a movement of clearing open; a concomitant of this relative openness is more porous, permeable boundaries with background compared with diametric structured spatial closure to background. Such permeable boundaries in concentric space pertain also to light, so a duality of an opening clearing and light permeation can coexist in a concentric spatial movement. The openness through which light illuminates is one modality of the relative openness of concentric space. The luminous and the open as clearing are mutually entwined in the concentric spatial movement.

As Capobianco observes, the later Heidegger often prefers reading *Lichtung* in terms of "to raise the anchor," that is, "to unburden . . . to lift"[74] rather than in terms of *lux*, light; and, in my view, this is also a correlate of a process of compression into a tightening, an increasing density in a closure process of diametric spatialization. This is the counterweighing down, the gravity, pressing into closure against the open expanse of concentric spatial movement. A thicker partition of diametric space as a process of concealment integrates concepts of closure, loss of permeability, such as for light, and tightened density as an anchor weighing down the expansive. The concept of attunement as "atmosphere in which we immerse ourselves . . . through and through,"[75] directly linked by Heidegger to being "concealed or hidden,"[76] is apt not only for concentric and diametric space but also for *integrating space, light, and lightness* as expansion contrasted with *blockage of light through compression as a heaviness of atmosphere.*

Capobianco highlights how Heidegger seeks a conception of a spatial Clearing (*Lichtung*) that is different from Plato's metaphysical trope of light. Likewise, a space and geometry is needed that is different from the traditional. Heidegger needs to offer a similar strategic response to space as he does for light, to excise it from traditional associations with Platonism and geometry, respectively, in order to open a different realm for both. These relative differences between concentric and diametric spaces bring geometry into a realm of time, motion, and movement "peopled by spaces too bright to see," to adapt Shelley in *Prometheus Unbound*.

IV. RETRIEVING A PRIOR SPATIAL REALM OF BEING AND THE HOLY FROM THE DIAMETRIC SPATIAL MIRROR IMAGE INVERSION OF THE SENSUOUS AND NON-SENSUOUS REALM UNDERPINNING THE BEYOND OF METAPHYSICS

The holy needs to be retrieved for Heidegger from a Western metaphysical tradition that glosses over originary experience and flattens understandings of truth. Allied with interrogation of projection as a different movement to that of cause-effect, where the latter is characterized by Heidegger as a "guiding thread" in the "dominance" of metaphysics,[77] the focus for current purposes is on a spatial precondition underpinning a central concern of Heidegger regarding the above/below metaphysical structure of the beyond in relation to the sensuous and supersensuous. This spatial precondition for the metaphysical can be uncovered as the mirror image inverted symmetry of diametric space.

Lévi-Strauss describes "symmetrical inversions"[78] in Mandan and Hidatsa myths and develops a view of diametric structural opposition as expressing qualities of inverted symmetry more generally. A mirror image is not an identical one but a left–right inversion. This diametric spatial process of inversion is pertinent to Heidegger's questioning of the metaphysical realm of the sensuous/non-sensuous inversion.

For Heidegger's commentary on Heraclitus' fragments 45 and 50, the sensible/not-sensible distinction is "the differentiation upon which all metaphysics is based."[79] Heidegger in *Fundamental Concepts of Metaphysics* treats traditional conceptions of metaphysics as "confused," "trivialized," and "unconcerned about the real problem of that which it is supposed to designate."[80] This confusion is between two "fundamentally different"[81] conceptions of the beyond, identified by Heidegger, the supra-sensuous and the non-sensuous. The non-sensuous determinations, such as "something, unity, otherness, differentiation" and "multiplicity," are ones which "lie out beyond every individual thing" and yet are "entirely different from God's lying beyond" in the realm of the supra-sensuous.[82] For Heidegger, from Aristotle and Aquinas onward, the metaphysical tradition offers "no mention of at all of any distinction or of any problem persisting between the supra-sensuous and unsensuous ['not accessible to the senses'] in their mutual and contrasting relation to the sensuous."[83]

Heidegger's subsequent reading of Nietzsche goes further with specific structural objections:

> A path must be cleared for a new interpretation of the sensuous on the basis of a new hierarchy of the sensuous and non-sensuous. The new hierarchy does not simply wish to reverse matters within the old structural order, now reverencing the sensuous and scorning the non-sensuous.[84]

Reversing relationships within a diametric opposition still rests within the same structure. Heidegger's vital point here is on the need to shift the very structure underlying the sensuous-non-sensuous diametric opposition, "A new hierarchy and new valuation mean that the ordering *structure* must be changed" (italics in original).[85] Heidegger needed to go further to recognize that this change in the ordering assumption structure is a *spatial questioning*. Diametric opposition is not only a projected *structure*, it is also a *space*.

Heidegger continues, "But what does that mean—the sensuous stands above all ? . . . But as long as the 'above and below' define the formal structure of Platonism, Platonism in its essence perdures," "the vacant niches of the 'above and below' are preserved, suffering only a change in occupancy."[86] However, the above and below are not vacant in another sense, as a relation of diametric space. *It is the diametric space that needs overcoming to offer a direct challenge to Platonic metaphysics.* While diametric spatial structures of inverted mirror image symmetry sustain key metaphysical divisions for a "beyond," it is the diametric spatial processes as movements that actively contribute to the glossing over and concealment of a more primordial truth of Being pertaining also to the holy.

Concern for current purposes is with a spatial mode of experience prior to the sensory, projected into language and thought, that does not seek to escape into the *meta*, that is, beyond, of the metaphysical; it is for a spatial mode of experience that shifts the diametric mirror image split spatial structure from being a supporting precondition underpinning the above/below hierarchy of the *meta*. Concentric space offers this different embedded spatial mode of relation modifying diametric spatial inversions.

To adapt Heidegger's words, a "concealed fundamental attunement"[87] is being sought, namely a concealed attunement of the breath to be awoken as an expansion and opening into concentric structured spatial experience;[88] the concealing process of diametric spatial movement also requires uncovering. The holy as lived experiential content is an expanded breath space, a "fluidating" of the breath in the body, bringing a spatial reconstruction of the breath–body, suprasensory–sensory relation into a concentric relation of breath within the body, in contrast to a split diametric spatial relation between a closed off breath displaced from body.

Capobianco points out that "breath" and "breathing in and out" is an overlooked theme in Heidegger, and that this theme plays a "prominent role"[89] in his 1944 lecture course on the primordial *Logos* of Heraclitus. Capobianco observes that Heidegger employs both the terms *der Atem* and the more poetic *der Hauch* to name breath, while Heidegger explicitly distinguishes this from simply air; "but he [Heidegger] does not clarify the broader, richer sense of 'breath' that he is suggesting,"[90] beyond a reaching out into the Open and bringing back from the Open.

It is further significant that Heidegger's discussion of Heraclitus' fragments 45 and 50 explores "the breath of life":

> Why is it that we consider both 'breath' and 'light' as having the same relation to the fundamental characteristics of the living thing? Light is the lightening— it is that which lightens and opens, and which as the bright, holds open. Breath grasped broadly and properly enough as not being limited to air, is the drawing-in and drawing-out, the emerging into the open and the pulling back in of the open . . . if we think of air as ether, then 'air' and 'light' coincide.[91]

Breath, breathing, light, lightening, and the open are intimately related for Heidegger. The further step is to incorporate not only space but concentric spatial movement.

A concentric relation of the breath as an inner circle within the outer circle of the body assumes a basic connection. It involves awareness of the breath in the body. A diametric relation of the breath to the body splits awareness of breathing, as a basic experience. Meditation, as an emptying of the self-conscious mind, invites a more intense awareness of the breathing process. This emphasis on breathing challenges a view of spirit as mind and reclaims the association between spirit and breath in a range of cultures. Spirit, as mind or intellect, contrasts with, for example, the Latin etymology of *spiritus* as breath and the Hebrew etymology of *ruach* uniting spirit and wind. This offers direct resonance with Hölderlin's "heaven's breezes" in his poem, *Contentment*, cited and discussed by Capobianco.[92]

It is notable also that the later Heidegger associates transition and breezes, "simple transitions relating to the while, transitions that are not present at hand in some empty vacuum, for over them draw lulling breezes,"[93] which as seen, is resonant with transition as a concentric spatial movement. These roots between breath, wind, and spirit are largely lost to an English association of spirit as mind and a German, or at least Hegelian, treatment of spirit as *Geist* or self-consciousness. Nevertheless, association between spirit and breath is implicit in English terms such as respiration.

Spirit as breath is still evident in, for example, Finno-Ugric languages. For example, spirit in Finnish is *henki* (breath) and spiritual (*hengillinen*) literally means breathful. Similarly, in Estonian, *hing* (spirit) is expressed through *hingama* (to breathe) and *hingeohk* (breath). In Russian, *Duch* means spirit, *Dusha* means soul, both of which have clear associations with *Dychanie* (breath) and *Dyshat* (to breathe). Jung notes that in the East "the psyche is . . . all important; it is all-pervading Breath, the Buddha-essence."[94] The mandala can be interpreted as a circular space opened in the structure of the heart for the awareness of the flow of the breath. A compressed circle, in other words, a line, expresses the closure of a space giving awareness of the breath flow.

Moving from diametric to concentric space as an unveiling process, a clearing of the membrane of differentiation in diametric space to the open center of concentric space emerges; the point of symmetry of concentric space is open at the co-center, whereas in diametric space it is a wall as the axis of symmetry. Heidegger's brief remarks of thanks for being awarded the Hebel Prize to celebrate the poet's 200th birthday, held in Wiesental, May 20, 1960, translated and commented on by Capobianco,[95] are as follows:

> Every being 'has a secret door' [*het e geheimi Tür*] into the mystery, through which Being comes forth and shines forth towards us. The calling of the poet is: to point to this 'secret door' in all things or even to guide us through it.[96]

Turning from line to circle is the opening of a secret door, a secret door of concentric structured space in the opening of the walls of diametric spatial boundaries. This opened door becomes the tunnel for the breath, the light of the breath. Heidegger's door is the lost circle opened and closed in its turning at right angles toward a line;[97] a line is a circle bereft of air, with its space dispelled and displaced. The walled center in diametric space expresses this line, for turning open into the clearing of the concentric spatial center, one without walls to allow permeability of light through the circle.

The closing off of diametric space is both a structure and content of experience, as with the closure of a forgetting that forgets itself, in Heidegger's *Basic Problems*, "Forgetting, in closing off the past . . . closes itself off for itself. The characteristic of forgetting is that it forgets itself."[98] This is a self-referential bringing together of foreground and background levels, structure, and content.

A similar process needs to be envisaged for the holy as a concentric space of illumination in relation to a concentric space of experience in authenticity. One concentric space as a structure houses the other concentric space as a content of experience, as radiance. Heidegger's commentary on Heraclitus' fragments 64 and 66 on fire and flame describes "the conjoined boundaries of its form" and "The instantaneity of enflaming."[99] This invokes not only concentric structured imagery of living fire, including a structural issue of *conjoined* concentric relations, but also relates this to a focus on the instant. Radiance of a fire or flame is a concentric spatial movement, a ripple effect through space. The radiance of the holy is immersed in the concentric space as a structure, a housing dwelling structure, *and is itself a concentric space as content*. In the concentric dwelling space of the authentic, a space is opened for the dwelling of a concentric light space, as a space within a space, in concentric terms as an expansive movement. The holy fuses structure and content into an assumed connection in experience, through the mediating mode of concentric space, so this space is not sheer mediation but also exhibits the common concentric structure in both structure and content of experience.

Space relates fundamentally to the pre-sensory, as a precondition for the sensory. Space can also be understood actively as an inner concentric dimension, within which senses are embedded, as an inner connective precondition. Without the medium of space, sound cannot be heard; without space to move through, the resistance of touch cannot be experienced. Such a concentric spatial mode of experience, prior to the sensory, can be located in the breath, as part of a shift from a mind–body (non-sensory–sensory) opposition to a breath–body opposition. This pre-sensuous mode of experience is not non-sensuous; concentric spatial relations can be projected also into and through the senses.

A self-referential questioning of concentric and diametric spaces asks, is there a *background relation itself* to concentric and diametric spaces? The questioning of Being at this level is as to the concentric, directional dimension of connection *between* concentric and diametric spaces rather than a diametric spatial split of non-Being governing the relations between foreground concentric and diametric spaces. As William J. Richardson highlights, it is a *question* of Being: "It is only when we comprehend the horizon of transcendence as both the unifying dynamism of sheer presence and as non-being that we understand it properly."[100] Both Richardson and this self-referential questioning of the background relation to concentric and diametric spaces accommodate this background as both a unified structure *and* possible non-unity. It is not a bias of presence toward a necessary synthesis. A neutral (or actively) non-interactive background space between diametric and concentric spaces *preserves a diametric relation between the two structures themselves*, whereas *a concentric background relation itself connects concentric and diametric spaces*. This shift in focus from Dasein to Being is a turn that is amenable to interpretation in terms of concentric and diametric spaces at both levels—at both the foreground level of Dasein's structures of Being and the background Being-level of the temporal interactive dynamic spatial relation itself between concentric and diametric spaces.

Foreground and background are relative terms; the foreground concentric and diametric spatial-phenomenological structures are themselves a background for the foreground content of lived experience of the holy. Three layers of concentric space have thus been uncovered as part of an expanding directional movement: (i) the background layer of Being mediating concentric and diametric spaces, (ii) concentric structures of Dasein's authenticity interacting with inauthentic diametric spaces, and (iii) lived experiential content as itself a concentric process. The holy is not a category (as diametric spatial side-by-sideness) but a living process emanating throughout these concentric spatial layers of Being.

The foreground concentric space of Dasein's authenticity is a receptacle for the background space of the holy that is itself also structured in concentric spatial terms. The concentric within the concentric as an expansive directional movement shapes the contours of the holy. This perspective eschews a form-content split in experience; the holy as a content of experience, as a shimmering light and radiance makes its way through the concentric structured space of authenticity.

Uncovering this hidden chamber of meaning for space and the holy in the assumption structure of Heidegger's texts, these multiple interlocking levels of concentric and diametric spaces are an interplay that takes place *both at and between* each level, as part of a fragile directional expansive movement toward embedded concentric spatial expansions. On this view, the holy is the concentric spatial directional movement at each of these levels in its tension with diametric spatial movements, as well as the concentric directional movement of expanse *between* all these levels—a vertical expanse. The holy is the concentric spatial directional animation as a vivifying principle to further "fluidate" the positional authentic concentric spatial structures as ways of being. The holy generates a series of expanding part–whole concentric spatial relations. The diametric spatial directional counter-movement of splitting, closure, and inversion at *and* between these various levels is the countervailing interactive process of concealment, assumed as a central principle across Heidegger's *oeuvre*.

NOTES

1. Martin Heidegger, *Being and Time*, trans. J. MacQuarrie and E. Robinson (Oxford: Basil Blackwell, 1927/1962). [BT]

2. Martin Heidegger, *The Basic Problems of Phenomenology*, trans. Albert Hofstadter (Bloomington & Indianapolis, IN: Indiana University Press, 1927/1988). [BPP]

3. BPP, 215.
4. BPP, 159.
5. Hans-Georg Gadamer, "The Idea of Hegel's Logic" in *G.W.F. Hegel: Critical Assessments*, Chapter 60, ed. Robert Stern (New York: Routledge, 1993), 221–42.
6. BPP, 159.
7. BPP, 168.
8. BPP, 284.
9. BPP, 286.
10. BPP, 22.
11. Paul Downes, *Concentric Space as a Life Principle Beyond Schopenhauer, Nietzsche and Ricoeur: Inclusion of the Other* (New York, London, and New Delhi: Routledge, 2020).
12. René Descartes, *Descartes: Philosophical Writings*, trans. E. Anscombe and P. T. Geach (London: Nelson, 1954), 200.
13. BPP, 21.
14. BT, 440.
15. BT, 488.
16. BT, 258–59.
17. BT, 259.
18. Jacques Derrida, *The Ear of the Other: Otobiography, Transference*, trans. and ed. C. V. MacDonald, trans. Peggy Kamuf (New York: Schocken Books, 1985); Derrida, *On Touching – Jean-Luc Nancy* (Stanford, CA: Stanford University Press, 2005).
19. Claude Lévi-Strauss, *Structural Anthropology*: Vol. 1, trans. C. Jacobsen and B. Grundfest Schoepf (Allen Lane: Penguin, 1963); *Structural Anthropology*: Vol. 2, trans. M. Layton (Allen Lane: Penguin Books, 1973/1977).
20. BT, 227.
21. Lévi-Strauss, *Structural Anthropology*: Vol. 2, 73.
22. BPP, 42.
23. See Ezra Delahaye "Re-enacting Paul: On the Theological Background of Heidegger's Philosophical Reading of the Letters of Paul," *International Journal of Philosophy and Theology* 74 (2013): 2–17.
24. Martin Heidegger, *Hölderlin's Hymn 'Remembrance'*, trans. William McNeill and Julia Ireland (Indiana: Indiana University Press, 2018), 110–12. [HHR]
25. Martin Heidegger, *The Fundamental Concepts of Metaphysics: World, Finitude, Solitude,* trans. William McNeill and Nicholas Walker (Bloomington and Indianapolis, IN: Indiana University Press, 1929/30), 67. [FCM]
26. Henning Nörenberg "The Numinous, the Ethical, and the Body: Rudolf Otto's "The Idea of the Holy" Revisited," *Open Theology* 3 (2017): 546–64, 551.
27. Nörenberg, 553.
28. Jean-Louis Chrétien, *Spacious Joy: An Essay in Phenomenology and Literature*, trans. Anne Ashley Davenport (New York: Rowman & Littlefield, 2019), 145. See also Paul Downes "Seeds of a Primordial Spatial Phenomenology: Chrétien's *Spacious Joy*," *Phenomenological Reviews* (2019).

29. Chrétien, *Spacious Joy,* 115.
30. Chrétien, *Spacious Joy,* 88.
31. Chrétien, *Spacious Joy,* 178.
32. BPP, 143.
33. BT, 84.
34. Gaston Bachelard, *The Poetics of Space* (Boston, MA: Beacon Press, 1964/1994), 212.
35. BPP, 245.
36. BPP, 289.
37. BPP, 290.
38. For a more detailed argument on concentric space as authentic structures of being and diametric space as inauthentic structures of being in BT, see Paul Downes *The Primordial Dance: Diametric and Concentric Spaces in the Unconscious World* (Oxford/Bern: Peter Lang, 2012).
39. BPP, 156.
40. BPP, 157.
41. BPP, 171.
42. BPP, 156.
43. BPP, 152–53.
44. BPP, 277.
45. BT, 81.
46. BT, 81–2.
47. BPP, 257.
48. BT, 416.
49. BT, 419.
50. BT, 381.
51. In BPP, 312.
52. HHR, 34, 153.
53. BPP, 260.
54. While Heidegger's original temporality embraces transition, he notes that "Aristotle assigns transitionary character to the now," BPP, 273. Likewise, "stretch" drawn from Aristotle is stated as "already originally present in the ecstatic character of temporality," BPP 270.
55. BPP, 244.
56. BPP, 242.
57. BPP, 270.
58. BPP, 243.
59. BPP, 248.
60. BPP, 249.
61. BPP, 252.
62. BPP, 253.
63. For an argument to situate concentric and diametric spaces as prior to metaphor, see Paul Downes "At the Threshold of Ricoeur's Concerns in *La Métaphore Vive*: A Spatial Discourse of Diametric and Concentric Structures of Relation Building on Lévi-Strauss," *Ricoeur Studies/Etudes Ricoeuriennes* 7 (2016): 146–63.

64. BPP, 288.
65. BPP, 306.
66. BPP, 288.
67. Lévi-Strauss, *Structural Anthropology*: Vol. 1, 152.
68. Lévi-Strauss, *Structural Anthropology*: Vol. 1, 152.
69. BPP, 267.
70. BPP, 283.
71. BPP, 284.
72. Richard Capobianco, *Heidegger's Way of Being* (Toronto: University of Toronto Press, 2014), 29.
73. Capobianco, *Engaging Heidegger,* 100.
74. Capobianco, *Engaging Heidegger,* 102.
75. FCM, 67.
76. FCM, 68.
77. HHR, 88.
78. Lévi-Strauss, *Structural Anthropology*: Vol. 2, 247.
79. Martin Heidegger, *Heraclitus. The Inception of Occidental Thinking and Logic: Heraclitus's Doctrine of the Logos,* trans. Julia Goesser Assaiante and S. Montgomery Ewegen (New York: Bloomsbury, 2018), 227.
80. FCM, 41.
81. FCM, 44.
82. FCM, 44–45.
83. FCM, 45.
84. Martin Heidegger, *Nietzsche, Vols I and II*, ed. David Farrell Krell, trans. D.F. Krell (New York: HarperCollins, 1991), 209.
85. Heidegger, *Nietzsche* Vol. 1, 209.
86. Heidegger, *Nietzsche* Vol. 1, 201.
87. FCM, 59.
88. This is to be distinguished from the later Heidegger's reference to attunement and the holy in relation to the festival, "the fundamental attunement for the festival, the awaiting of the festive, and that is, of the holy," HHR, 110 or linked to "the holy in its own fatherland," HHR, 111.
89. Capobianco, *Heidegger's Way of Being,* 87.
90. Capobianco, *Heidegger's Way of Being,* 87.
91. Heidegger, *Heraclitus,* 226.
92. Capobianco, *Heidegger's Way of Being,* 32.
93. HHR, 90.
94. Carl Jung, "What India Can Teach Us?" in *Psychology and Religion: West and East.* CW 11 (1939): 110.
95. Richard Capobianco, See "Heidegger on Hebel: The Inexhaustible Depth of "Things" in *Heidegger's Being: The Shimmering Unfolding* (Toronto: University of Toronto Press, 2022)
96. Capobianco, "Heidegger on Hebel" GA 16: 565–67, trans. and commentary by Capobianco (see previous note).

97. See Downes, *Primordial Dance* for an argument regarding temporality and care in BT and their relation to concentric space as a circular spatial movement and diametric space as a linear spatial movement.

98. BPP, 290.

99. Heidegger, *Heraclitus,* 122–23.

100. William J. Richardson, *Heidegger: Through Phenomenology to Thought* (The Hague: Martinus Nijhoff, 1963/1974), 148.

Notes on the Text and Heidegger's *Gesamtausgabe*

All chapters in this volume use the convention of writing Heidegger's "Being" with a capital "B." This is an orthographical convention in the English-language Heidegger scholarship that goes back to the late 1950s and early 1960s, and is followed here. The capital "B" "Being" was employed by the late preeminent Heidegger scholar William J. Richardson in his groundbreaking commentary *Heidegger: Through Phenomenology to Thought* (Kluwer), first published in 1963. Yet he was certainly not alone in employing this convention, and over the years many other eminent commentators and translators have found the convention useful. For a discussion of the philosophical intentions and justifications for this convention, see Ch. 3 in Richard Capobianco, *Heidegger's Being: The Shimmering Unfolding* (Toronto: University of Toronto Press, 2022).

All references in the essays to Heidegger's *Gesamtausgabe* ("Collected Works") cite the volume and page in this form: (GA + volume number: page number). What follows is a comprehensive (but not yet complete) bibliographical list of the published volumes in the *Gesamtausgabe*. Bibliographical information for the English translations that are used by the authors in their essays can be found in their Endnotes.

MARTIN HEIDEGGER'S *GESAMTAUSGABE* PUBLISHED BY VITTORIO KLOSTERMANN, FRANKFURT AM MAIN:

GA 1. *Frühe Schriften* (1912–1916). Ed. Friedrich-Wilhelm von Herrmann, 1978.

GA 2. *Sein und Zeit* (1927). Ed. Friedrich Wilhelm von Herrmann, 1977.

GA 3. *Kant und das Problem der Metaphysik* (1929). Ed. Friedrich-Wilhelm von Herrmann, 1991.
GA 4. *Erläuterungen zu Hölderlins Dichtung* (1936–1968). Ed. Friedrich-Wilhelm von Herrmann, 1981, 2012 (rev. ed.).
GA 5. *Holzwege* (1935–1946). Ed. Friedrich-Wilhelm von Hermann, 1977.
GA 6.2 *Nietzsche II* (1939–1946). Ed. Brigitte Schillbach, 1997.
GA 7. *Vorträge und Aufsätze* (1936–1953). Ed. Friedrich-Wilhelm von Herrmann, 2000.
GA 8. *Was heißt Denken?* (1951–1952). Ed. Paola-Ludovika Coriando, 2002.
GA 9. *Wegmarken* (1919–1961). Ed. Friedrich-Wilhelm von Herrmann, 1976, 1996 (rev. ed.).
GA 10. *Der Satz vom Grund* (1957). Ed. Petra Jaeger, 1997.
GA 11. *Identität und Differenz* (1955–1963). Ed. Friedrich-Wilhelm von Herrmann, 2006.
GA 12. *Unterwegs zur Sprache* (1950–1959). Ed. Friedrich-Wilhelm von Herrmann, 1985.
GA 13. *Aus der Erfahrung des Denkens* (1910–1976). Ed. Hermann Heidegger, 1983, 2002 (rev. ed.).
GA 14. *Zur Sache des Denkens* (1927–1968). Ed. Friedrich-Wilhelm von Herrmann, 2007.
GA 16. *Reden und andere Zeugnisse eines Lebensweges* (1910–1976). Ed. Hermann Heidegger, 2000.
GA 18. *Grundbegriffe der aristotelischen Philosophie* (1924). Ed. Mark Michalski, 2002.
GA 19. *Platon: Sophistes* (1924–1925). Ed. Ingeborg Schüßler, 1992.
GA 20. *Prolegomena zur Geschichte des Zeitbegriffs* (1925). Ed. Petra Jaeger, 1979, 1988 (2nd, rev. ed.), 1994 (3d, rev. ed.).
GA 21. *Logik. Die Frage nach der Wahrheit* (1925–1926). Ed. Walter Biemel, 1976, 1995 (rev. ed.).
GA 24. *Die Grundprobleme der Phänomenologie* (1927). Ed. Friedrich-Wilhelm von Herrmann, 1975.
GA 25. *Phänomenologische Interpretation von Kants Kritik der reinen Vernunft* (1927–1928). Ed. Ingtraud Görland, 1977.
GA 26. *Metaphysische Anfangsgründe der Logik im Ausgang von Leibniz* (1928). Ed. Klaus Held, 1978, 1990 (2nd rev. ed.), 2007 (3d rev. ed.).
GA 27. *Einleitung in die Philosophie* (1928–1929). Ed. Otto Saame and Ina Saame-Speidel, 1996, 2001 (rev. ed.).
GA 28. *Der deutsche Idealismus (Fichte, Schelling, Hegel) und die philosophische Problemlage der Gegenwart* (1929). Ed. Claudius Strube, 1997.
GA 29/30. *Die Grundbegriffe der Metaphysik. Welt—Endlichkeit—Einsamkeit* (1929–1930). Ed. Friedrich-Wilhelm von Herrmann, 1983.

GA 31. *Vom Wesen der menschlichen Freiheit. Einleitung in die Philosophie* (1930). Ed. Hartmut Tietjen, 1982, 1994 (rev. ed.).

GA 32. *Hegels Phänomenologie des Geistes* (1930-31). Ed. Ingtraud Görland, 1980.

GA 33. *Aristoteles, Metaphysik Θ 1–3. Von Wesen und Wirklichkeit der Kraft* (1931). Ed. Heinrich Hüni, 1981, 1990 (2nd rev. ed.), 2006 (3d rev. ed.).

GA 34. *Vom Wesen der Wahrheit. Zu Platons Höhlengleichnis und Theätet* (1931–1932). Ed. Hermann Mörchen, 1988, 1997 (rev. ed.).

GA 35. *Der Anfang der abendländischen Philosophie: Auslegung des Anaximander und Parmenides* (1932). Ed. Peter Trawny, 2011.

GA 36/37. *Sein und Wahrheit* (1933–1934). Ed. Hartmut Tietjen, 2001.

GA 38. *Logik als die Frage nach dem Wesen der Sprache* (1934). Ed. Günter Seubold, 1998.

GA 39. *Hölderlins Hymnen "Germanien" und "Der Rhein"* (1934–1935). Ed. Susanne Ziegler, 1980, 1989 (rev. ed.).

GA 40. *Einführung in die Metaphysik* (1935). Ed. Petra Jaeger, 1983.

GA 41. *Die Frage nach dem Ding. Zu Kants Lehre von den transzendentalen Grundsätzen* (1935–1936). Ed. Petra Jaeger, 1984.

GA 42. *Schelling: Vom Wesen der menschlichen Freiheit (1809)* (1936). Ed. Ingrid Schüßler, 1988.

GA 43. *Nietzsche: Der Wille zur Macht als Kunst* (1936–1937). Ed. Bernd Heimbüchel, 1985.

GA 44. *Nietzsches metaphysische Grundstellung im abendländischen Denken: Die ewige Wiederkehr des Gleichen* (1937). Ed. Marion Heinz, 1986.

GA 45. *Grundfragen der Philosophie. Ausgewählte "Probleme" der "Logik"* (1937-38). Ed. Friedrich-Wilhelm von Herrmann, 1984.

GA 46. *Zur Auslegung von Nietzsches II. Unzeitgemäßer Betrachtung "Vom Nutzen und Nachteil der Historie für das Leben"* (1938–1939). Ed. Hans-Joachim Friedrich, 2003.

GA 47. *Nietzsches Lehre vom Willen zur Macht als Erkenntnis* (1939). Ed. Eberhard Hanser, 1989.

GA 48. *Nietzsche: Der europäische Nihilismus* (1940). Ed. Petra Jaeger, 1986.

GA 49. *Die Metaphysik des deutschen Idealismus. Zur erneuten Auslegung von Schelling: "Philosophische Untersuchungen über das Wesen der menschlichen Freiheit und die damit zusammenhängenden Gegenstände" (1809)* (1941). Ed. Günter Seubold, 1991, 2006 (2nd rev. ed.).

GA 50. *Nietzsches Metaphysik; Einleitung in die Philosophie—Denken und Dichten* (1941–1942, 1944–1945). Ed. Petra Jaeger, 1990, 2007 (2nd rev. ed.).

GA 51. *Grundbegriffe* (1941). Ed. Petra Jaeger, 1981, 1991 (rev. ed.).
GA 52. *Hölderlins Hymne "Andenken"* (1941–1942). Ed. Curd Ochwadt, 1982.
GA 53. *Hölderlins Hymne "Der Ister"* (1942). Ed. Walter Biemel, 1984.
GA 54. *Parmenides* (1942–1943). Ed. Manfred S. Frings, 1982.
GA 55. *Heraklit* (1943, 1944). Ed. Manfred S. Frings, 1979, 1987 (rev. ed.).
GA 56/57. *Zur Bestimmung der Philosophie* (1919). Ed. Bernd Heimbüchel, 1987, 1999 (rev., expanded ed.).
GA 60. *Phänomenologie des religiösen Lebens* (1918–1921). Ed. Matthias Jung, Thomas Regehly, and Claudius Strube, 1995, 2011 (rev. ed.).
GA 61. *Phänomenologische Interpretationen zu Aristoteles. Einführung in die phänomenologische Forschung* (1921–1922). Ed. Walter Bröcker und Käte Bröcker-Oltmanns, 1985, 1994 (rev. ed.).
GA 62. *Phänomenologische Interpretationen ausgewählter Abhandlungen des Aristoteles zu Ontologie und Logik.* (1922). Ed. Günther Neumann, 2005.
GA 63. *Ontologie. Hermeneutik der Faktizität* (1923). Ed. Käte Bröcker-Oltmanns, 1988.
GA 64. *Der Begriff der Zeit* (1924). Ed. Friedrich-Wilhelm von Herrmann, 2004.
GA 65. *Beiträge zur Philosophie (Vom Ereignis)* (1936–1938). Ed. Friedrich-Wilhelm von Herrmann, 1989, 1994 (rev. ed.).
GA 66. *Besinnung* (1938–1939). Ed. Friedrich-Wilhelm von Herrmann, 1997.
GA 67. *Metaphysik und Nihilismus* (1938-39, 1946–1948). Ed. Hans-Joachim Friedrich, 1999.
GA 68. *Hegel* (1938–1939, 1942). Ed. Ingrid Schüßler, 1993.
GA 69. *Die Geschichte des Seyns* (1938–1940). Ed. Peter Trawny, 1998, 2012 (rev. ed.).
GA 70. *Über den Anfang* (1941). Ed. Paola-Ludovika Coriando, 2005.
GA 71. *Das Ereignis* (1941–1942). Ed. Friedrich-Wilhelm von Herrmann, 2009.
GA 73.1 and 73.2. *Zum Ereignis-Denken* (1932–1970s). Ed. Peter Trawny, 2013.
GA 74. *Zum Wesen der Sprache und Zur Frage nach der Kunst* (1935–1960). Ed. Thomas Regehly, 2010.
GA 75. *Zu Hölderlin—Griechenlandreisen* (1939–1970). Ed. Curd Ochwadt, 2000.
GA 76. *Leitgedanken zur Entstehung der Metaphysik, der neuzeitlichen Wissenschaft und der modernen Technik* (1935–1955). Ed. Claudius Strube, 2009.
GA 77. *Feldweg-Gespräche* (1944–1945). Ed. Ingrid Schüßler, 1995, 2007 (2nd rev. ed.).
GA 78. *Der Spruch des Anaximander* (1942). Ed. Ingeborg Schüßler, 2010.

GA 79. *Bremer und Freiburger Vorträge* (1949, 1957). Ed. Petra Jaeger, 1994.
GA 80.1 *Vorträge 1915 bis 1932.* Ed. Günther Neumann, 2016.
GA 81. *Gedachtes.* Ed. Paola-Ludovika Coriando, 2007.
GA 82. *Zu eigenen Veröffentlichungen* (1936–ca. 1950). Ed. Friedrich-Wilhelm von Herrmann, 2018.
GA 83. *Seminare: Platon—Aristoteles—Augustinus* (1928–1952). Ed. Mark Michalski, 2012.
GA 84.1. *Seminare: Kant—Leibniz—Schiller* (1931–1936). Ed. Günther Neumann, 2013.
GA 86. *Seminare: Hegel—Schelling* (1927–1957). Ed. Peter Trawny, 2011.
GA 87. *Nietzsche: Seminare 1937 und 1944.* Ed. Peter von Ruckteschell, 2004.
GA 88. *Seminare (Übungen) 1937/38 und 1941/42: 1. Die metaphysischen Grundstellungen des abendländischen Denkens; 2. Einübung in das philosophische Denken.* Ed. Alfred Denker, 2008.
GA 89. *Zollikoner Seminare* (1959–1969). Ed. Peter Trawny, 2017.
GA 90. *Zu Ernst Jünger* (1934–1954). Ed. Peter Trawny, 2004.
GA 94. *Überlegungen II–VI (Schwarze Hefte 1931–1938).* Ed. Peter Trawny, 2014.
GA 95. *Überlegungen VII–XI (Schwarze Hefte 1938–1939).* Ed. Peter Trawny, 2014.
GA 96. *Überlegungen XII–XV (Schwarze Hefte 1939–1941).* Ed. Peter Trawny, 2014.
GA 97. *Anmerkungen I–V (Schwarze Hefte 1942–1948).* Ed. Peter Trawny, 2015.
GA 98. *Anmerkungen VI-IX (Schwarze Hefte 1948/49–1951).* Ed. Peter Trawny, 2018.
GA 99. *Vier Hefte I und II (Schwarze Hefte 1947–1950).* Ed. Peter Trawny, 2019.
GA 100 *Vigiliae und Notturno (Schwarze Hefte 1952/53–1957).* Ed. Peter Trawny, 2020.
GA 101 *Winke I and II (Schwarze Hefte 1957–1959).* Ed. Peter Trawny, 2020.

Index

absence of the holy, 113, 138, 153
Agamben, Giorgio, 87
aletheia: and the clearing (*Lichtung*), 13, 20; and Greek tragedies, 140, 143, 145; as name for Being, 2; spatial-phenomenology of the holy, 159–60, 163
Allen, W. S., 29
all unifying One (*alles einigende Eine*), 11
Anaximander, 2, 13, 65
Anthropocene, 144, 152, 162
apeiron, 2, 13–14
Aquinas, 133, 174–75
Aristotle, 154, 166, 168–70
atheism, 10, 20, 133

Bachelard, Gaston, 166
Barklay, William, 138
Baudelaire, Charles, 95
Being: and color, 63–79; and concentric and diametric spaces, 163; and the divine, 48–49, 51–52, 100–101; and dwelling and nature, 16–17; *Es gibt*, 2, 7, 131, 132; the Greek experience of, 65; and Hölderlin, 27–32, 34, 40, 108, 109; and the holy, 132; and language, 3–4, 31–32, 35, 38, 93, 96; as *Logos*, 2, 35, 38; manifold names, 2; and metaphysics, 3–4; names for, 2; as nature, 27–36; and phenomenology, 1–2; and restraint, 46–48, 50; rift (*Riss*), 39; silence, 97; the specific illumination of, 172; and the work of art, 52–53, 55–57
Being and Time (Heidegger): compared to *What is Metaphysics*? (Heidegger), 125–26, 159; Mitchell, 117, 119
Being-as-the holy, 1–4. *See also* the holy (*das Heilige*)
Benveniste, Emile: *Dictionary of Indo-European Concepts and Society*, 86–88; significance, 94–95; signification, 86–90, 92, 95; silence as holy, 97, 99
Bergson, Henri, 169
Bernasconi, Robert, 39, 144, 147
Blanchot, Maurice, 31–32, 34–35
Braig, Carl, 63
Buber, Martin, 45

Capobianco, Richard: the ability to hear the ancient names of Being, 152; on *Antigone* in *Engaging Heidegger*, 150; Being as *Logos*, 35; on breath and breathing, 176; on the clearing (*Lichtung*), 173–74; on *deinon*, 148; on Heidegger after "the turn" (*die Kehre*), 2, 137; on

191

Heidegger's elucidation of Hebel, 177; on Heidegger's *On the Islands of the Aegean*, 19; *Heidegger's Way of Being*, 28; on Hölderlin's late poem "Autumn", 27–28; nature as the crowning wreath, 100–101; on the perdurance of nature, 143–44; on *physis*, 140, 141, 143; on recovering the "Greek experience", 20

Chrétien, Jean-Louis, 164

Christianity: and belief in God, 6; and Heidegger, 64, 110, 113; and Hölderlin, 111; and the holy, 121, 138; and the last god, 10, 20; and philosophy, 105, 108, 139; Plato, 139

Claudel, Paul, 164

Claxton, Susanne, 1

the clearing (*Lichtung*): and awe, 17–20; and the divine, 52; Eckhart, 11; Eliade, 12, 23; and flight of the gods, 5, 6, 9–11, 19–21; Hölderlin, 5, 8, 27; Husserl, 5; *The Idea of the Holy...its Relation to the Rational (Das Heilige....Verhältnis zum Rationalen)* (Otto), 5–6, 8; *kosmos*, 7, 13–14; the last god, 10–12, 20; and light, 173; *Logos*, 27; *physis*, 13, 14, 17–19; regioning/that-which-regions (*Gegend*), 5, 13–16; *Theogony* (Hesiod), 7, 12; and wonder, 18–20

Crowe, Benjamin, 19, 118

Dasein: historicality and temporality, 143; measure-taking, 146–47; side-by-sideness, 167

das Gestell (enframing), 138

das Heilige (the holy). See the holy (*das Heilige*)

the death of God, 5–7, 20, 34, 108

de Man, Paul, 30–31

Derrida, Jacques, 35, 37, 129, 161

Descartes, René, 167

the divine: and the clearing (*Lichtung*), 52; compared to the holy, 139; and dwelling, 57–58; effort for, 48–49; and *Ereignis*, 49–50, 60; mindfulness (*Achtsamkeit*), 45–47, 56–59; ontological effort, 45–51, 54, 55; presencing of, 51–52; and preservation of the work of art, 56–57; and renunciation, 46, 47; and restraint, 46–48, 50; steadfastness (*Inständigkeit*), 46, 51, 55; Van Gogh, 53

dwelling: awe and, 18–20; as basic character of the human being, 58; the holy and, 13; nature and, 14–17; and poetizing (*Dichtung*), 137; in the presence of the holy, 138; the unsayable, 35

Eckhart, Meister, 11, 35, 38–39, 41

Eliade, Mircea, 12

Enneads (Plotinus), 45

Ereignis: compared to *aletheia*, 73–74; and the divine, 49–50, 60; the holy, 98, 138, 153; silence and, 97

flight of the gods, 5, 6, 9–11, 19–21, 138

forgetting of Being (*Seinsvergessenheit*), 2, 5, 94, 112

the fourfold (*das Geviert*), 15

Franke, William, 36–37

Gadamer, Hans-Georg, 33, 160

George, Stefan, 39, 120, 121

German idealism, 90, 167

Goethe, Johann Wolfgang: and color, 64; definition of the holy, 85; *The Four Seasons*, 86, 91, 94, 99–100; and the holy, 89–90, 94

Gray, John, 18, 152

Harries, Karsten, 38

Hegel, Georg Wilhelm Friedrich: *Aesthetics*, 85, 94; idealism of, 119, 131, 167; on the tower of Babel as holy, 85–86, 94; unveiling, 160

Heidegger, Martin: and *Antigone* (Sophocles), 65–66, 147–52; and Christianity, 64; compared to Benveniste, 95, 99; compared to Goethe, 99; *Confessions* (St. Augustine), 107; and Heraclitus, 65, 154, 174, 177–78; and medieval mysticism, 64, 106; and Nietzsche, 107, 108, 175; and Otto, 18, 105–7, 113; and Parmenides, 2, 65; and Pindar, 64, 68–72; and St. Paul, 163; and the technological age, 111–12

hen (the One), 2

Heraclitus, 2, 15, 17, 65, 154, 174

Hölderlin, Friedrich: and Christianity, 32, 33, 111; feasts and festivals, 129; the flight of the gods, 6, 20–21, 138; fundamental attunement (*Grundstimmung*) in poetry of, 89–91; and Greek tragedies, 145–46; the holy measure in poetry of, 146; nature as the holy, 27–28; and Nietzsche, 107; and *physis*, 141; and poetizing (*Dichtung*), 9, 17–18, 41, 137, 151, 154; as prophet of a new revelation, 110, 112; on silence, 41

the holy (*das Heilige*): arrival of, 98; Blanchot, 31–32, 34–35; Capobianco, 27–28; Derrida, 35, 37; and dwelling, 34; Eckhart, 35, 38–39, 41; etymology of, 88–89, 99–100; Franke, 36–37; and the gladsome (*das Heitere*), 2–3, 8–9; and the gods, 28, 31; Goethe's definition of, 85; Harries, 38; as immediate, 32; and the joyful one, 2–3; Jung, 33; Kant, 6; Kazemi, 35; Mersch, 39; the mystical (*das Mystische*), 35–39; nature as, 27–29; Pindar, 29, 32; and poetizing (*Dichtung*), 86, 92–99; and religious and spiritual sensibility, 2–3; and renunciation, 39; rift (*Riss*), 39, 57; Rumi, 36; Schutz, 35; and silence, 34–36, 39–41, 96–99; as the source (homecoming), 3; Tilghman, 38; and the unsayable, 31, 35–39, 41

Husserl, Edmund, 1, 5, 64, 106, 119

The Idea of the Holy...its Relation to the Rational (*Das Heilige....Verhältnis zum Rationalen*) (Otto), 64

Jaspers, Karl, 110
the joyful one, 2–3
Judaism, 110, 113, 114, 138
Jung, Carl, 33, 164, 177

Kalary, Thomas, 48
Kant, Immanuel: *Critique of Pure Reason*, 164–65; and the holy, 6, 107; *Kant and the Problem of Metaphysics* (*Kant und das Problem der Metaphysik*) (Heidegger), 8; spatial-phenomenology of the holy, 163–65, 167, 170
kosmos, 2
Kristeva, Julia, 95

the last god, 10–12, 20, 51–52, 127
Levinas, Emmanuel, 114
Lévi-Strauss, Claude, 162–63, 165, 171, 174

Marion, Jean-Luc, 133
McNeill, William, 140, 149, 153
Mersch, Dieter, 39
Mitchell, Andrew, 117, 127
modernity: approach to the holy, 113; and enframing (*Gestell*), 119; and nihilism, 5
Mörike, Eduard, 73
the mystical (*das Mystische*): Eckhart, 38–39, 41; and the unsayable, 35–39; Wittgenstein, 36–41

Nancy, Jean-Luc, 101, 127
Neoplatonism, 3, 121, 129
Nieli, Russell, 37

Nietzsche, Friedrich: the death of God, 5–7, 20, 34, 108; and Heidegger, 107, 108, 175
nihilism: the death of God, 6, 19, 20, 34; and Heidegger, 108, 110–11; and modernity, 5, 20

Otto, Rudolf: *The Idea of the Holy... its Relation to the Rational (Das Heilige....Verhältnis zum Rationalen)*, 5–6, 8, 64, 97–98, 105, 106; music and silence to express the holy, 97–98; the numinous, 5, 18, 64, 68, 98, 164; phenomenology of the holy, 106–7

Parmenides, 2, 29, 65
phenomenology of religion, 5–6, 18, 106–7
physis: and the clearing (*Lichtung*), 13, 14, 17–19; and Greek tragedies, 139–41, 143–46, 149–52; and Hölderlin, 27, 141; as name for Being, 2
Pindar: *5th Isthmian*, 64–67, 71–73; *8th Pythian*, 73, 79; and Heidegger, 64, 68–72
Plato: *chora* in *Timaeus*, 13–14; the holy in *Euthyphro*, 138–39; light and, 173–74
Plotinus, 45
poetizing (*Dichtung*): and dwelling, 137; Hölderlin, 9, 17–18, 41, 137, 148, 151, 154; and the holy, 86, 92–99; thinking and, 109–10, 113; and wonder (*thaumazein*), 18, 20
Prometheus Bound (Aeschylus), 141–43
Prometheus Unbound (Shelley), 174

the question of Being (*die Seinsfrage*): Aquinas, 133, 174; and artworks, 124–26; *Being and Time* (Heidegger), 16, 122, 126; Capobianco, 131; the clearing (*Lichtung*), 127, 128; Crowe, 118; Derrida, 129; and enframing (*Gestell*), 119; George, 120; Goethe, 131; Hegel, 119, 131; Hölderlin, 129; Husserl, 119; Kant, 131; Marion, 133; metaphysics, 129, 130, 132; Mitchell, 127, 129; Nancy, 127; Silesius's rose, 130–32; Young, 119

Richardson, William J., 178
Rilke, 137
Rumi, 36

salvation (*Rettung, Heil*), 9, 33, 71–72, 78, 88, 113, 114
Schoenbohm, Susan, 140
Schutz, Alfred, 35
Silesius, 68, 130
Socrates, 69, 138
the source (*der Ursprung*), 2–4, 148, 151
Staiger, Emil, 73
St. Bonaventure, 63

Tilghman, B. R., 38
Tractatus (Wittgenstein), 27
Trakl, Georg, 63, 65, 99, 120
the turn (*die Kehre*), 1, 137

uncanniness, 12, 13, 68, 120, 126, 128, 149
un/ground (*Ab-grund*), 7–9

Van Gogh, Vincent, 53, 126
Vernant, Jean-Pierre, 147

Welte, Bernhard, 114
Windelband, Wilhelm, 107
Wittgenstein, Ludwig: and the limits of language, 36–41; *Tractatus*, 27, 37, 39

Young, Julian, 119

zoe, 2

CONTRIBUTORS

Editor: **Richard Capobianco** is professor of philosophy and Meehan humanities scholar at Stonehill College, Massachusetts.

Lawrence Berger, Ph.D. philosophy, taught business studies and ethics at the University of Pennsylvania and the University of Iowa and is currently an independent scholar.

Paul Downes is associate professor of psychology, Dublin City University, and affiliate professor at the University of Malta.

John Krummel is associate professor of religious studies at Hobart and William Smith Colleges.

Sazan Kryeziu is assistant professor of English and American literature at the University of Gjakova "Fehmi Agani" in Kosovo.

James M. Magrini, Ph.D., is an instructor in philosophy and ethics at the College of Dupage, Illinois.

Ian Alexander Moore is assistant professor of philosophy at Loyola Marymount University in Los Angeles, CA.

Joeri Schrijvers is extraordinary professor at the School of Philosophy at North-West University Potchefstoom, South Africa.

Elias Schwieler is associate professor of education at Stockholm University, Sweden.

Holger Zaborowski is professor of philosophy at Erfurt University, Germany.

www.ingramcontent.com/pod-product-compliance
Lightning Source LLC
Chambersburg PA
CBHW021849300426
44115CB00005B/83